Harvard Historical Monographs

XLVIII

Published under the direction
of the Department of History
from the income of
The Robert Louis Stroock Fund

JOHN FISKE

The Evolution of a Popularizer

Milton Berman

HARVARD

UNIVERSITY PRESS

Cambridge · 1961

920
F541b
94728

To My Mother

ACKNOWLEDGMENTS

This study has benefited greatly from information contained in Fiske's manuscripts about his activities and the public reception of them. For granting access to their collections of manuscripts and books, I would like to thank the librarians and administrators of the following libraries and archives: the Boston Public Library, the Cornell University Archives, the Houghton and Widener Libraries of Harvard University, the Harvard University Archives, the Henry E. Huntington Library and Art Gallery, the Johns Hopkins University Library, the Library of Congress, the Missouri Historical Society, the New York Public Library, the Princeton University Library, the Department of Special Collections of the University of California at Los Angeles, the William L. Clements Library of the University of Michigan, the University of Southern California Library, and the Archives of the Washington University of St. Louis.

For consent to publication of quotations from manuscripts in their collections, I am indebted to the Cornell University Archives, the Houghton Library of Harvard University, the Harvard University Archives, the Henry E. Huntington Library and Art Gallery, the Library of Congress, the William L. Clements Library of the University of Michigan, and the Department of Special Collections of the University of California at Los Angeles.

I am especially grateful to Fiske's grandchildren, James Brooks Fiske, John Fiske, and Susan Willard Flint, for their kind permission to print quotations from the unpublished manuscripts of their grandfather.

Many individuals aided me in locating useful sources, among

whom the late Rollo Walter Brown, Patrick D. Hazard, John E. Higgins, the late Mark Antony DeWolfe Howe, Mark DeWolfe Howe, Howard Mumford Jones, and Samuel Eliot Morison deserve special mention. Frank Freidel read an earlier version of this book and provided gratifying encouragement. Donald Fleming, Max Hall and Miss Kathleen Ahern gave me detailed criticisms of the entire manuscript.

Above all, I am indebted to Oscar Handlin, who brought this topic to my attention and directed the doctoral dissertation upon which this book is based, and whose patient and illuminating criticisms helped me greatly in preparing the present text.

M.B.

CONTENTS

ILLUSTRATIONS

following page 66

John Fiske in the Sixties
> From the Harvard Class of 1863 Album, through the courtesy of the Harvard University Archives.

John Fiske in the Eighties
> From an engraving in J. S. Clark, *The Life and Letters of John Fiske* (Boston, 1917).

John Fiske in the Late Nineties
> From the *Outlook* (August 3, 1901).

JOHN FISKE

LIST OF ABBREVIATIONS USED IN FOOTNOTES

JF   John Fiske.
Abby   Abby Morgan Brooks Fiske, John Fiske's wife.
HHL   Henry L. Huntington Library and Art Gallery, San Marino, California.
HMCo   Houghton, Mifflin and Company Letter Books, Harvard University Library.
HUA   Harvard University Archives.
HUL   Harvard University Library.
LC   Library of Congress.
PUL   Princeton University Library.
WUA   Washington University Archives, St. Louis, Missouri.

CHAPTER ONE

MODEL BOY
INTO VILLAGE INFIDEL

When John Fiske died on July 4, 1901, the nation mourned the passing of a great man. Newspapers from coast to coast carried the news of his death; literary, religious, and historical periodicals printed highly flattering estimates of his contributions to American philosophy, science, history, and religion. "The death of John Fiske came to a very large part of the people of the land he loved and served so well with a sense of personal loss," mourned the *Book Buyer*. The London *Athenaeum* termed him "a man of rare ability who was an honour to his country and to literature." The *American Historical Review* noted that he was "without doubt deservedly the most popular historical writer in America," and agreed with the literary journals that his death was "a grave loss to American historical writing." The religiously oriented *Outlook* confidently expected future generations to reaffirm its high estimate of his worth and assured its readers that "certain of his books will be in more demand in the future even than now." [1]

During his lifetime famous scientists and philosophers praised Fiske's writings. Charles Darwin complimented the early books. "I never in my life read so lucid an expositor (& therefore thinker) as

[1] *Book Buyer*, 23:15 (August 1901); London *Athenaeum*, July 20, 1901, p. 95; *American Historical Review*, 7:187 (October 1901); *Outlook*, 68:619 (July 13, 1901).

you are," he wrote Fiske in 1874, providing a quotation which thereafter appeared on many book-jackets and lecture programs.[2] Herbert Spencer and Thomas Henry Huxley valued Fiske's efforts and aided his career. While not blind to Fiske's limitations, these men approved the body of his work, much of which popularized ideas they themselves had put forward earlier.

Fiske's work drew favorable attention from leaders of American religious thought, especially in the last two decades of the nineteenth century when he successfully expounded the theological implications of his ideas. Impressed by the praise of scientists and attracted by the respectful tone with which Fiske spoke of religion, preachers and troubled laymen hailed him as a scientific defender of the faith.

The steady drumbeat of press notices that Fiske used to arouse interest in his coast-to-coast lecture tours, and which his publishers found effective in selling his books, heavily affected the public image of him. Interviews, biographical sketches, remarks in book reviews, and announcements of lectures—all described Fiske as a child prodigy who had mastered a multitude of languages and almost all knowledge before entering college, and who had since matured into a profound scholar. He was portrayed as a jovial, warmhearted, hard-working man, traveling endlessly across the country to enlighten his fellow citizens. His early work had contributed greatly to the theory of evolution, and he now applied his vast knowledge of science and history to teaching the mass of Americans the meaning of their past and the truth of traditional religious ideas.[3]

---

[2] Charles Darwin to JF, Dec. 8, 1874, HHL (a table of abbreviations used in citations appears on the page following the table of contents). All letters are quoted from original manuscripts when these are available; they therefore differ, sometimes widely, from the versions found in the heavily edited printed editions of Fiske's correspondence.

[3] The myth of Fiske's childish precocity and mature profundity can be sampled in: "Well Equipped Historian," *Critic,* 26:310 (Apr. 27, 1895); O. E. Dana, "John Fiske," *Journal of Education,* 45:239–240 (Apr. 15, 1897); S. Waterman and J. W. Hanson, Jr., *Famous American Men and Women* (Chicago, 1896), 218–219; A. M. Davis, "John Fiske," in American Academy of Arts and Sciences, *Proceedings,* 37:665–678 (August 1902); G. Gunton, "John Fiske," *Gunton's Magazine,* 21:161–164 (August 1901); F. H. Head, *John Fiske* (Chicago [1902?]); W. D. Howells, "John Fiske," *Harper's Weekly,* 45:732 (July 20, 1902); W. D. Quint, "John Fiske in Cambridge," *New York Times Saturday Review,* Oct. 15, 1898, pp. 688–689;

The full flowering of this legend did not come until 1905, when Elbert Hubbard apotheosized him in one of his "Little Visits to the Homes of Great Scientists." Hubbard, accepting and embellishing the popular image of Fiske, told his readers that at seven Fiske read Caesar and Josephus in the original, and discovered for himself that the famous passage in Josephus on Jesus of Nazareth was a late interpolation. At nine, reported Hubbard, Fiske spoke Greek with an Attic accent; before he was out of knee breeches he kept a diary in Spanish, spoke German at table, and read German philosophers in the original language. Before entering college he could read Hebrew and Sanskrit, and so great was his fame that Harvard admitted him by acclamation and waived all entrance requirements. Hubbard credited Fiske with three great scientific discoveries; that the length of a pigeon's bill increased as the size of its feet increased, that white tomcats with blue eyes were always deaf, and that the extent of mental development in any animal was dependent on the length of its infancy. Hubbard used the last to explain Fiske's failure to produce work as great as his early talents promised—he had matured too early.

Hubbard informed his readers that Fiske first won a reputation by giving substitute lectures for an absent Harvard professor, in the course of which he brilliantly surveyed all of natural history. Admitting that Fiske was not an original discoverer, Hubbard yet insisted that he "comes as near being a great scientist, perhaps, as any man that America has ever produced." Most valuable of all were Fiske's contributions to religion. "John Fiske made the science of Darwin and Wallace palatable to orthodox theology, and it is to the earnest and eloquent words of Fiske that we owe it that Evolution is taught everywhere in the public schools and even in the sectarian colleges of America today." [4]

Even in the obituary chorus of praise, however, doubting voices could be heard. Some who were sure of his greatness found it difficult to specify the nature of his achievement. The *Dial*, while laud-

Frank Waldo, "John Fiske: an American Scholar," *Education*, 22:331–339 (February 1902).

[4] Elbert Hubbard, "John Fiske," *Little Journeys to the Homes of Great Scientists*, 17:135–151 (December 1905); quotations from pp. 144, 146.

ing his histories, objected that his religious writing was "flavored with sophistry." The *Outlook*, praising his religious writing, admitted that as a historian he was "rather an interpreter than an original thinker or investigator." Rollo Ogden in the *Nation* described Fiske as primarily a popularizer, but one whose talents in this field were so great that he had to be called "a prince of his art." Even before Fiske's death disciples of rival scholars had become contemptuous. When J. B. McMaster published a new volume, his disciple, Frederick D. Stone, was reported to have said, "Now we shall soon have something from John Fiske." [5]

In 1901 the most negative assessments came from specialists evaluating Fiske's contribution to their fields of study. George Louis Beer, a historian, criticized Fiske's work as lacking in creative power, relying on the research of others, and tending to ignore social forces while concentrating upon political and military narrative. Because of these defects, "though a man of brilliant talents, of vast learning, Fiske's name will never stand conspicuous in the list of American philosophers and historians." Albert Bushnell Hart paid tribute to Fiske's services as an interpreter of other writers, but judged his attempts at generalization and originality unsatisfactory. "He has after all done no more than to tell better what other men painfully toiled to tell as best they could," Hart concluded. Thus it "seems inevitable that Fiske's work will not be accepted as foundations on which future historians will build." [6]

After 1901 unfavorable opinions became predominant. The appearance of a brief biography by T. S. Perry in 1905, a two-volume life and letters by J. S. Clark in 1917, and a volume of letters edited by his daughter, Ethel F. Fisk, in 1940, stimulated repetitions of the earlier reactions, with the chorus of scholarly rejection tending more and more to outweigh praise by book reviewers. Although Fiske's name continues to appear in histories of American philosophy and literature, and in accounts of American historical writing, most references are brief and frequently derogatory. [7]

[5] Chicago *Dial*, 31:48 (July 16, 1901); *Outlook*, 68:619 (July 13, 1901); *Nation*, 73:27 (July 11, 1901); E. P. Oberholtzer, "J. B. McMaster," *Pennsylvania Magazine of History and Biography*, 57:26 (January 1933).

[6] G. L. Beer, "John Fiske," *Critic*, 39:117 (August 1901); A. B. Hart, "The Historical Services of John Fiske," *International Monthly*, 4:568 (October 1901).

[7] See reviews of these books.

Fiske "was neither a profound scholar nor an original thinker in either [philosophy or history]," said James Truslow Adams in the brief sketch he contributed to the *Dictionary of American Biography,* which in effect summarized the standard scholarly evaluation of Fiske. However, "the lucidity and charm of his style made him unrivalled as a popularizer," Adams explained. "In the historical field, Fiske was solely a popularizer, and in spite of his strong adhesion to evolution his historical writing was not, as has so often been claimed, philosophical. Far from making any original contribution of material or interpretation, he merely narrated conspicuous facts, and he did that not authoritatively, but with a charm of style rare among American historians. He never got below the surface and his reliance upon secondary works not seldom involved him in errors of fact." [8]

Neither the popular nor the scholarly view provides an adequate assessment of Fiske's real contribution to American life and thought. Both fail for the same reason; they examine Fiske as if he were essentially a philosopher or historian, while Fiske's importance actually lay in what he contributed to popular culture. Uncritical acceptance of publicity releases distorted the image of Fiske held by most of his contemporaries. Scholars helped correct this by revealing the sources from which Fiske drew his ideas and demonstrating his factual errors. But tributes to his charming prose style fail to answer the key questions raised by his career. They do not adequately explain how Fiske won his success, why he was so widely praised; nor do they explain the relation of his career to the important intellectual and social developments of his day.

The present work is an attempt to deal with these problems by narrating the facts of Fiske's life as they appear in his personal correspondence and published writings, and by showing how his life interacted with contemporary developments in the fields of science, philosophy, religion, and history. His religious thought and its relation to his time is a convenient unifying thread, since it connected the various areas in which he worked, affecting his view of science and history, and helping attract popular attention. Studying Fiske's life to see how he came to say what he did, how he went about com-

[8] J. T. Adams, "John Fiske," *Dictionary of American Biography,* VI (New York, 1931), 422–423.

municating with his audience, and how and why they responded to him, should provide not only a more realistic view of Fiske's career but, hopefully, also some insight into the way a significant part of the American population reacted to the intellectual and social changes of the age.

II

John Fiske grew up in Middletown, Connecticut, the home of his mother's family. In this quiet New England town along the banks of the Connecticut River, where no factories had yet come, and where ocean-going sailing ships still occasionally docked, Fiske spent his childhood and early youth, until his departure for college.

During Fiske's youth Middletown proudly remembered its eighteenth-century greatness. In that earlier day the aggressive energies of its merchants had made it the major port of Connecticut, despite its location well up the Connecticut River from Long Island Sound. In population and wealth, Middletown then compared favorably with Hartford and New Haven. From its wharves foodstuffs, cattle, and lumber were exported to the West Indies in return for tropical produce, including molasses for the local rum distillery. Shipyards echoed along the waterfront, busy with orders from New York merchants and Nantucket whalers. Even after the American Revolution, the town retained sufficient trade for the new nation to locate the customs house for western Connecticut there, and in 1817 the Second Bank of the United States considered it significant enough to open a branch.

But the tightening of British imperial control over the sugar islands after the end of the Napoleonic wars destroyed the West Indies trade. The town relied on water transport while other areas turned to railroads. The result was a sharp decline in relative importance. Few factories came, and by mid-century the major use of the port was to ship brownstone from local quarries to New York City. In Fiske's youth the town rested quietly in the doldrums. Although no absolute decline in wealth was yet visible, its competitors for preeminence had long surpassed it and energetic young men left home to seek their fortunes in the large cities or in the West.[9]

[9] D. D. Field, *Centennial Address with Historical Sketches of . . . Middletown*

In Middletown the Fisks (John did not add an "e" to his name until 1860; he was baptized Edmund Fisk Green in 1842 and changed his name to John Fisk in 1855) had an honored place. The head of the family had achieved almost hereditary succession to the office of town clerk. Four Fisks, three of them named John, occupied the office nearly continuously from 1722 to 1847. The incumbent in 1840, the John Fisk who was the great-grandfather of the subject of this study, lived in one of the better sections of the city in a large house with ample grounds overlooking the Great Bend of the Connecticut River. With him were his second wife, his widowed daughter (Mrs. Polly Bound), and his granddaughter (Mary Fisk Bound). Their life was leisurely and did not lack culture. The house was well supplied with religious literature befitting a family of pious Congregationalists and over the year editions of the classics of English and European literature, as well as standard historical works and school textbooks in mathematics and science, had been added to the bookshelves.[10]

John Fiske's father, Edmund Brewster Green, came to Middletown in 1833 to attend Wesleyan University. Although the son of a Quaker merchant of Smyrna, Delaware, Green affected Southern standards of dress and speech attractive to the young ladies of Middletown, among them Mary Fisk Bound. He completed the scientific course of study offered at the University, but did not take a degree, leaving Wesleyan in the middle of his senior year to study law in the office of a practicing attorney.

In 1840 Green abandoned the law for a career in journalism, becoming editor and part owner of the *New England Review,* a weekly Whig journal published in Hartford. Feeling now able to support a family, he married Mary Bound on September 14, 1840, and moved with her to Hartford where their only child, Edmund Fisk Green, was born on March 30, 1842.

The *Review* proved a financial failure and Green could not provide for his wife and child. Early in 1843 he sold out his interest to

and its Parishes (Middletown, 1853), pp. 61–63, 124, 152–158. A. Brainerd, *Middletown Illustrated* (Westchester, Conn. [1877]), pp. 9–13. JF, "The Story of a New England Town," *Atlantic Monthly,* 86:730–734 (December 1900).

[10] JF to Abby, Jan. 19, 1862; Manuscript Autobiographical Notes, HHL.

try his luck as journalist in New York City. Since Green was unable to support the infant, his grandmother and great-grandfather took him to Middletown. There, in a household of elderly people, he passed his childhood and early youth.

Green found earning a living in New York as arduous as it had been in Hartford. His wife taught in a school for young ladies to supplement her husband's income from the *Saturday Review* and other Whig organs. After the victory of Zachary Taylor as Whig presidential candidate in the 1848 elections, Green moved to Washington where he became secretary to Henry Clay and enlisted the Senator's aid in his search for a government office. But this, too, failed, and in 1850 he disappointedly returned to New York.

Attracted by news of the Gold Rush, Green decided to try his luck in California. In December 1850 he left New York, intending to cross the isthmus of Panama and continue on to San Francisco. Finding conditions in Panama ripe for the establishment of an English newspaper, Green remained there and started the *Panama Herald*. Except for a brief trip back to the United States in the spring of 1852, Green never saw his wife or son again; on July 11, 1852, he died of cholera in an epidemic that swept over Panama.

During these years Mrs. Green remained in the New York area as a schoolteacher, seeing her son, who continued to live with his grandparents, only during brief visits home. The major influences on the young boy's life were the elderly people among whom he lived—his great-grandfather until his death in 1847, his great-grandfather's second wife ("the ancient Mrs. Fisk," the young boy called her), his grandmother, and his grandmother's second husband, Elias Lewis. With these last three he continued to live until he left Middletown for college in 1860.[11]

Young Edmund was a model boy. Spoiled by the old people, with no close friends among children of his own age, he lived a serious, quiet life, and early developed an interest in books that led his elders to regard him as a child prodigy. He learned to read before beginning formal schooling and soon began to explore the well-stocked

[11] *Alumni Record of Wesleyan University* (Hartford, 1883), p. 350. JF to Abby, Jan. 19, 1862, HHL. Charles Fisk Bound, "Personal Reminiscences Concerning John Fiske," manifold copy in HUL.

shelves of the large house. By the time he was twelve he had read widely in history and English literature, as well as in the Greek and Latin classics. When he was fifteen a friend of the family stored a piano in the house on which the boy taught himself to play; many pleasant hours were spent alone with his music.

From the first he much preferred to be alone or with his elders rather than associate with the rough and noisy town boys who terrorized him on the streets and in school, teasing him for his effeminate manners, tearing his neat clothes, and defacing his books. In the evenings he liked to sit with his grandmother, watching her embroider and sew, and telling her of his reading during the day. Sometimes he took a hand in the work, embroidering several cushion covers for her. He also learned to sew and enjoyed helping the village seamstress during her regular visits to the Fisk household to make the family clothes. His outdoor exercise took the form of lonely walks about the quiet outskirts of the village, or rows on the placid rivers near Middletown.[12]

The quiet days of his childhood in Middletown, disturbed only by occasional fights with boys, entranced the youth. He was not at all happy when his mother decided upon a second marriage. Edwin Wallace Stoughton, a successful New York lawyer and friend of her first husband, proposed to Mrs. Green in 1854. After some discussion with her family, she accepted him and the two were married in Middletown in March 1855.

This marriage, which greatly improved his mother's financial position, benefited her son as well. Mr. Stoughton provided the funds to remove the boy from the Middletown schools, where the other students baited him, to a boarding school in Stamford, Connecticut, which prepared for Yale College. Yet his letters showed much jealousy and discontent. He was lonely in boarding school and pleaded with his mother to visit him often. Rarely did he refer to his stepfather; and his references to his own father were often defensive. When he mentioned the winter of his mother's remarriage, he rhetorically exclaimed, "Oh that its recollections could be blotted out." All through Fiske's life his relations with his stepfather re-

---

[12] JF to Abby, Jan. 19, 1862; JF to his mother, Aug. 9, 1854; Manuscript Autobiographical Notes, HHL. Bound, "Reminiscences," 3–10.

mained uneasy. He tended to underestimate or forget the benefits his stepfather conferred on him and accused Stoughton of being jealous of him.[13]

Shortly after his mother remarried, Edmund legally changed his name to John Fisk, taking the name of his recently deceased great-grandfather at the request of his grandmother. He was now the only living male descendant in his line and she did not want her father's name to die out. The young boy continued to make his home in Middletown with his grandmother, going there during vacations rather than to New York.[14]

At the Betts Academy at Stamford, John continued his career as a model boy, standing at the head of his class and carrying off all prizes for composition and declamation during his two years there. Outside the classroom he avoided his schoolmates and abstained from all sports. During the required play periods "he would don his overcoat in cold weather, stand in some sheltered spot during the recess, and at the first signal, would hastily make his way back into the schoolroom." He continued his independent reading, going on with his exploration of the classics of world literature and history.[15]

III

The orthodox Congregational Calvinism of Connecticut saturated the religious atmosphere of young John's home and school. But by the 1850's Connecticut Calvinism had already begun to depart from its original strict adherence to the concepts of an omnipotent God arbitrarily saving or damning wholly sinful and helpless men, who worked out their destinies in a universe which passively awaited His dramatic interventions. Although doctrinal changes were held to a minimum, shifts in the concepts of God, Man, and the Universe, and of their interrelations altered the significance of dogmas, while keeping them verbally intact.

In the seventeenth century New England theology had empha-

---

[13] JF to his mother, May 7, 1855, Jan. 2, 1857; JF to Abby, Jan. 19, 1862, HHL (quotation from letter of Jan. 2, 1857).

[14] JF to his mother, Apr. 26, 1855, Jan. 4, 1856; JF to Abby, Jan. 19, 1862, HHL.

[15] F. W. Osborn, "John Fiske as a Schoolboy," *Education,* 22:206–208 (December 1901), quotation from p. 206. JF to his mother, Apr. 4, 1857; JF to Abby, Jan. 19, 1862, HHL.

sized the power and sovereignty of God and the weakness of man. By the mid-nineteenth century new meanings had become attached to the old terminology. Even those who labored mightily to maintain the old system had inevitably modified it. Jonathan Edwards restated and reinvigorated Calvinist doctrines; yet his own emphasis on revivals and the experience of conversion encouraged attitudes that diverged from his theological position. Revivalistic practice, especially as it developed in the nineteenth century, called upon man actively to turn to God, and did not completely match the view of man that considered him entirely helpless. Edwards' successors stressed the ability and power of man to attain salvation and affect the world in which he lived, while continuing to speak of him as helpless in contrast to God.

Eighteenth- and nineteenth-century science inevitably affected the view of the universe held by theologians. While verbally battling against rationalism, they came themselves more and more to accept the idea that much of nature could be explained in reasonable, uniform terms which man could comprehend. They did not adopt, as rationalists did, a closed system or block universe which excluded miraculous interventions by God, but they did place major emphasis on arguments from design in which the regular and successful functioning of the universe demonstrated God's mind and hand at work. This was still pious, yet it had come a long way from the older view which found its evidence of God's plan in earthquakes, plagues, and other dramatic interruptions of the regular course of nature.

The position of God in such a universe was not clearly worked out. Orthodoxy could not accept a "clockmaker God" who started the universe and thereafter abstained from further intervention. But if regularity and uniformity were signs of the foresight and power of God, irregularities and interventions might be termed signs of lack of foresight and power. Few dealt explicitly with this problem. More often thinkers tried to combine both sides of the argument, to see in uniformity and law the designing mind of God, and to see in areas where no clear pattern could be discerned evidence of direct intervention that proved the immediate concern of God for man. Biology, where science could as yet explain little, provided a favorite field for analogy. Organic nature showed regularity in the sense that each species had been constant since the moment of creation; yet it also demonstrated divine intervention, since each species was the direct result of God's will with no intermediate laws or forces intervening between the creature and his maker. In the close adaptation of life to environment the pious mind found direct proof of the omnipotence and benevolence of God.

Not only the relation of God to the universe, but also his relation to man was no longer simple. When revivals put emphasis on the power and ability of man to achieve good, to make himself worthy of God, it became harder to believe that this effort was irrelevant to God. The older concept of an incalculable, unpredictable Deity who damned thousands and saved a few for incomprehensible reasons of his own became more difficult to believe. Orthodox theologians rarely overtly faced the question of whether some way could be found to state the relation of God to man in a uniform, predictable manner, as had already been done with the relation of God to the universe. Most of them continued to use modified versions of the doctrines associated with God's incomprehensible omnipotence, while their preaching in effect assured listeners that the acts of man mattered, that goodness would be saved while evil was punished. These tendencies were then still operating below the level of consciousness, but by the end of the century became visible even to defenders of orthodoxy.[16]

In debates and religious controversies of the last half of the nineteenth century, enemies of orthodoxy attacked the verbal positions to which the Calvinist denominations were formally committed and ignored the actual practices that ruled in daily religious life and preaching. Defenders of orthodoxy frequently found themselves in the embarrassing position of trying to sustain doctrines from which they had already begun to deviate in their everyday religious life.

In this religious atmosphere John Fiske grew up, listening to preachers who insisted on the utter depravity and helplessness of man while calling on him to take steps to save himself, and who theologically based all salvation upon faith while urging their parish-

[16] See Frank W. Foster, *A Genetic History of New England Theology* (Chicago, 1907), George P. Fisher, *History of Christian Doctrine* (New York, 1896), pp. 394–418, and G. Frederick Wright, *Story of My Life and Work* (Oberlin, Ohio, 1916).

ioners to daily good works as a means of pleasing their God. His grandmother and the rest of his family formally avowed these doctrines and John, as a model boy, followed early in their footsteps. He regularly attended services and prayer meetings and sang in the choir of the North Congregational Church of Middletown to which his family belonged.

The experience of conversion occupied a central position in the religious life of the period. With major doctrines stressing the need for man to undergo the saving action of God's grace out of his own free will, the peak of religious life and experience became the moment in which weak, depraved man found it possible to dedicate his life to Christ and experienced an assurance that his action was acceptable. All revival practices were organized to aid the achievement of this ecstatic experience. With the grace of God now aiding his corrupt will, the life of the believer should alter and good deeds abound. Piety and ethical conduct should mark his behavior and set him apart from the unsaved who depended solely on their unaided will to guide their daily lives.

In October of 1856, at the age of fourteen, a year after his mother's remarriage, Fiske responded to the environment in which he was raised and underwent a conversion experience. His age was not unusually low. From the early teens pressure for conversion was heavy; since youth was a time of great temptations, there could be no better moment to turn to Christ for assistance. The few letters that survive from the period immediately following Fiske's conversion breathe the air of sanctity. He formally joined the North Congregational Church, sang in the choir, taught Sunday School and Bible class, and took part in the singing and exhortation at prayer and revival meetings. He considered undertaking as his life's work the tracing out of God's providence as shown in history. For New Year, 1857, he sent his mother a pious wish: "May we live so that in future years, we may look back upon it as one spent in the service of the meek and lowly Jesus. . . . Mother, I wish you many 'Happy New Years' and that we may meet to spend a happy eternity in Heaven is the prayer of your son." [17]

This mood apparently lasted through much of 1857 and 1858, fed

[17] Manuscript Autobiographical Notes: JF to his mother, Jan. 2, 1857, Mar. 27, 1858, HHL. Manuscript Class Book, Harvard Class of 1863, p. 275, HUA.

by an upsurge of emotion as the last of the great national revivals swept the country in these years. But as revival fever waned, so too did Fiske's fervor. His new status had had little effect on his life or behavior. John continued to live much as before, still devoting twelve or more hours a day to his books. His conversion and Sunday School preaching did not make him any more attractive to his contemporaries than had high grades or neat clothing. Nor did it cure his emotional failings; the pious New Year's letter quoted above contained slighting allusions to his mother's remarriage and other indications that religion had not diminished his jealousy of his stepfather.

The religious view of the world failed to satisfy Fiske intellectually. Although at the time he expressed little direct dissatisfaction with New England theology, the eagerness with which he adopted the views of the "positivists" as soon as they were brought to his attention and the terms in which he praised them indicated the lack he felt in his earlier opinions. He acclaimed Alexander von Humboldt's and Henry Thomas Buckle's simple, uniform explanation of all phenomena, in implicit contrast with the dualistic view of the world that he was abandoning. Humboldt's *Cosmos* showed "vast learning & comprehensive thought," he told his mother, and assured her that "Buckle's system is founded on a very broad & comprehensive generalization." The search for a unified view of the universe that would bring the totality of phenomena into easily comprehensible generalizations became a recurrent theme in Fiske's intellectual pursuits for the rest of his life.[18]

IV

As Fiske's intellectual horizons broadened, two young men in Middletown, John Langdon Dudley, the minister at the South Congregational Church, and George Litch Roberts, a student at Wesleyan University, strongly attracted him.

Dudley had read widely in the literature of German idealism and American Transcendentalism. He considered himself a disciple of Fichte and followed his master in stressing ethical and emotional aspects of religion rather than doctrine. Although Dudley had not

[18] JF to his mother, Oct. 8, 1858, Nov. [15], 1859, HHL.

yet carried his divergence from orthodoxy to the degree that would later lead to his dismissal by a Congregational church in Milwaukee and his enlistment in the Unitarian ranks, his sermons formed a striking contrast to those of the Reverend Jeremiah Taylor in the North Church where John's family regularly attended. As he began to draw away from orthodoxy, John split his Sunday devotions between the two churches, often attending the North Church in the morning to sing in the choir and going for the evening services to Dudley's South Church. "Black John," as Fiske came to call Dudley, soon won his respect and affection. In later years, after the minister had moved to Wisconsin, Fiske always remembered to visit him when his lecture tours brought him that way. When first married, he insisted that his wife express her admiration of "Black John's" sermons. In 1884 he dedicated his *Excursions of an Evolutionist* to Dudley in gratitude for the time when he "used to listen with delight to your preaching and come to you for sympathy and counsel in my studies." [19]

Stimulated by Dudley, Fiske turned away from pious supporters of orthodoxy and began to read books that questioned the religious ideas on which he had been brought up. In 1858 he carefully read Hugh Miller's *Testimony of the Rocks,* which demonstrated how geology supported the orthodox theory of creation, and James Barr Walker's *God Revealed in the Process of Creation and by the Manifestation of Jesus Christ.* By 1859, however, Fiske preferred Horace Bushnell's *Nature and the Supernatural* and Theodore Parkers' *Discourse of Religion.* These last two writers each stimulated important changes in American religious thought. Bushnell, who remained within the official bounds of the Calvinist churches while carrying out his revisionary work, had a greater influence on American Protestantism as a whole, but Parker's work most impressed Fiske.

Both men attacked what they considered objectionable in the religious world about them. But Bushnell desired to reform pre-

[19] JF to his mother, Aug. 2, 1858, November 1859, Dec. 8, 1863; JF to Abby, Sep. 15, 1872, Apr. 22, 1891, HHL. JF to Abby, Feb. 18, 1881, LC. JF, "Dedication" to *Excursions of an Evolutionist* (Boston, 1902). *Christian Register,* 73:794 (Dec. 6, 1894).

vailing practices, whereas Parker tended to reject them outright. In his very influential *Christian Nurture,* Bushnell provided a theoretical base encouraging a stress upon the careful upbringing of children in religious faith and morality rather than the agonies of conversion and revivalism. His *Nature and the Supernatural, Together Constituting One System of God* interested Fiske more since it tried to interpret the universe according to a unified system. Bushnell carried further the tendency in American Calvinism to think of the world as a consistent whole. His two books proved very useful to Protestants of all denominations after the Civil War, for they provided a means of adapting to the decline of belief in revivals and the challenge of science. But for Fiske, as his reading in science increased his knowledge, Bushnell's synthesis was not finally convincing. He grew increasingly critical of Bushnell's attempt to use analogies from nature to prove the cosmological necessity of redemption by Christ; Bushnell's influence on Fiske did not last.[20]

As a Unitarian rebelling within a sect that had already cast off much of Calvinism, Parker was more radical than Bushnell. Fiske found him more attractive. Parker dropped most of the characteristic doctrines of Christianity as "transient" and stressed what he termed "absolute" religion—belief in God, in immortality, in morality. Since these could be intuitively verified, Parker thought they were clearly absolute truths. Parker shocked his contemporaries by asserting that "if Christianity be true at all, it would be just as true if Herod or Catiline had taught it." He argued that "when it is said that the doctrines of religion . . . rest on their own authority . . . then if all the evangelists and apostles were liars; if Jesus were mistaken in a thousand things; if he were a hypocrite; yes, if he never lived, but the New Testament were a sheer forgery from end to end, these doctrines are just the same, absolute truth." [21]

While Dudley widened Fiske's religious horizons, George Litch Roberts introduced him to the positivists. The two had met when

---

[20] Horace Bushnell, *Nature and the Supernatural* (New York, 1858), *Christian Nurture* (New York, 1861). T. T. Munger, *Horace Bushnell* (Boston, 1899). JF, Manuscript List of Books Read, 1858–1859; Manuscript Autobiographical Notes, HHL.

[21] Theodore Parker, *A Discourse of Matters Pertaining to Religion* (Boston, 1907), quotations from pp. 217, 239–240; *The Transient and Permanent in Christianity* (Boston, 1908), pp. 1–39.

singing in the church choir shortly after Fiske returned to Middletown from Stamford. Despite the fact that Roberts was five years
older, they found each other stimulating companions and began to
take long walks every evening during which they discussed their
readings in recent works of science and philosophy. After becoming
a lawyer, Roberts put his interest in science to practical uses; he
became a leading patent attorney employed by the Bell Telephone
Company and the American Telephone and Telegraph Company.
But while at Wesleyan, Roberts' interest, like that of Fiske, took the
form of a search for a comprehensive world-view which would
render the universe and man's place in it easily intelligible. In May
1859 Roberts brought Fiske a copy of the first volume of Henry
Thomas Buckle's *History of Civilization in England*. Fiske de-
voured it, deeply impressed by the attempt to explain political and
mental behavior in terms of physical causation. Here at last was a
theory which promised to unify the physical and intellectual worlds
and make both meaningful.[22]

Buckle stimulated the two young men to search further for a
physical rather than a religious explanation of the universe. Together
they ransacked Middletown, avidly borrowing every scientific book
they could locate. The list of books read by Fiske in 1858-59 included
surveys of many branches of science, but that which impressed him
most was Alexander von Humboldt's *Cosmos*. Here he found an
attempt to present a unified view of all nature, "in which all phenomena and energies are revealed as one entity pulsating with inner
life." [23] Fiske also revelled in Goethe's *Faust*, which he found more
fascinating than current events. When the Civil War broke out in
1861, he wrote "What's war when a fellow has 'Kosmos' on his shelf,
and 'Faust' on his table?" [24] The Faustian attempt to grasp the
meaning of the universe expressed with poetic fervor and power an
aspiration akin to his own.

As Fiske's reading in science and the philosophy of science pro-

[22] *Who Was Who in America* (Chicago, 1942), I, 1040. JF to Abby, Jan. 19,
1862; Manuscript List of Books Read, 1858–1859, HHL.

[23] Helmut de Terra, *The Life and Times of Alexander von Humboldt* (New York,
1955), p. 370, quoting from Humboldt's introduction to Vol. I of *Cosmos*.

[24] JF to G. L. Roberts, April 1861, quoted in J. S. Clark, *Life and Letters of John
Fiske*, 2 vols. (Boston, 1917), I, 237. (The manuscript of this letter could not be
found.)

gressed, as he dipped into the writings of John Stuart Mill and George Henry Lewes, he was inevitably drawn to Auguste Comte's *Positive Philosophy,* the work whose title gave rise to the then popular epithet, "positivist," applied to all thinkers who explored the philosophic implications of the new scientific advances. At first reading, Comte's system seemed to Fiske to provide what he had been searching for. Comte supplied what Buckle had awakened his appetite for, what Humboldt's too exclusively physical description of the universe failed to achieve completely. Here was a thinker who not only saw the need for, but appeared to succeed in, carrying out the unification of all knowledge into one simple comprehensible scheme. "I am now reading . . . Comte's Positive Philosophy, translated by Miss Martineau," he noted late in 1859. "During the remainder of the winter I hope to study principally . . . the studies which lie at the foundation of a Positive Education." Beginning to believe that science was the discipline of the future, he seriously considered abandoning the usual literary college course for which he had been preparing and taking a scientific degree instead.[25]

His exploration of the work of the positivists drew Fiske further and further from the beliefs of his youth. By the spring of 1869 he could write his mother: "I have only kept up my relations with the North Church to please Grandmother. What further use could there be in it? Is it honest for me to go and sit there on communion-day & eat that bread, &c., while feeling it all mummery? Is it honest for me to sing hymns which I don't believe in?"[26]

Outwardly he remained a model boy, studying hard and singing in the choir. But he could not resist talking of his intellectual discoveries and word soon spread around Middletown that the bright young Fiske boy had turned infidel. His grandmother turned a deaf ear to all stories, even refusing to believe the Reverend Mr. Taylor when he came to speak to her about it. Not until she asked John and heard him boldly avow that he did not believe in the divinity

[25] Quotation from Manuscript List of Books Read, 1858–1859, HHL. JF to his mother [January 1861], Feb. 2, 1860, HHL. Auguste Comte, *The Positive Philosophy, Fully Translated and Condensed by Harriet Martineau* (New York, 1858). Woodbridge Riley, "La philosophie française en Amérique; ii, Le positivisme," *Revue philosophique,* 87:369–423 (Mai-Juin, 1919).

[26] JF to his mother, Mar. 20, 1860, HHL.

of Christ or the inspiration of the Bible did she accept the story as
true. When she did, Fiske's position became very uncomfortable.
His grandmother began to treat him as if he were slightly insane.
The town drew itself away from him on the streets as if he were an
"imp of darkness." Taylor tried unsuccessfully to argue with the
young man, but John arrogantly assured his mother that "error
needs an abler head than his [Taylor's] to sustain it." His mother
wrote expostulating with him, but John exasperatingly replied, "You
feel as the Hindu parent does when the missionary takes away her
son to Christianity," and even tried to convert her from her old
faith. "I wish you would let me reason with you on the subject, for
I hate to have my dear mother fettered by what I deem a very un-
happy system of superstition." Since the situation in Middletown
had become very uncomfortable for him, he asked permission to
move to Cambridge and continue his preparation for college there.[27]

Fiske informed a minister who tried to argue with him that he
had "found a religion better suited to my needs than Christianity,"
and over and over proudly referred to himself as an "infidel." [28]
By infidel, however, he did not mean atheist. At no time did Fiske
question the existence of God or the value of morality. Fiske accepted the beliefs which Parker called the absolute truths of religion
(except, perhaps, for immortality, on which he did not then comment). He rebelled only against orthodox Calvinist dogma in its
most extreme form. To that extent he rejected Christianity. That
there could be any other definition of Christianity did not occur
to him. The Calvinists among whom he grew up were sure that
Theodore Parker had placed himself outside the Christian pale
and were deeply suspicious of Horace Bushnell. Fiske was an infidel in the same sense as they.

Yet Fiske was certain he had gone beyond and improved on Bushnell and Parker. Under the stimulus of his admiration for Dudley,
Fiske had explored their positions, but had concluded that they were
neither scientific nor comprehensive enough. Their view was still
too irrational, claimed too much for the supernatural, and did not
explicitly organize the facts of the world. Fiske complained of Bush-

[27] *Ibid.*
[28] JF to J. E. Barnes, Apr. 9, 1860, HHL.

nell's "total ignorance of physical science," and, although he did not openly attack Parker, knowledge of science was not a strong point of the Unitarian's position. To Fiske neither Bushnell's modernized theology nor Parker's religious version of Transcendentalism provided the concrete and comprehensive world view he sought. In May 1860, when he was eighteen, he described how he had arrived at a position which satisfied him. "I . . . read 'Kosmos' and the 'Positive Philosophy.' This was an era in my life. . . . [I] found both a philosophy & a religion which met all my wants, & filled me with such joy as I had never known before." Despite his rejection of the Calvinist conversion philosophy, Fiske described his reaction to scientific thought in terminology that might be used by a revivalist urging men to come forward for Christ.[29]

Fiske's infidelity did not involve social radicalism. He felt he occupied a satisfactory social position and saw no reason to desire any changes. Though insisting that ethics were central to all religion and part of his new view as well as of Christianity, Fiske put no stress on duty or responsibility. He shifted because of intellectual, not social, discontent, and he went on accepting Christian ethics as practiced in Middletown as the highest possible formulation. He assured his mother that he would not deviate from that standard of conduct.

At each stage of his intellectual progress Fiske had been certain that he now believed the absolute truth. After his conversion, it was Calvinist Christianity. As he began to doubt the tenets of his childhood faith, he held fast to the Reverend Mr. Dudley. As he pushed on, positivism became the peak of all the history of thought. Nothing more clearly indicated the strength of his inner need for security than his continuous insistence on attaining absolute certainty.

Lonely and isolated, with most of his growing energies concentrated on his intellectual life, he felt it necessary always to be in the right, to turn in perfect examination papers at all times. Scientific support, which he thought he had found in positivism, seemed the most secure position possible. In his rhapsodies on the views he adopted, Fiske never asked whether absolute certainty was fully compatible with a scientific, experimental way of thinking, for Fiske

[29] JF to J. E. Barnes, May 1860, HHL.

thought of science not as a method of investigation but as a source of absolute truth. At every stage Fiske felt completely sure that he had actually attained greater insight into ultimate truth than anyone else around him, an attitude at the root of his public rejection of Middletown religious beliefs and the superior air which he assumed when his open defection from Calvinism precipitated a family crisis.

CHAPTER TWO

A SPENCERIAN
AT HARVARD

John Fiske's growing interest in science and scholarship affected his educational ideas as well as his religious development. During the same years, 1857 to 1859, in which he explored the writings of the positivists and rejected orthodoxy, his scholastic ideal underwent radical changes as he sought ways to satisfy his ambitious dreams of intellectual success.

Fiske originally intended, when he returned to Middletown from the Betts School in April 1857, to engage a tutor for the spring and summer, enter Yale in the fall, and take his degree by nineteen. A friend of the family recommended the Reverend Henry M. Colton, but Fiske's first impression was decidedly unfavorable. Colton charged high fees and laughed at the boy's previous preparation. Fiske decided to study with him only because he was assured that Colton's recommendation would secure almost certain admission to Yale and because his grandmother reassured him about the cost.[1]

Within a week he was enthusiastic about Colton's methods. A language scholar of some repute who had edited several texts, Colton insisted that his students do more than just memorize conjugations and limp their way through a translation. It was not unusual for him to keep his small group of boys working an entire morning

---

[1] JF to his mother, May [17?], 1857, May 23, 1857, HHL.

over one third of a page of Greek. He demanded that the students achieve a clear, flowing translation of each passage and also analyze every word to trace its etymology and compare its root with similar words in Latin, Hebrew, Sanskrit, French, and German. "Although I have been with him only three days, I can already see the beautiful and wonderful relations between these parallel languages," John enthusiastically assured his mother.[2]

Colton gave Fiske his first direct contact with a world of scholarship beyond that of drilling young boys to pass college entrance examinations. Although Yale did not require French and German for entrance, the men Colton trained had a basic knowledge of both and benefited thereby. This introduction to comparative linguistics gave Fiske his first taste of the new science of philology, which attempted to reduce the apparently unrelated details of language to a carefully ordered developmental pattern. Fiske never lost the interest in linguistics and philology which this early training stimulated.

Under Colton's influence Fiske changed his plans. Impressed by stories of men who entered Yale young and ruined their health by overwork, he now proposed to stay with Colton for a year or two, then go on studying on his own while teaching school, and wait to enter Yale until he was over twenty-one or twenty-two. With this preparation he expected to "take the valedictory, and render myself immortal—*for a Yale valedictorian is immortalized*." He assured his mother that this deviation from his earlier plan would work out for the best. "I have but one life to live & I cannot live too well. I cannot learn too much, nor take too high a niche in the Temple of Fame. . . . *I do want to stand high in college & I can't do that if I enter now*."[3]

Fiske remained with Colton two years, studying not only the languages Colton required but also branching out on his own. He diligently continued his Greek and Latin preparation for college, mastered French and German, and in addition picked up a smattering of Sanskrit and Hebrew. On his own he studied Spanish, Italian, and Portuguese. In both 1857 and 1858 he attended the Yale commencement exercises and familiarized himself with campus and

[2] JF to his mother, May 26, 1857, HHL.
[3] JF to his mother, May 26, 1857, HHL (italics in source).

student life. In July of 1859 he passed the Freshman examinations at Yale, but in mid-August he urgently wrote to his mother for permission to stay out of college another year and then try for admission to Harvard with advanced standing.[4]

It was at this juncture that he had moved sharply away from the faith of his childhood. Most Middletown men (including the Fisks) went to Yale; none had gone to Harvard since the seventeenth century. Yet Yale, a citadel of orthodoxy, was distasteful to John once he publicly rejected the faith in which he had been raised. In contrast, Harvard's reputation for "infidelism" made it appear a more congenial atmosphere in which to spend his college years. Harvard also offered more work in languages and science. Yale permitted the election of only one semester of work in any modern language; Harvard provided a comparatively wide choice. When his mother objected to the laxity of Harvard, John assured her that he would not need discipline to keep him studying. While agreeing that Harvard was "a bad place for a careless scholar," he argued that it was "unequalled in facilities for an ambitious one." [5] There he could carry on his efforts to train himself as a scientist and linguist. He received his mother's consent to continue studying on his own and try for Sophomore standing at Harvard the following year.

II

On May 18, 1860, Fiske arrived in Boston, staying with a friend of the family, Judge Benjamin R. Curtis, until he finally settled his plans. From the beginning John found Boston and Cambridge congenial. On his first Sunday he went with Judge Curtis to the Unitarian services at King's Chapel where he greatly enjoyed the elaborate music and unfamiliar ritual. He joyfully described the relaxed way the Curtis family observed Sunday, in implicit contrast with the rigid Sabbath at Middletown. George Roberts, who had now entered the office of a Boston lawyer, welcomed him, and the two friends

[4] JF to his mother, Aug. 1, 1857, Aug. 2, 1858, Dec. 28, 1858, July 26, 1859, [August] 1859; JF to Abby, Jan. 19, 1862, HHL.

[5] JF to his mother, [August] 1859, HHL. "List of College Graduates from Middletown," appended to D. D. Field, *Centennial Address* (Middletown, 1853), pp. 219–255. *Yale University Catalogue, 1859–1860. Harvard University Catalogue, 1859–1860.*

wandered through the Boston bookstores where John feasted his eyes on works by admired positivist writers—J. S. Mill, H. T. Buckle, Herbert Spencer, Alexander Bain, Charles Darwin, and Sir Charles Lyell—piled up awaiting purchasers.[6]

Judge Curtis accompanied Fiske to Cambridge, helped him find and furnish a room near the College Yard, interviewed President Cornelius C. Felton to make sure that John's plans met all college regulations, and located the best tutor in Cambridge, who shocked Fiske by asking for a dollar an hour. At two hours a day this would come to $172 by the first of September, more than the cost of two years' tuition at Harvard. After his mother approved paying this much—his stepfather had offered to meet all the costs of Fiske's education, including tutoring—he settled down to regular study in preparation for the entrance examinations at the end of August.[7]

When Fiske arrived in 1860 Cambridge was still a rural village. Open fields extended in all directions, and a mighty elm, which rose where the subway kiosk now stands, dominated Harvard Square. The horsecars to Boston ran only on weekdays, and the time consumed by the eight-mile trip behind plodding horses kept the journey in the category of a minor excursion. The Harvard Square shopping area was self-sufficient; Fiske seems rarely to have shopped in Boston except for books. While Cambridge had many bookstores, nothing there equalled the magnificent stock in the Little, Brown or Ticknor, Fields sales rooms.[8]

To Fiske, however, Cambridge did not seem at all rural. Though in size and physical appearance it might be inferior to Middletown, its intellectual resources and activity thrilled the young man. On the quiet streets he might see Louis Agassiz or Asa Gray, or perhaps even "encounter, with a thrill of pleasure not untinged with awe, Longfellow and Lowell walking side by side." [9] In June he and Roberts called on George Ticknor, who welcomed the young men in a library which seemed to Fiske "the most splendid room of the

[6] JF to Lizzie Wilcox, May 25, 1860; JF to his mother, June 17, 1860, HHL.

[7] JF to his mother, May 28, 1860, Manuscript Autobiographical Notes, HHL.

[8] JF, "Cambridge as Village and City," in *A Century of Science* (Boston, 1902), pp. 298–301. All citations to Fiske's books are to the 1902 collected edition, unless otherwise indicated.

[9] *Ibid.*, p. 301.

kind I was ever in. It is full of beautiful paintings & fine statuary . . . besides an immense collection of books: the Spanish books alone could be counted in thousands instead of hundreds." Ticknor's offer to permit him to use the library any time he desired delighted Fiske. In September Fiske and another student traveled to Concord on a sightseeing trip, in the course of which they met and had tea with Ralph Waldo Emerson, sitting in awe as the great man talked with them about science and history, and told anecdotes about Carlyle and others of his friends. "I listened to him as to an oracle," he reported, and he was certain that he could never forget that day.[10]

Above all he raved about the Harvard College Library. The librarian, John Langdon Sibley, gave Fiske access to the locked philology alcove where he found all the great classic authors of the field, Jacob Grimm, Franz Bopp, Wilhelm von Humboldt, many impressive volumes on Asiatic languages that he had not even heard of, "and so many other books that I was nearly driven wild by the sight of them." He grimly determined to master them all.[11]

Stimulated by his surroundings and the opportunities offered by the Cambridge and Boston book shops, Fiske went on a buying spree that drew pained protests from his mother. In the first three months at Cambridge, he spent more than $400, much of it on books, a sum he insisted was not excessive since he had been able to purchase so many bargains.[12]

Despite his outside activity, Fiske's preparation for his entrance examinations went forward steadily. He studied continuously through the summer until his health broke down in August and a doctor ordered him home to Middletown to rest the last two weeks of the month. Although unable to complete the final review he had planned, Fiske passed the Freshman examinations on August 30 and 31 and the advanced standing examination the following day. On September 1, 1860, the Faculty voted to admit him to Harvard College as a Sophomore.[13]

---

[10] JF to Lizzie Wilcox, June 24, 1860, Sept. 16, 1860, HHL.

[11] JF to G. L. Roberts, quoted in J. S. Clark, *Life and Letters of John Fiske,* 2 vols. (Boston, 1917), I, 141–142.

[12] JF to his mother, Sept. 9, 1860, HHL.

[13] JF to his mother, Aug. 15, 1860, Aug. [28?], 1860, [Sept. 4, 1860], HHL. Harvard University, Manuscript Faculty Records, XVI, entries of Aug. 31, 1860 and Sept. 1, 1860, HUA.

In the college catalogue for the year 1860-61 the printer added an "e" to the Fisk name, so that it now read John Fiske. His mother protested the change, but John overrode her objections. "I thought it would look better & more finished," he told her, and also explained that it was already too late to make any changes in the catalogue. "The e will be fastened on by usage here in College and there will be no getting rid of it as I see. I don't see why it isn't my grandfather's name still; & I am utterly unable to see the falsehood in taking an e under the circumstances." Thereafter John spelled the family name Fiske, writing the names of all his mother's ancestors and relatives that way.[14]

III

Despite the high hopes with which Fiske began his college career, and his early enchantment with Cambridge and Harvard, he found his three years there disappointing. Although Harvard's curriculum had seemed to him superior to Yale's, in practice the studies in which he felt the greatest interest either were not given at all or were handled on a very elementary level. The bulk of the courses covered subject matter that he had already studied independently before coming to Harvard.

Ancient languages still largely dominated the curriculum; science and modern languages had only begun to squeeze their way into the offerings. Almost the entire program was prescribed. No electives were permitted in the first two years. In each of the last two years one elective course could be taken for credit; while a second elective could be taken each year, it did not count toward the rank score of the student. All courses were assigned to a specific year and could only be taken then. Even though the Greek and Latin courses included most of the great works of the ancient world, classroom drill concentrated on language rather than on the meaning of the work studied, and few professors took as broad a view of linguistics in their classes as Colton had done with his students.

Greek and Latin were required in each of the first three years and in the Senior year they were replaced by philosophy and history. While mathematics and science were among the assigned courses,

<hr/>

[14] JF to his mother, Sept. 9, 1860, HHL.

the work was on a very simple level. They were taught by lectures supplemented by textbook reading. Laboratory work was available only to postgraduate students.

Modern language courses were few and elementary. The only work in English literature was Professor Francis Child's semester in Anglo-Saxon, required in the Sophomore year. Two years each of French and German were included among the elective studies, and Professor James Russell Lowell offered two years of Spanish and one of Italian.[15]

This curriculum, although more liberal in its offerings than that of any other American university, provided little that was new to Fiske. His studies in science, mathematics, history, and philosophy had already covered more ground than the college required of degree candidates. Only in languages did he find new material. He was introduced to Anglo-Saxon in Professor Child's course. As his two permitted electives Fiske chosen Spanish and Italian. If class work added little to what he had already learned under the stimulus of Colton's tutoring, he did benefit from the reading groups in Dante and Cervantes that Lowell provided for interested students.[16]

Much of the work offered was simple drill and recitation, with little inspiration or understanding communicated to the student, except where an outstanding instructor managed to establish special rapport with some of the undergraduates. Unfortunately, no teacher affected Fiske in this manner. "I am clear that I owe absolutely nothing to Harvard except the friendships formed while there," he wrote in 1884, without too great exaggeration. The only faculty member with whom he formed a close relation, Ephraim W. Gurney, then tutor in Greek and Latin, was more a contemporary with similar interests in positivism than a respected older guide.[17]

---

[15] *Harvard University Catalogue,* 1860–61, pp. 29–31; 1861–62, pp. 31–32; 1862–63, pp. 32–33. *Annual Report of the President of Harvard University,* 1860–61, pp. 17–24; 1861–62, pp. 17–24; 1862–63, pp. 15–24. S. E. Morison, *Three Centuries of Harvard* (Cambridge, Mass., 1936), pp. 344–355. Henry James, *Charles W. Eliot,* 2 vols. (Boston, 1930), I, 205–235.

[16] Harvard University, Manuscript Record of Absences from and Tardiness at Recitations and Lectures, 1861–1863, HUA. JF to Editor, Feb. 13, 1889, *Critic,* 14:92 (Feb. 23, 1889).

[17] JF, Manuscript Autobiographical Notes, HHL.

Fiske's classmates also gained little from a curriculum that had no relation to their future careers or present educational needs. Among the one hundred and five graduates in 1863, fifty-seven had decided on their careers; of these twenty-one planned to become lawyers, sixteen to enter business, and thirteen to train as doctors. Neither law nor medicine then required any undergraduate preparation, nor did the course work aid a career in business. Only the four men intending to teach and the three planning to enter the ministry could be considered to have prepared for careers while at Harvard.[18] For the great majority of the students, the four college years were primarily a pleasant interlude in which to grow up among a group of congenial contemporaries. The most valuable parts of their education came outside the classroom, in such activities as the literary societies in which they explored the resources of English and American literature and thought, and in the games and drinking bouts where they learned to hold their own among their contemporaries.

Fiske took little part in the rich and varied extracurricular activity which engrossed most of his classmates in the leisure time left by a study program that made little demand on them. He ignored sports and, despite his interest in music, failed to join either of the two musical societies. Nor does his name appear in the lists of members of the two science clubs. He joined only one of the six literary and social clubs, the O.K. Society (more active classmates commonly participated in several). His major participation in college life was his service as one of the editors of the undergraduate *Harvard Magazine* in his last year, and the contribution to it of several minor essays during the time he was on its board. He participated little in the social life of his class. Although his friends in the O.K. Society secured his election as Class Supper Odist, Fiske stayed away from the all-night affair at which his song was sung.

Instead of joining in the vigorous social and intellectual life of his class, Fiske preferred to undertake a schedule of outside reading and study that kept him at his desk twelve to sixteen hours a day. To his classmates the sight of the six-foot, slender, bespectacled youth with poetically flowing hair, continually intent on his books, seemed queer

---

[18] "List of Future Plans," in Harvard Class of 1863, Manuscript Class Book, p. 941.

and amusing. In the elaborate Mock Parts worked up by the Class of 1863 as a parody on Commencement Exercises, his classmates assigned Fiske an oration on the theme:

> "Though studying doth please his mind
> He still takes pleasure in a quiet grind."

Fiske's younger friend, Thomas Sergeant Perry, later described "seeing him when he was a student at Cambridge, and how I gazed upon his gaunt frame and pallid face with awe; for he was said to read and study fifteen hours a day, and to be far advanced in atheism;—a sort of Cambridge, Massachusetts, Faust." [19]

To carry on his interest in linguistics, Fiske worked out by March of his first year at Harvard a study schedule which kept him busy from 7:15 in the morning to 11 at night, with two-and-a-half hours each day set aside for meals and exercise. In addition to the Greek, Latin, mathematics, chemistry, and botany he studied for his courses, he allotted time each week to Spanish, Sanskrit, German, Italian, Hebrew, and Danish, as well as to the Anglo-Saxon he had begun the previous semester. Later he would find time to begin, at least, the study of Icelandic, Dutch, Provençal, Roumanian, Zend, Gothic, and Russian. His efforts gave him a background for comparative linguistics matched by very few Americans.[20]

He also undertook heavy reading in philosophy and history. In his first year at Harvard he discovered Herbert Spencer and thereafter the works of the man who became his intellectual mentor bulk large on his reading list, along with the writings of other positivists.[21]

Harvard's disciplinary system caused Fiske difficulty. Since academic work filled up little of the student's time, while college regulations still minutely specified the behavior considered necessary for a gentleman and a scholar, maintenance of discipline became a vexatious problem for the Harvard Faculty. Students were justifiably

---

[19] Harvard Class of 1863, Manuscript Class Book, pp. 165–170, 935–937; Manuscript Mock Parts, Class of 1863, HUA. T. S. Perry, "John Fiske: an Appreciation," *Atlantic Monthly,* 89:630 (May 1902).

[20] JF to Lizzie Wilcox, Mar. 10, [1861], HHL.

[21] JF to Abby, Jan. 19, 1862; Manuscript Autobiographical Notes, HHL.

resentful of the harsh, picayune regulations and the arbitrary manner in which they were applied, and took advantage of their leisure time to think up ways to "bend" the regulations to the maximum. The result was a state of war between Faculty and student. Most Faculty meetings of these years were devoted to discussing disciplinary rather than academic affairs.

The vengeful attitude of the Faculty can be seen in the penalties it imposed. For offenses less serious than those which led to suspension or expulsion, it deducted points from the grade scale used to record academic achievement and to determine class rank. The marking system assigned points for each recitation or exercise; a perfect recitation was worth eight points, while a perfect composition or oration earned twenty-four. Examinations were infrequent, and most grades were based on the accumulation of these day-to-day scores. The marks were totaled at the end of the term and reached into the hundreds for each course. The running total through the four years of college decided class rank. A student of the class of 1863 could have accumulated 27,218 points by the end of his Senior year, and the class valedictorian actually had 24,883. Disciplinary offenses, like cutting class without an excuse, missing morning chapel or Sunday church, failing to hand in an assigned exercise, smoking in the College Yard, or any other of a host of possible infractions of college regulations, were punished by the deduction of points from the grades the student had accumulated in his academic work. If a student missed six recitations or ten morning prayers, he was reported to the Faculty, which then voted to give him a "private admonition," consisting of the deduction of thirty-two points from his grades. Cutting twelve recitations or twenty prayers was punished by a "public admonition," or sixty-four points off the grade scale.[22]

Fiske ran badly afoul of this system, partly due to his resentment of compulsory chapel, but even more to his disappointment at the quality of instruction which led him to cut classes extensively. Despite his later statements to the contrary, his grades in the first year

[22] Harvard University, Manuscript Faculty Records, XVI; Manuscript Record of Absences, . . . , 1861–1863, HUA. Mark DeWolfe Howe, *Justice Oliver Wendell Holmes: the Shaping Years* (Cambridge, Mass., 1957), pp. 35–39.

were good but not outstanding. In his first semester he received 2,012 points before deductions out of a possible 2,477, or eighty-one per cent; since the valedictorian managed to accumulate only 2,219, or ninety per cent, Fiske's grade can be considered a solid (or perhaps even a high) B in terms of today's grading system. However, in the following semester, when he intensified his outside study program, his grades tumbled to seventy-three per cent of maximum. His first-year grades placed him twenty-ninth in his class, sufficiently high for President Felton to advise him to apply for a scholarship, but not high enough for him to win one. In his second or Junior year, they went still lower, dropping to sixty-four per cent the first semester and fifty-seven per cent the second. This was low enough for him to receive a condition and be forced to stand an examination in Tacitus in the fall of 1862. In his last year, when his studies were upset by an attack of measles which cost him several weeks of class work, he remained at about sixty per cent. This record placed Fiske forty-seventh in his class of one hundred and five graduates. Translated into modern terminology from the point scale in which they were recorded, his grades (before disciplinary deductions) indicate that he was a B student his first year and a C student thereafter.[23]

Fiske's frequent absences from class, a habit that grew out of his disappointment at the quality of Harvard instruction and his decision to devote most of his time to outside study, was the major reason for his low academic standing. Deductions resulting from

[23] Harvard University, Manuscript Record of Absences, . . . , 1861–1863; Manuscript Rank Scales, 1861–1863, HUA. JF to his mother, Apr. 2, 1861, July 24, 1862, HHL. Fiske later blamed his relatively low academic standing on deductions from his grade score. On 1 April 1870 he wrote his mother: "The amount of my deductions for absences &c., was above 5000. Omitting these from the amount, and calculating my rank *on my examinations* alone, I should have stood first for senior year, and fourth or fifth for the whole course. My average percentage for senior year was almost unprecedentedly high." (HHL, italics in MS.) Even ignoring the fact that examinations were rare at Harvard, the figures do not bear out Fiske's contentions. Fiske had 3,646 points, before deductions, in his Senior year as compared with 5,455 accumulated by the valedictorian. In his three years at Harvard, Fiske had 1,506 points deducted due to disciplinary action; 850 were penalties for cutting class, 200 were for parietal rule violations, and 456 were for cutting prayers and other offenses against compulsory chapel. Unless Fiske counted points he could have earned had he been present and known the work, his statement does not make sense, and on this criterion all students would be entitled to a perfect score whenever they cut class.

the punitive disciplinary attitude of the Faculty merely intensified the adverse results of Fiske's behavior, for they meant that he not only lost the points he could have made had he recited successfully, but also had additional points subtracted from the total he had already earned by previous recitation.

Fiske's religious attitude involved him in an uncomfortable situation during his Junior year. Harvard required its students to attend church twice each Sunday, as well as weekday morning chapel. Each church in Cambridge had a special section set aside for Harvard students where monitors checked the roll to be sure all attended; Fiske normally attended the Episcopal Church on Sundays. On October 13, 1861, he was reported to the Faculty for reading a volume of Comte during divine service, an act which infuriated the conservative Unitarians on the Faculty, who were already suspicious of Fiske as a proclaimed non-Christian. The next day the Faculty voted to punish him with a "public admonition," which consisted simply of deducting sixty-four points from the grade scale.

This light punishment did not satisfy President Felton, who thought such a gross insult to religion deserved at least suspension, if not expulsion. After calling in Fiske for an interview that was highly unsatisfactory to him, he wrote bitterly to Fiske's mother that "through conceit of superior wisdom he avows himself an infidel," and warned her that if he persisted in disrespectful behavior or tried to spread infidel ideas he would be expelled. In answer to his mother's expostulations, John promised to take care not to get expelled and assured her that he had no desire to propagandize his opinions. He admitted his fault in being rude, but tried to excuse himself on the ground that he had not realized how reading in church would seem to a believer. He told her that "it has for many years been the custom for students to read at the Episcopal Church. It is always done. Most of the students do it Sunday after Sunday, & I only did it twice." He also claimed that "the three upper classes . . . are swarming with infidels of all sorts, but principally Parkerites," and named ten among the twenty Faculty members whom he believed shared the same opinions.[24]

[24] Harvard University, Manuscript Faculty Records, XVI, meeting of October 14, 1861; Mrs. M. F. B. Stoughton to President C. Felton, Oct. 19, 1861 (Harvard College Papers, XXVIII, 344), HUA. JF to his mother, Oct. 21, 1861, HHL.

IV

The frigid reception of Fiske's religious heresies at Harvard was intensified by the suspicion which recent developments in science and the philosophy of science had raised in the religious mind. Charles Darwin's *Origin of Species,* which advanced an explanation of organic nature that seemed to remove all trace of purpose from the universe and to contradict the common religious tendency to see in the adaptation of life to environment proof of God's beneficent interest in the world, was only the latest such development. Every religious periodical that reviewed Darwin rejected his ideas and refuted his proofs to its own satisfaction. There was little to differentiate Unitarians from orthodoxy on this issue, and James Amory Lowell's words in the Unitarian *Christian Examiner* might have appeared in the most orthodox quarterly: "It adopts, or at least suggests, views on the modes of action of the Creator, and on the ways of Providence, that are repugnant to the most cherished feelings and hopes of man." Lowell rejected in advance any attempt to prove it compatible with religion. "It is in vain that the apologists of this hypothesis might say that it merely attributes a different mode and time to the Divine agency." [25]

Asa Gray, professor of botany at Harvard and an orthodox Congregationalist layman, argued persuasively the latter view, but had little influence as long as religious leaders thought they could easily refute Darwin. The attitude of most American scientists, who either hesitated to accept Darwin at first or else followed Louis Agassiz in vigorously rejecting the theory, encouraged this belief. Feeling certain of their ground, most of the early religious reviewers did not explore the religious significance of evolution, but rather tried to reject it on scientific grounds—drawing the bulk of their objections from the difficulties in his own theory that Darwin had raised in his book and tried to answer. [26]

[25] J. A. Lowell, "Darwin's Origin of Species," *Christian Examiner,* 68:449, 463 (December 1860).

[26] Asa Gray, *Darwiniana* (New York, 1876), *Letters,* J. L. Gray, ed., 2 vols. (Boston, 1893), II, 457–458, 479–480, 656. A. H. Dupree, *Asa Gray* (Cambridge, Mass., 1959), ch. XIV, XV. Louis Agassiz, *Essay on Classification* (London, 1859); *American Journal of Arts and Sciences,* 2nd ser., 30:142–154 (July 1860). *Baptist Quarterly Review,* 2:257–274 (July 1868). *Methodist Quarterly Review,* 42:335–339

In the seventies, however, no holds would be barred as a vicious onslaught against Darwin became a central preoccupation of much of the religious press. By then, support for Darwin had grown among the younger generation of scientists and laymen who, when they read Darwin for themselves, discovered that he had answered most of the objections raised by his critics. When his *Descent of Man* (1871) threatened to bring humanity within the explanatory scheme of evolution, Darwin became a major object of religious attack. But until the seventies, most religious apologists thought they had adequately refuted Darwin and preferred to attack what seemed to be more significant targets. "Positivism" was a more frequent subject of religious polemic; attacks on Buckle, Spencer, Comte, and physical science occupied more space in religious periodicals than discussions of biology.

To Fiske, as well as to his elders, Darwin appeared to be only one, and by no means the most important, of the positivist writers. In letters written in the 1860's Fiske rarely mentioned Darwin, except when he listed the "works of all the English Positivists." [27] His great enthusiasm was Herbert Spencer, who seemed in process of providing the comprehensive unification of all thought and experience for which Fiske still searched.

During his first exploration of the Boston book stores in June, 1860, Fiske discovered the prospectus of Herbert Spencer's projected series of volumes while browsing in Ticknor and Fields' "Old Corner Book Store." In it he learned that a man he already revered as one of the leading English positivists had under way a massive scheme to unite the partial views of Mill and Buckle and Humboldt into a comprehensive synthesis which would also solve the problems of religion. Unlike Darwin, Spencer did not limit himself to biology; rather, he tried to use evolution as a philosophical principle explaining the laws controlling the entire universe. In Part I of his "First Principles," which would open the series by presenting the basic ideas underlying all phenomena, Spencer promised to begin by

---

(April 1860), and 43:605–627 (October 1861). *American Church Review*, 17:169–198 (July 1865). *American Presbyterian Review*, 2:326–344 (May 1861). *New Englander*, 18:516–519 (May 1861). See below, Chapter Six.

[27] JF to his mother, June 17, 1860, HHL.

showing "the only possible reconciliation of Science and Religion." This would be followed by a section expounding the "ultimate principles . . . true not of one class of phenomena but of *all* classes of phenomena; and which are thus the keys to all classes of phenomena." As the series continued he intended to build on the basic principles laid down in the first work an exposition of the principles of biology in two volumes, then erect on the basis of biologic laws a two-volume exposition of the principles of psychology. These in turn would furnish the foundation for a three-volume survey of sociology, which would then lead to the capstone of the whole work, two volumes establishing the principles of morality upon a firm, scientific basis. Inorganic sciences would be excluded in order to bring the project down to a feasible size. Each of the four multivolume works would begin with a survey of the data of the field being considered, then go on to extract inductively from the data the laws governing them. He would then demonstrate that these laws logically followed from the basic principles, primarily the "law of evolution," which "First Principles" would expound as the key to understanding all phenomena.[28]

Fiske was overjoyed at the prospect and wrote enthusiastically to his mother urging her to persuade Mr. Stoughton to subscribe to Spencer's series. "I consider it my duty to mankind as a Positivist to subscribe," he told her. "If I had 2,000,000 I would lay 1,000,000 at Mr. Spencer's feet, to help him execute this great work." [29]

The appearance of the first installments in October 1860 and January 1861, with their reconciliation of science and religion, so pleased Fiske that he went on to devour the earlier works of Spencer which had been referred to in footnotes to the prospectus. In July 1861 he read the one-volume edition of *The Principles of Psychology* which Spencer had published in 1855. This, he informed his mother, was "the profoundest work I ever read. . . . The author has discovered a great law of evolution in nature, which underlies all phenomena, & which is as important & more comprehensive than

[28] JF to his mother, June 24, 1860, HHL. Quotations from Spencer's prospectus, printed with the prefatory matter in most editions of *First Principles* (italics in source).

[29] JF to his mother, June 24, 1860, HHL.

Newton's law of gravitation." He urged his mother to get it at once. "I have had an 'intellectual drunk' over it," he boasted. In August he went on to read *Social Statics;* the volumes of essays which Appleton had published in America soon followed.[30]

Fiske was not alone in his reactions. Many of his contemporaries were also entranced by the sweep of Spencer's world-view in which, as a Belgian admirer phrased it, "the fluctuations of the Exchange are thus subject to the same law as the passage of a comet; while the victories of Alexander and the works of Shakespeare are reducible to the same factors as the Falls of Niagara and the spots on the sun." While professional philosophers like Josiah Royce would later complain of Spencer's "beautiful logical naïveté" in believing that "if you found a bag big enough to hold all the facts, that was an unification of science," most of Spencer's contemporaries found his simplicity and comprehensiveness awe-inspiring. His books sold in enormous quantities, especially in America, and he became the most widely read and admired philosopher of his day.[31]

The key to Fiske's enthusiasm is the comparison with Newton, which appeared again and again in his later writing. Here was a work professedly scientific, basing itself on facts rather than on metaphysics, yet which produced even more comprehensive generalizations than the sweep of Newtonian physics. Fiske desired to find laws which would be as broad as possible and bring the whole universe into one logical pattern. He had rejected Connecticut Congregationalism because its theology failed to satisfy his quest for a simple, uniform explanation of the world. Spencer, more than any other "positivist" he had read, seemed to accomplish this.

And Spencer went even further. His great system began with a section on religion which, with its doctrine of the Unknowable as the basic assumption of both science and religion, seemed to Fiske to solve the problem of the place of religion and its relation to science by providing an unassailable function for religion that almost put it at the basis of all thought.

---

[30] JF to his mother, July 21, 1861, Aug. 12, 1861, HHL.
[31] Eugene, Comte Goblet d'Alviella, *The Contemporary Evolution of Religious Thought* (London, 1885), p. 41. Josiah Royce, *Herbert Spencer* (New York, 1904), p. 115. Herbert Spencer, *Autobiography,* 2 vols. (New York, 1904), II, 113, note.

Yet if almost from his first glimpse of Spencer's prospectus, Fiske enrolled himself as a disciple his adherence was neither blind nor unqualified. In the next few years he treated Spencer as one of many positivists, the leading and most satisfactory member of the school, but not one above correction by the works of the others. Indeed, Fiske's insistence on using the term "positivist" greatly annoyed Spencer, who despised Comte and desired to disassociate his ideas from those of the Frenchman. Not until 1870, after a long correspondence with Spencer on this point, did Fiske drop the use of the name "positivist," and even then he chose the term "Cosmic Philosophy" to describe his approach, rather than the less sweeping "Synthetic Philosophy" that Spencer preferred.[32]

Fiske deviated from his master in his tendency to lay greater stress on religious implications, a trait he shared with many of Spencer's American admirers. While Spencer later declared that he had placed the theological section of his work at the beginning only to disarm suspicions that he might be a simple materialist, Fiske and many others, both admirers and critics, took these ideas to be the foundation upon which the physical synthesis rested. Spencer was annoyed by the tendency of many critics to attack Part I of *First Principles* while ignoring the larger Part II of the work, which to Spencer seemed an independent piece of reasoning of greater importance than the preliminary material. While Fisk admired both parts, as his thought developed he tended to stress religious implications since these were more relevant to his immediate needs.[33]

V

Before the end of his first year at Cambridge, Fiske met and fell in love with the girl who would become his wife. Abby Morgan Brooks came to Cambridge in the spring of 1861 to visit her brother James, a lawyer practicing in Boston who resided in the same Cambridge boarding house as Fiske. Her beauty impressed John as he saw her about the house and walking around Cambridge with her brother. She seemed very refined, stately in her carriage, and with

[32] See below, Chapter Five.

[33] Spencer to JF, Feb. 2, 1870, HHL. Spencer, *Autobiography,* II, 85–87; "Postscript," to Part I, *First Principles* (6th ed., New York, 1900), pp. 109–110.

a mobile face, blue eyes, and dark brown curls that took his fancy. When Abby asked her brother and friends who the slender young man with the poetically flowing hair was, she was told that he was a deep scholar who spent all day and night at his books, and an arch infidel.

Abby did not find his appearance or his fearsome reputation disturbing. One evening while John sat on the front veranda smoking, she asked Mrs. Woods, the housekeeper, to introduce her. In five minutes John was sure he was deeply in love and horrified to learn that her visit was over and that she would leave for her home in Petersham, Massachusetts, the next day. He sat down and wrote a long letter to her asking her to correspond with him but, believing that Abby would return to Cambridge in the fall, never sent it. He was disappointed the following September to learn from Mrs. Woods that Abby planned instead to go to Chicago to visit her other brother, John Brooks, who was a lawyer there.[34]

Faced with the prospect of not seeing Abby again, John decided on heroic measures. He obtained a leave of absence from Harvard and departed for Petersham to visit Abby before she left on her western trip. He found her delighted to see him, but reluctant to agree to his suggestion that they correspond while she was away in the west. Although making it clear that she was not engaged to anyone, she insisted that there was some mysterious reason why she should not undertake to correspond with any young man. Nothing that he could say in the following days moved her from her tantalizing position.

While he remained in Petersham John had an opportunity to meet most of Abby's family. She was the daughter of a Petersham lawyer, Aaron Brooks, who had died in 1845 leaving his widow to bring up their two boys and two girls. Mrs. Brooks had used the money left by her husband to see that both sons, James and John Brooks, were trained as lawyers. Despite the fact that all the children were reputed to have some money in their own right, economically speaking the family was unquestionably on the way down, and there was some talk of selling the family home to make ends meet. Thus, economic-

[34] JF to his mother, Jan. 2, 1862; JF to Abby, June 17, 1861 [typed copy, marked "never sent" in JF's hand], HHL.

ally as well as socially, the Brooks and Fisk families occupied a similar position—people of old New England stock who had achieved professional status but now found it difficult to maintain as the economic opportunities in their home towns contracted. Unlike the orthodox Congregational Fisks, the Brookses attended the Unitarian church of their town.[85]

John returned to Cambridge taking what satisfaction he could from Abby's promise to see him there in November before leaving for Chicago. During the second afternoon of her visit in Cambridge, she explained that she had promised her brother John not to correspond with any young man without his permission. In the course of this conversation he learned that she was already twenty-two years old; he himself would not be twenty until the following March, but the difference in age did not disturb him in the least. He was in a whirl all week, and "went to bed and dreamed that I was being married to Abby Brooks—she robed in the blue silk dressing gown which I had just seen her with." [36]

In December Abby wrote from Chicago that her brother John had given his consent to their correspondence. Not until then did John mention Abby to his mother. On December 15 he wrote a brief letter promising that when Mrs. Stoughton came to Boston over Christmas he would tell her more about this girl with whom he was in love. When Mrs. Stoughton found it impossible to come, John sat down and on January 2, 1862, brought his mother up to date on his courtship by writing an enormous letter that recounted the affair day by day. He urged her to permit them to become engaged immediately and to marry soon after.[37]

Mrs. Stoughton's answer and the correspondence with John that followed have not survived, but it is easy to imagine her reaction. However, by March, after assuring his mother that he could support a wife after graduation, John won her consent to an engagement. The marriage would not take place until John had completed his education and begun a career.[38]

[85] JF to his mother, Jan. 2, 1862, HHL.
[36] JF to Lizzie Wilcox, Nov. 24, 1861, Nov. 27, 1861, HHL (quotation from letter of November 24).
[37] JF to his mother, Dec. 15, 1861, Jan. 2, 1862, HHL.
[38] JF to his mother, Mar. 9, 1862, July 5, 1862, HHL.

Writing to his friends, Fiske ecstatically described the week early in March in which Abby came to Cambridge and accepted his engagement ring. They met every day, playing music and singing together, and comparing notes on their religious views. John enthusiastically informed his Middletown friends that "she is almost as much of a *heathen* as I am. She is very glad that I am *not* a Christion—so that we will get along together admirably on that point." He took her walking in Cambridge. "How the fellows stared at us! how meekly they took off their hats as they passed!" he boasted. "How they turned around & looked at us after they had passed! how aghast they have eyed me since! I felt very proud as well as very happy." Perhaps his classmates thought the "Cambridge Faust" was parading a mistress, for although John told such close friends as E. W. Gurney of the engagement, he apparently preferred to keep it a secret from the rest of Harvard. The only reference to it in the autobiographical sketch Fiske contributed to the manuscript Class Book compiled by the Class of 1863 reads: "My life has been fraught with romantic adventure, never exceeded in strangeness by any novel, but I am not at liberty to recount my adventures." [39]

During the months that followed, John and Abby corresponded freely and saw each other often. John wrote her voluminous letters describing his intellectual likes and dislikes, urging her to study languages and read the authors he admired. In May 1862 he spent two weeks in Petersham, taking Abby on walking excursions over the hills, joining her at the piano in the evenings, and reading Tennyson with her. John brought along his copy of *First Principles* and introduced Abby to it while he was there. Apparently her reaction was satisfactory, for he wrote to her brother James, who had gone to Paris to serve as a secretary in the American mission there, that he had "seen her eyes sparkle over the toughest analytic passage in Spencer, & I think that will do. I have no fault to find with her intellect or acquirements." [40]

When Fiske's interest in the Civil War finally awoke, Abby was

[39] JF to Mary Wilcox, Mar. 9, 1862, HHL (italics in source). Harvard Class of 1863, Manuscript Class Book, p. 275, HUA (in JF's hand).

[40] JF to Abby, Mar. 30, 1862, June 13, 1862; JF to his mother, June 3, 1862; JF to James Brooks, May 26, 1862, HHL.

the confidante to whom he expressed his reactions. At first he had not felt involved; he had not been affected by the current of reform which stimulated so many of his elders, nor did he feel emotionally drawn to a defense of the Union—he was much more interested in the history and development of Asia or Greece than that of the United States. The war seemed distant and much less exciting than the reading matter on his desk. "What fools people make of themselves about this confounded war!" he wrote in April of 1861. "Why, I forget there is a war half the time. What's war when a fellow has 'Kosmos' on his shelf and 'Faust' on his table?" [41] Not until the fall of 1862 did the war catch his imagination. Tactical and strategic details of the fighting particularly fascinated him. He hung large maps of the battlefronts in his room, with pins marking the positions of the armies, and subscribed to the New York *Times* to keep informed of troop movements. When Lincoln issued the preliminary emancipation proclamation, Fiske hailed it with delight and proclaimed himself an abolitionist. He read widely in books on military strategy and fancied himself an expert. [42]

Fiske's interest in the war intensified when his stepfather and his mother, who were Northern Democrats, began to denounce Lincoln furiously for his emancipation moves. Fiske almost automatically took opposing views from his stepfather, and he now had a further reason—these were also the two who were frustrating his desire for an early marriage by insisting that he be able to support a family. "It is disheartening to hear treason from the lips of one's dearest friends," he complained to Abby while visiting his mother. "I am afraid New York will vote for Seymour—& what is Democracy but treason? Here is Judge Curtis—[a traitor?]—Mr. Stoughton is another [traitor?]—my mother is another [traitor?]. It is enough to make one weep tears of blood." [43]

Despite the violence of his criticism of his mother, Fiske never felt personally involved in the war. At no time did he consider enlisting and joining in the fighting he mapped so carefully. Although

---

[41] JF to G. L. Roberts, April 1861, quoted in Clark, *Life and Letters*, I, 237.

[42] JF to Abby, Sept. 7, 1862, Sept. 24, 1862, May 8, 1863, May 12, 1863, HHL.

[43] JF to Abby, Nov. 3, 1862, HHL (the bracketed words have been partially erased in the surviving manuscript).

not many of his classmates left college to fight, quite a few volunteered before the war ended. All four southerners in the Class of 1863 served with the Confederate forces, one dying before Richmond in 1863. Among his northern classmates, forty-nine served in various ranks from private to captain, and eight were killed in action. Since less than half his classmates joined the military, Fiske's position was not in any way unique. He sharply rejected any thought that he might serve. "Why are you so troubled about my being drafted?" he asked his mother. "The paper says, None who have any defect of speech hearing or VISION will be drafted. . . . Besides, I could get a substitute. *I* shouldn't go—bless me!!!!!!!!!!!!!!" [44]

His classmates might view him as a grind, but to Fiske his own life, as the comments in his Class Book indicated, was full of hidden romance. He was a rebel defying the authority of orthodoxy, college officials, his mother, and his stepfather in a battle for truth and freedom. Superior to those around him, he was sure that no ordinary person could understand him; and he spent most of his time buried in his books and in his dreams of glory. His ambitious yearning for distinction found little satisfaction in college affairs. Rather, he chose to master all knowledge, certain that once he had accumulated great stores of erudition, he would win renown and immense financial reward by revealing to the world truths that no one had even suspected. His romantic image of himself was most directly realized in his successful courtship of Abby. In her he found a partner who would help him sustain his vision. But Abby's adoration was not enough. He wanted the world to agree, and set out to convince his country that he was a great writer and thinker by publishing in leading national magazines.

VI

In June of 1861, stimulated by the publication of the second volume of Buckle's history, and by stories that E. H. Sear's *National Quarterly Review* paid five dollars a page to contributors, Fiske decided to write a long essay review of the work. Buckle's first volume

[44] JF to mother, Aug. 9, 1863, HHL (italics in source; the sentence ends with thirteen exclamation points). Harvard Class of 1863, *Class Report*, VIII (1913), 151–152.

had stimulated Fiske to question his own religious views when he read it in the spring of 1859, for it then seemed to him that Buckle had accomplished his aim of doing "for the history of man something equivalent, or at all events analogous, to what had been effected by other inquirers for the different branches of natural science." Fiske was fascinated when Buckle pointed out that actions of men had predictable statistical regularity, even in such emotional acts as suicide and murder, or such random acts as the number of undirected letters sent annually through the British Post Office. Buckle's attempts to show causal relations between history and physical or mental laws greatly excited Fiske. Here was a system which made the life of man as much a subject of law as Humboldt's *Cosmos* had the physical universe.[45]

But as he sat down that summer to work on his essay, Fiske became dubious. Buckle had concluded that European civilization could not be explained by the operation of simple physical agents, such as climate, that served to illuminate the course of lesser civilizations like those of Egypt, India, or Central America; for a high civilization the operation of mental laws was more important. Buckle then investigated these mental laws, or truths, separating them into moral and intellectual laws. Moral laws, he argued, were more stable, while intellectual truths showed growth over the course of man's history. Since he saw no evidence that man's natural faculties had altered, Buckle turned to this moving agent, the march of mind, as the cause of progress in history. It was this law of progress which Fiske began to question and finally rejected.

That summer, as he worked along on his essay, Fiske first read Spencer and accepted with acclamation his "law of evolution." The bulk of his essay turned into a detailed criticism of Buckle's law of progress from a Spencerian viewpoint. Fiske's attack centered upon the statement that moral truths do not change. This was incompatible with the law of evolution, and Fiske tried hard to prove that there had been a real moral advance. He argued that there were moral truths which had not been disclosed until recently, citing as an example "the moral law that governments shall not interfere

---

[45] Henry T. Buckle, *History of Civilization in England,* 2 vols. (London, 1857–1861), I, 6; see also, I, 36–137 and II, 255–259. JF to his mother, June 28, 1861, HHL.

with trade," which was not discovered until the eighteenth century and was still not wholly accepted. Here Fiske closely followed Spencer, whose *Social Statics,* which Fiske read for the first time while writing his review, set forth an extreme laissez-faire position. Fiske also used Spencer's version of the Lamarckian concept of the inheritance of acquired characteristics as a weapon with which to criticize Buckle. Fiske argued that virtue was not only heritable (an idea that Buckle had questioned) but, since environment modified inheritance, that inheritance altered, making it possible for man's moral faculties to progress. As he wrote, Fiske's refutation of Buckle became quite polemic in tone.[46]

Fiske discovered other "laws of progress" in Buckle which he accepted and praised. But what Buckle called the most important factor, "the triumph of the mental laws over the physical," Fiske vigorously rejected. Only by substituting Spencerian evolution for Buckle's view did he arrive at a law of progress which satisfied him.[47]

Fiske finished the essay in September of 1861, boasting that "the view I take of Buckle's work is entirely new." He was greatly pleased when E. H. Sears accepted the article for the December *National Quarterly Review.* This success helped sustain Fiske's self-esteem that fall during the troubles with the Harvard Faculty over reading Comte in church, but it proved no help for his pocketbook, for Sears insisted that he never paid for uncommissioned work.[48]

Even more ambitious was Fiske's "Evolution of Language," published in the October 1863 *North American Review,* then the leading intellectual magazine of the country. In it he tried to demonstrate how Spencer's version of evolution could help the science of philology. In the first half of the nineteenth century, students of language led by Jacob Grimm, Franz Bopp, Wilhelm von Humboldt, and August Schleicher founded the study of comparative grammar and began to propose laws which would organize the diverse facts of human speech into orderly patterns. The generalizations they ad-

---

[46] JF, "Mr. Buckle's Fallacies," in *Darwinism and other Essays* (Boston, 1902), pp. 136–195 (quotation from p. 162). JF to his mother, July 21, 1861, Aug. 12, 1861, Sept. 30, 1861, HHL.

[47] Buckle, *History,* I, 207–208. JF, "Mr. Buckle's Fallacies," pp. 138–139, 189–195.

[48] Quotation from JF to his mother, Sept. 30, 1861; see also JF to his mother, Jan. 2, 1862, HHL. *National Quarterly Review,* 4:30–63 (December 1861).

vanced explained relations between languages and permitted classifications into great families. These men were able to show historical
growth within some families, as in the case of Indo-European, which
included Sanskrit, Greek, Latin, and the languages of modern Europe. But they could not do this for all tongues. The most influential
classification, that of August Schleicher, arranged all world languages by word structure, but did not demonstrate developmental
connections between its great classes.

Fiske believed that he could show such connections. He accepted
Schleicher's system as expounded by Max Müller in his popular
London *Lectures on the Science of Language* (1861). This divided
all languages into three great types, the Monosyllabic, like Chinese,
in which words mostly consisted of single roots; the Agglutinative
(containing most Asiatic languages), which formed words by adding roots together; and the Amalgamative (including Semitic and
Indo-European), which inflected roots and joined affixes and suffixes
so completely that independent meanings of these word elements
were often forgotten. Applying Spencer's evolutionary system, Fiske
tried to show that this was not merely a descriptive classification but
also a developmental progression, with Chinese as the most primitive
type of language and Indo-European (or Aryan, as Fiske followed
Müller in terming this language group) as the most advanced and
civilized. Fiske argued that all languages had passed through these
stages, or would do so if they progressed. In his demonstrations
Fiske used impressive citations from many esoteric languages, dis-
playing amazing erudition for a youth of twenty-one. Interspersed
through the scholarship were florid passages praising Herbert Spencer and enthusing over the significance of the work he and others
like him had undertaken. Fiske concluded: "When generalization
has gone on till the most remote phenomena are seen to be allied,
when in all parts of the universe the order of evolution is ascertained
to be the same, then absolute community of causation will have been
established, Ahriman will be vanquished by Ormuzd, and science
and religion will be in complete accord." [49]

Fiske was very proud of this article. It won him praise from Her-

[49] JF, "Evolution of Language," *North American Review,* 97:450 (October 1863).
Otto Jespersen, *Language* (New York, 1922), pp. 19–99.

bert Spencer himself for the "power of independent thought" Fiske had shown in applying Spencer's law of evolution to territory with which Spencer was unfamiliar.[50] Linguistics fascinated Fiske because it was a science of man in an advanced state. Although it dealt with an area in which freedom of the will was present, its subject matter followed laws and permitted predictability, so that in these significant respects it was on a par with physical science. In his law of progress Fiske felt he had found the key to all orderly processes of development; therefore he tried to show that the scientifically verifiable laws of linguistics fitted his over-all generalization and thus confirmed its validity.

This seemed a road to the establishment of a large-scale science of man, one that would explain his behavior in rational terms. To Fiske the idea of making the study of linguistics his career was very attractive. This was at the same time the area of his greatest proficiency, and also a field in which he felt it possible for him to make a lasting contribution to human knowledge. But there seemed no way to earn a living by doing so. As his days as an undergraduate drew toward a close, Fiske began to search for a career that would permit him to marry Abby as soon as possible, while also providing time to pursue his scholarly studies.

[50] Herbert Spencer to JF, Mar. 26, 1864, HHL.

CHAPTER THREE

SEARCH FOR A CAREER

Searching for a career that would support his projected marriage preoccupied Fiske during his last year at Harvard. His mother and stepfather did not object to his choice of a wife. They were willing to help the young couple, but insisted that John should at least have made a start in a profession before he married. Since he needed their aid, he had no choice but to accept.

Fiske's dependence on his stepfather irritated him. Mr. Stoughton had given him a generous allowance while he was an undergraduate, but his expenditures always exceeded his allowance. Each quarter he was tempted by enough interesting book bargains and side excursions to Petersham or Middletown or New York to exhaust his money before the next payment came due. Urgent appeals for help to his mother and grandmother were frequent. All through his college years (and long after as well), these two women formed the habit of slipping a five or ten dollar bill into their letters. Fiske complained to Abby that his mother had not complied with his last request since "she says I never write her an affectionate letter except when I want money!!!!" [1]

Fiske felt he was undertaking important work which deserved support. Most successful scholars in the 1860's had independent in-

---

[1] Quotation from JF to Abby, Mar. 29, 1863, HHL. JF to his mother, Jan. 11, 1861, May 12, 1861, Apr. 11, 1862, Apr. 11, 1864; JF to James Brooks, Jan. 21, 1863, May 13, 1863, HHL.

comes, without which success in their careers was almost impossible. They earned little or nothing from their writing; frequently new knowledge could be published only if the author paid the costs. Money had to be laid out in the course of their investigations. Even securing access to the books needed for an intensive study of any subject took money in a day before any university or public library had adequate facilities for advanced work. Fiske's scholarly goals involved him in financial problems; books were a major item among his expenditures.

The attitude of his mother and stepfather now forced Fiske to think seriously about how he could support a family. College trained only for the ministry and teaching. Fiske despised the ministry and would have liked to be a teacher, but Abby wanted him to be a lawyer, the profession of her father and brothers which would assure her the social and financial position to which she was accustomed. This was also the choice of his mother and Mr. Stoughton, himself a successful lawyer who had become wealthy from his profession.

Fiske had agreed to this idea in June of 1862, when Abby first suggested it, but in July he wrote his mother, "I can not *bear* the idea of studying *Law:* I *detest* it with my whole soul." He was afraid the law would prevent him from carrying out his scholarly ambitions. He wanted to continue his linguistic studies and find a way to apply them to the study of early civilization, a project which he estimated would take six years to carry out. But he could not earn a living from this. He proposed to find a job as a teacher. If Harvard would appoint him Tutor (then the lowest full-time position), the salary combined with the income from Abby's inheritance would provide sufficient money to live on and give him time to go on with his own work. He had already discussed this with Abby and assured his mother that now "Abby had rather have me a tutor." [2]

In January 1863 he thought this position would be easy to secure. He wrote his prospective brother-in-law, James Brooks, that his rank had risen from seventy-second to third or fourth in his class, and thus he stood well in the eyes of the Faculty. A Tutorship, he assured James, would enable him to carry out his desire to become

[2] Quotations from JF to his mother, July 5, 1862, HHL. JF to his mother, Mar. 9, 1862, June 28, 1862, HHL.

an author of the "English positive-stamp." But his expectations proved too optimistic. In March, E. W. Gurney, who had been sounding out the Faculty on his behalf, told him Harvard would not hire him.[3]

The only explanation of the refusal which Fiske passed on to Abby was that the Faculty still held against him the infidel attitude he had shown by reading Comte in church the year before. But other reasons for the decision are easy to discern. The Faculty knew that Fiske's academic standing did not put him at the top of his class. Even more important, his area of greatest competence was of no use to Harvard as long as the curriculum remained unaltered— Francis Child, the outstanding linguist of the Faculty, still spent most of his time correcting Freshman themes. Fiske's knowledge of Zend or Gothic or Sanskrit was meaningless since such subjects were not offered. In modern languages the college could hire teachers who had studied in the countries whose language they proposed to teach. Work in pre-history, the field into which Fiske desired to branch out from his linguistic studies, was not considered necessary for undergraduates. Fiske could only have taught elementary courses in Greek and Latin, positions for which any Harvard graduate was qualified. But Harvard needed drillmasters to discipline the students more than it needed scholars. The College made little use of the scholars already on the Faculty and saw no need to subsidize the development of another, especially when they distrusted his religious radicalism.[4]

With Harvard unattainable, Fiske turned to the idea of teaching at lower levels, applying for a vacancy in the Boston Latin School. He expected to hear by August and, if he got the place, had his mother's consent to marry. Otherwise he would be forced to postpone the marriage "indefinitely for two or three months until I find some permanent place of the sort." [5]

When the Boston position failed to materialize, he applied to other schools and came close to getting a job in Charlestown. He was sure

[3] JF to James Brooks, Jan. 21, 1863; JF to Abby, Mar. 8, 1863, HHL.

[4] JF to Abby, Mar. 8, 1863, HHL. William James. *C. W. Eliot,* 2 vols. (Boston, 1930), II, 14–15.

[5] JF to James Brooks, May 13, 1863, HHL.

he was the first choice of the school authorities, but they put off a definite decision until a few days before school opened in September, by which time an experienced teacher applied and was immediately hired.[6]

After all possibility of a teaching position had vanished, Fiske turned to the alternative which his mother and stepfather opened to him. He agreed to attend Harvard Law School and prepare for admission to the Bar. Since this had been the course Abby preferred from the first, she agreed to delay the marriage until he became a lawyer. On this condition Stoughton undertook to finance his studies for the two years they normally took, but Fiske did not care to wait that long and determined to complete the work needed to secure admission to the Bar in half the time. This plan was possible since he had only to present a certificate from a practicing attorney that he had diligently prepared himself, and then pass a written examination.[7]

Fiske kept up his linguistic and historical studies while in the Law School. It was easy to do so because of the way the school was then organized. Justice Joseph Story had attempted unsuccessfully in 1829 to set up the Law School as a graduate study, with an intensive organized program designed to keep college graduates occupied for three years. Students entering without a bachelor's degree were to take five years of course work before earning a law degree. But the school had not been able to hold to this ambitious standard in an age when it was more common to study for the Bar by apprenticeship in the office of a successful lawyer than to go to law school. By the time Fiske entered, requirements were very simple. Any student paying a $50 fee for three terms received the Bachelor of Laws degree automatically, without any examination or other check on what he had learned.[8]

In return for the fees, the Law School permitted students to attend

---

[6] JF to James Brooks, Sept. 17, 1863, HHL.

[7] JF to Abby, Sept. 17, 1863; JF to his mother, Sept. 19, 1863, Apr. 11, 1864, HHL.

[8] *Annual Report of the President of Harvard University, 1875–76*, pp. 28–29. *Harvard University Catalogue, 1863–64*, p. 64. Roscoe Pound, "The Law School," in *Development of Harvard University*, S. E. Morison, ed. (Cambridge, Mass., 1930), pp. 490–498. Mark DeWolfe Howe, *Justice Oliver Wendell Holmes: the Shaping Years* (Cambridge, Mass., 1957), pp. 176–207.

a series of lectures on various topics in law given by the three professors, Joel Parker, Theophilus Parsons, and Emory Washburn, who then composed the entire faculty. Professor Parsons gave the elementary lectures on Blackstone and on Kent's Commentaries each year. All three professors taught advanced courses covering important subjects at least once every other year, so that all students might hear them during their residence in the school; topics considered less significant might only be given once in three or more years. While Fiske attended the Law School the three professors offered some twenty advanced courses in such fields as Constitutional Law, Partnership, Shipping and Admiralty, Equity, Corporations, International Law, Contracts, Evidence, Pleading, and Domestic Relations.[9]

It is unlikely that Fiske made much use of his privilege of auditing lectures. When he first registered at the school in October 1863, he dutifully listened to Parson's lectures on Blackstone, Parker on Bailments, and Washburn on Real Property, but thereafter his letters indicate that he spent most of his time following the course of reading recommended in the Law School catalogue. If he sat in on other lectures he did not think enough of them to mention the fact in his detailed letters to Abby. Nor did Fiske participate much in the other major activity offered by the Law School, the moot courts organized by both the Faculty and by student clubs in which practice in arguing cases could be gained. Fiske mentioned only two moot court cases, and one of these came after he had passed his Bar examination.[10]

A week after he started his law study, Fiske was enthusiastic. "I am perfectly enchanted and carried away and *electrified* with Blackstone . . . ," he assured Abby. "I scarcely ever read anything so interesting in my life. I get so engrossed in it that I can hardly leave it to go to bed. I never knew what I was talking about when I professed a dislike for the law." He set himself a rigorous study sched-

---

[9] *Harvard University Catalogue, 1863–64,* pp. 62–63. *Annual Report of the President of Harvard University,* 1863–64, p. 25; 1864–65, p. 17.

[10] JF to Abby, Oct. 7, 1863, Oct. 11, 1863; JF to his mother, Nov. 14, 1863, May 26, 1864, Oct. 8, 1864, HHL. *Harvard University Catalogue, 1863–64,* pp. 66–69.

ule, trying to devote six hours a day to law books and four hours to science or history. By April he had completed the reading of some eight thousand pages in law books, covering most of the most important suggestions of his advisers.[11]

His reading kept him abreast of new books. John W. Draper's *History of the Intellectual Development of Europe* caught his fancy and aroused an interest in the Arabian civilization which Draper admired. Fiske went on to read the *Koran,* which failed to impress him, as well as historical works on the Arabs. The new book that most excited him was Sir Henry Maine's *Ancient Law.* "I have passed through an Era and entered upon a new Epoch of my Life," he told Abby. Maine gave Fiske what his Harvard law professors ignored, a view of the philosophy and history of his subject. Maine applied to the history of Roman and Greek law the idea of development which so excited Fiske, trying to show a steady progress from an emphasis on status to an emphasis on contractual obligations as civilization advanced. "It has thrown all my ideas of Law into definite shape," said Fiske. "It has suggested to me many new and startling views of social progress." This was the study of law placed on a scientific basis and Fiske's enthusiasm knew no bounds. "It is perfectly GLORIOUS! I am going to read it over and over until I know it by heart. And I am going to get you posted up so that you can read it," he wrote Abby.[12]

Even while he was in the Law School, Fiske tried to build up his connections with magazines. When Charles Eliot Norton took over the editorship of the *North American Review* in 1863, he approached Fiske as a possible contributor of book notices, and printed his review of the American reprint of John Stuart Mill's *Political Economy* in the January 1864 issue. Norton rejected as too uncritical Fiske's next contribution, a highly flattering review of E. L. Youmans' textbook on chemistry. However, the *Atlantic Monthly* accepted the notice for its August number, opening a new outlet for future work.[13]

[11] Quotation from JF to Abby, Oct. 11, 1863, HHL. JF to his mother, Nov. 14, 1863, Apr. 10, 1864, HHL.

[12] Quotations from JF to Abby, Jan. 3, 1864, HHL. JF to Abby, Dec. 29, 1863, May 6, 1864, May 11, 1864, HHL. H. S. Maine, *Ancient Law* (London, 1861).

[13] JF to Abby, Nov. 1, 1863, Dec. 11, 1863; JF to his mother, Apr. 10, 1864, HHL.

Fiske's meeting with E. L. Youmans in October of 1863 provided personal contact with the wider group of Spencerian disciples in America. While in Boston raising money to underwrite a reprint of Spencer's *Essays* in America, Youmans learned that the essay on language, which had already attracted his attention, had been written by "a young *atheist!* in Cambridge named Fiske." George Litch Roberts, whom Youmans also tracked down, brought him to Fiske's rooms in Cambridge, where Youmans was highly complimentary, expressing his amazement that a young man of twenty-one had written the learned essay. Youmans fascinated the two young men with his descriptions of the "positivist" writers of England, whom he knew personally. When Fiske visited New York in March 1864, Youmans introduced him to the Spencerian circle there, including Draper, Henry Ward Beecher, the partners of the Appleton publishing house, and Manton Marble, editor of the New York *World*.[14]

Youmans encouraged Fiske to open a correspondence with Spencer. Fiske and Roberts had already considered expressing their admiration directly, but had felt too young and unknown to do so. Now Youmans urged them on and wrote Spencer describing the work of Fiske in applying the principle of evolution to language, and of Roberts trying to do the same for jurisprudence. "They are brimful of fire and enthusiasm, and may be relied on for important assistance," he told Spencer. Spencer wrote appreciatively to Youmans, who showed the letter to Fiske.[15]

Fiske finally wrote Spencer in February 1864, sending copies of his essays on Buckle and on language. He assured Spencer that "the influence of your writings is apparent alike in every line of my writings and every sentence of conversation. So inextricably have they become intertwined with my own thinking, that frequently on making a new generalization, I scarcely know whether to credit myself with it or not," Spencer responded warmly, "It is very refreshing to me to meet with so much sympathy as that expressed in

[14] Quotation from JF to Abby, Nov. 1, 1863, HHL. JF to Martha Brooks, Mar. 13, 1864, HHL.

[15] E. L. Youmans to H. Spencer, Nov. 23, 1863, printed in JF, *E. L. Youmans* (New York, 1894), pp. 164–165. Spencer to Youmans, *ibid.*, pp. 173–174.

your letter," and encouraged him to go on with his intention of working out a complete theory of the origin and evolution of language. This response delighted Fiske. He sent the letter on to both his mother and Abby, urging them to "treat it as carefully as if it were a scroll of Al Korân just *tumbled* from the prophet's pen (which he didn't use by the way as he couldn't write)." [16]

Fiske depended almost entirely on his own reading to prepare for the Bar examination. Aided by a phenomenal memory, which later permitted him to recite on the spur of moment entire chapters of Dickens for the entertainment of his friends, Fiske completed his work in less than half the time usually taken to prepare for the Bar examination. For the first six months of his study he divided his efforts between law and other interests, but during the last three months he concentrated almost solely on law, devoting eleven or more hours a day to it, and reading in thirty-seven volumes of law during his nine months of preparation. In July 1864 he persuaded a lawyer to certify that he had spent two years studying law and on the strength of this was admitted to the examination on the seventh of July. He passed easily.[17]

II

Fiske had already obtained his stepfather's consent to his marriage as soon as he was admitted to the Bar, so no obstacle now remained. Stoughton agreed to continue his allowance, and even offered to take the young lawyer into his office, but Fiske preferred to stay in Cambridge. Stoughton's generosity greatly aided Fiske, who still showed the same attitude toward money that had involved him in financial difficulties during his college days. In mid-June, when he was immersed in preparations for the Bar examination and for his forthcoming marriage, he could not resist "the most gigantic book bargain that was ever heard of," one hundred and thirty volumes containing the works of most of the classic Italian writers, for $52. That he looked on fourteen volumes of the *Opere di Baldinucci* and

[16] JF to Spencer, Feb. 14, 1864 (draft copy); Spencer to JF, Mar. 26, 1864; JF to his mother, Apr. 28, 1864 (italics in source), HHL.

[17] JF to Abby, July 1, 1864; JF to his mother, May 18, 1864, July 13, 1864, HHL. Franklin H. Head, *John Fiske* (Chicago, [1902?]), p. 11.

thirteen volumes of the *Opere di Gallileo* as "nearly all books that I shall eventually need and should have got anyway in course of time," indicates how little his ambitions were attached to a career in law.[18]

During July and August plans for the marriage advanced rapidly. New dresses were made up for the ladies. Abby's sister Martha came back from a visit to brother James in Paris with gifts for everyone. The young couple reserved the recently opened Appleton Chapel at Harvard for the wedding ceremony. On September 6, 1864, the two were married by Abby's uncle, Edmund Willson, with Professor A. P. Peabody of Harvard assisting.[19]

After the marriage they settled down temporarily in an apartment in the rooming house where Fiske had lived as an undergraduate. There Fiske relaxed from his rigorous studies of the preceding year by reading Dickens and Hawthorne, teaching Abby Italian and French, and taking her to operas and concerts. John registered for a third term at the Harvard Law School to qualify for his Bachelor of Laws degree and took part in his second moot court case early in the fall.[20]

In October Fiske began to spend most of the day in the office of a Boston lawyer, in order to "learn the practice," and discussed with his relatives the prospects of setting up a law office either in Petersham or Middletown. He assured James Brooks, "I hate the city & always have—I love the country & always have." Stoughton continued to help, making the fledgling lawyer his Boston representative in a case which had New England ramifications and promising more of such work in the future. In January 1865 Fiske shifted to the office of David P. Kimball, doing odd jobs such as drawing up deeds, suing for small sums, and looking up cases in order to gain experience.[21]

The death of Abby's uncle broke up the Petersham household,

[18] Quotations from JF to Abby, June 16, 1864, HHL. JF to his mother, May 18, 1864, June 3, 1864, HHL.

[19] JF to his mother, July 22, 1864, Aug. 14, 1864, Oct. 8, 1864, HHL.

[20] JF to James Brooks, Oct. 2, 1864; JF to his mother, Oct. 8, 1864, Nov. 2, 1864, HHL.

[21] Quotations from JF to James Brooks, Oct. 2, 1864, Oct. 23, 1864, HHL. JF to Shepherd Gilbert, Dec. 4, 1864; JF to his mother, Jan. 25, 1865, Feb. 14, 1865, HHL.

and the Brooks homestead was put up for sale. Abby's mother, sister, and brother joined forces with the young Fiskes in renting a furnished house and acre of ground in the suburban Jamaica Plain section, from which John commuted to his downtown office by horsecar each day. His first child, Maud, was born on July 21, 1865.[22]

Fiske's law career did not progress well. In May, Kimball's partner returned from an absence and Fiske's services were no longer needed. He opened an office of his own in Boston, but made little attempt to bring in business. Aside from work sent him by Stoughton, Fiske appears to have secured only one case of his own. Much of his time he devoted to his old love, the study of languages. While in Jamaica Plain Fiske aroused the interest of the liberal Unitarian minister, William R. Alger, in the choir of whose Boston church he and George Roberts sang each Sunday, and Alger used his influence with the Unitarian *Christian Register* to place there a lengthy article by Fiske entitled "Problems in Language and Mythology." This was an essay-review of Max Müller's *Lectures on the Science of Language,* in which Fiske took Müller to task for not using Spencerian patterns of evolution, although praising his work in the study of myth, which Fiske thought would soon make it possible "to deal with these fossil relics of ancient thought as successfully as the geologist now deals with the stony texts which are scattered over the crust of the globe." Fiske aided Alger in the preparation of a new edition of the minister's massive *Critical History of the Doctrine of a Future Life,* checking the manuscript for minor errors.[23]

Fiske had tried two ways of earning money to support a scholarly career without success. He had failed to get a teaching job and now he found the law unremunerative. A third alternative seemed possible. The appearance of national magazines able to pay writers for their contributions made free-lance writing appear a possible means of earning a livelihood. Fiske turned optimistically to this expedient, hoping it would permit him to earn money from his scholarship; he would now try to present his knowledge in a popular dress. He

[22] JF to his mother, Mar. 15, 1865, Mar. 29, 1865, HHL.
[23] JF to his mother, Mar. 29, 1865, May 13, 1865; JF to Lizzie Wilcox, July 1, 1865, Feb. 15, 1866, HHL. *Christian Examiner,* 78:368–383 (May 1865); quotation from p. 383.

started again on the lengthy review of Draper's *Intellectual History* he had dropped the previous year and began to cultivate the society of men who might clear his path to leading periodicals. He went frequently to Cambridge to look up Ephraim Gurney, Chauncey Wright, James Russell Lowell, Charles Eliot Norton, and others among the concentration of editors and writers around Harvard.[24]

Norton printed a brief review of the new edition of J. S. Mill's volume on Comte, written at Fiske's suggestion, in the January 1866 *North American Review*. Fiske's second proposal, a brief notice of W. E. H. Lecky's *History of the Rise and Influence of the Spirit of Rationalism in Europe,* did not work out as well. Instead of the short notice Norton expected, Fiske produced a lengthy essay that ran thirty printed pages in its final form. Fiske had tried to modify his previous style, as well as to stress colorful aspects of his topic, such as witchcraft and religious persecution, rather than the application of Spencerian evolution to history, in order to produce an essay "of an entirely popular character & the most interesting of anything I have written." But Norton found the article much more than he had bargained for and returned it unused after Fiske refused permission to cut it. Again Alger came to Fiske's assistance, getting the *Christian Examiner* to print the article in its September 1866 issue.[25]

To take advantage of his contacts with advanced thinkers in England, Fiske offered G. H. Lewes, editor of the *Fortnightly Review* and a leading English disciple of Comte, a lengthy article on the "Laws of History." This was to be a discussion of causation and progress in history, in the course of which Fiske planned to use his material on Draper's history of Europe's intellectual development to show the ineffectiveness of Draper's idea of change in history when compared with ideas based on the Spencerian concept of evolution.[26]

Fiske hoped to republish all these articles in a volume of essays showing the application of evolution to history, philosophy, religion,

---

[24] JF to his mother, May 23, 1865, June 22, 1865, HHL.

[25] Quotation from JF to his mother, Dec. 25, 1865, HHL. JF to G. L. Roberts, May 28, 1866, HHL. JF to C. E. Norton, Nov. 18, 1865, Nov. 20, 1865, Dec. 14, 1865, Jan. 20, 1866, May 22, 1866, HUL.

[26] JF to his mother, Dec. 16, 1865, Jan. 10, 1866, HHL.

language, and mythology, through which he hoped to acquire a scholarly reputation. Each essay, therefore, had to serve two purposes, to arouse popular interest and to win scholarly approval. Even this early Fiske had begun to struggle with the problem of doing both simultaneously, a dilemma which faced him in all his serious work. In part his difficulty can be explained by the absence of scholarly quarterlies (very few were founded this early) which left general circulation magazines as Fiske's major channel for getting into print; but even more significant was his need to earn money from his writing.

Lewes agreed to take two articles on the laws of history for the *Fortnightly* at a price which Fiske estimated would come to $193.60 in gold, or $270 in greenbacks. This encouraged Fiske to reveal to his parents his discontent with the law. Although doubtful of Fiske's chances of earning a living by his writing, Stoughton finally agreed to continue his subsidy while Fiske tried to build a career of full-time free-lance writing.[27]

When the lease on the Jamaica Plain house ran out in April 1866, the Fiske and Brooks families parted company. Fiske would have preferred to move back to the intellectual atmosphere of Cambridge, but his subsidizers insisted that he live in the country where he was less likely to contract heavy debts while trying to earn a living from free-lance writing. Early in April, John and Abby and Maud left for Middletown, where John's grandmother welcomed them to her house. Fiske was now definitely committed to earning his living by writing and he settled down in his boyhood home confident that he would soon demonstrate to his doubting stepfather that he could earn both money and reputation from his writing.[28]

III

The going was not easy. Shortly after the move to Middletown, Norton infuriated Fiske by his refusal to publish the article on Lecky as written, and in retaliation Fiske stopped sending Norton articles. This, however, temporarily blocked one of his major sources of

[27] JF to his mother, Jan. 20, 1866; JF to Shepherd Gilbert, Jan. 20, 1866; JF to G. L. Roberts, Sept. 28, 1866, HHL.

[28] JF to his mother, Mar. 21, 1866, Apr. 15, 1866, HHL.

income, and Fiske soon began searching for some way to renew his association with Norton without backing down. He requested Gurney to tell Norton of Fiske's great success with English journals, and to see if he could persuade Norton to request some articles, thus permitting Fiske to set his own terms.[29]

At first Fiske's opportunities for publication in England seemed excellent. Lewes not only agreed to take the two articles on the laws of history, but also expressed interest in three other articles Fiske suggested. In September 1866 he printed a short reply by Fiske to an orthodox defense of religion which Fiske entitled "Miracles No Proof." Herbert Spencer sounded out his English friends on Fiske's behalf and elicited an expression of interest from the editor of *Macmillan's Magazine* in a new article on the evolution of language which Fiske planned. The elation induced by this success in England lasted Fiske through his stay in Middletown, although the success later proved to be more one of promise' than performance. After accepting the two articles on history, Lewes resigned as editor of the *Fortnightly;* his successor proved uninterested in Fiske's essays. Part I of "The Laws of History" was finally printed in the *Fortnightly* for September 1868, but Fiske received only half the sum he expected in payment. Part II never appeared there, nor did any subsequent articles. Fiske did not complete the essay on language for several years, too late to send it to England.[30]

More immediately remunerative were the opportunities Gurney opened to Fiske in Boston and which Youmans arranged in New York. At Gurney's suggestion, Ticknor & Fields printed an essay on university reform by Fiske in the *Atlantic Monthly*. Gurney introduced Fiske to the Boston newspaper world and, after he became an editor of the *North American Review* in 1868, helped Fiske re-establish himself in that market. Through Youmans' intervention the *Nation* commissioned Fiske to write minor reviews, and the

[29] JF to James Brooks, Sept. 22, 1866, HHL.

[30] G. H. Lewes to JF, Aug. 24 ,1866; H. Spencer to JF, June 19, 1866, Oct. 17, 1868; JF to James Brooks, Oct. 24, 1866, HHL. JF to Manton Marble, Mar. 25, 1869, LC. Part II finally appeared in the *North American Review,* 109:197–230 (July 1869); the essay on language appeared there, too, in 109:305–367 (October 1869).

New York *Post* took one brief article. The most productive of all the opportunities Youmans opened to Fiske was with Manton Marble, editor and publisher of the New York *World*.[31]

Marble was one of the leading figures in the Spencerian group in New York and greatly interested in various forms of intellectual radicalism. His paper employed many of the more advanced thinkers as reporters and editorial writers, among them David Goodman Croly, the most vocal of American followers of Comte. Along with the political news and comments in which Marble followed a strongly Democratic line, attacking the Civil War and assailing all Republican plans for Reconstruction, the *World* also gave much attention to Spencerian views on the relation of the government to the economy. The scientific support Spencer provided for the idea that under no circumstances should there be any intervention by government in business, as well as Spencer's vigorous attack on protective tariffs, fitted well with Marble's political views. Marble also showed much interest in religious change. He regularly printed reports of scientific discoveries and sermons by leading ministers dealing with the problem of adapting religion to the new universe of science.[32]

Marble's opinions pleased Fiske. He had reluctantly turned down an offer from the Boston *Advertiser,* secured through the intervention of Gurney, to write regular columns for them, since the *Advertiser* was a strongly protectionist organ whose views Fiske felt he could not support. In contrast, Fiske and Marble were in almost complete agreement. Fiske fully agreed with the Spencerian position on laissez faire. And, as his stepfather began to shift away from his earlier support of the Democratic party and expressed approval of the acts of the Grant administration, Fiske dropped the ardent anti-Democratic views he had espoused during the war. It was now easy for him to join Marble in excoriating all the works of the

[31] JF to James Brooks, Aug. 26, 1866, Sept. 22, 1866; JF to G. L. Roberts, May 18, 1866; JF to Abby, Oct. 21, 1867, Oct. 22, 1867, HHL.

[32] Manton Marble, Manuscript Autobiographical Sketch, Marble Papers, LC. "Manton Marble," *Harpers' Weekly,* 14:81–82 (Feb. 5, 1870). New York *World,* 1869–1873. M. C. Phelan, *Manton Marble* (Washington, D.C., 1957).

Republican party. Fiske felt fully at home in the pages of the *World* and soon sent great quantities of material pouring down on Marble.[33]

Fiske's first two contributions were long reviews, one of Spencer's *Principles of Biology,* and the other of Ernest Renan's *Lives of the Apostles.* His lavish praise of Spencer and his presentation of scholarly support for "infidel" religious positions apparently pleased Marble, who encouraged Fiske to contribute heavily to the *World.* Although Marble did not accede to Fiske's boldest request, that he carry a regular weekly column in which Fiske could take over all book reviewing for the paper, he did print more than twenty-five long essay-reviews in the next two years.[34]

The books examined ran the gamut of serious literature from poetry to proposals for classroom discipline reforms. Fiske tried to adapt for a newspaper audience heavy scholarly articles similar in theme to those he contributed to quarterlies. Many of the subjects, like the three-part review of Longfellow's translation of Dante, were suggested by Fiske. His favorite subjects—linguistics, history, science, and religion—were all represented. Fiske later boasted of his ability to include praise of Herbert Spencer in unexpected contexts; at the time, he was equally proud of his skill in propagandizing for "infidelism" without arousing the overt wrath of the orthodox. In these years he first explored the technique of milking out financial gain from his work by using the same item many times over. Not only were many of his articles for the *World, Nation,* and *North American* intended for later inclusion in volumes of essays, but he occasionally composed more than one version of the same review. He contributed reviews of W. D. Whitney's volume on language to both the *Nation* and *North American,* praised Youmans' *The Culture Demanded by Modern Life* in both the *World* and *Nation.* Only the fact that all of his material was printed anonymously permitted this duplication.[35]

---

[33] JF to Marble, May 4, 1867, LC. *Dictionary of American Biography,* s.v. Edwin Wallace Stoughton.

[34] JF to Marble, May 29, 1866, Aug. 1, 1867, Feb. 17, 1867, LC. JF to G. L. Roberts, Aug. 12, 1866, HHL. New York *World,* May 19, 1866, Aug. 14, 1866.

[35] New York *World,* Nov. 23, 1867, Jan. 31, 1867, May 31, 1867, June 27, 1867, and July 21, 1867. Reviews of Whitney in *Nation,* 5:369–370 (Nov. 7, 1867), and

The writing style Fiske adopted for the *World* had curious elements. In trying to adapt the scholarly essay-review to a popular audience he interspersed graphic descriptive passages with long analytic sections advancing Spencerian or radical religious ideas, and buttressed the articles with citations of little-known historical events and scraps of esoteric languages. These anomalies bothered some of his readers, and one suggested that Fiske should better concentrate on scholarship. "He will press a point with great skill & lots of learning," his critic remarked, "which the readers of newspapers generally care little or nothing about and have not time to read if they wanted to." [36] But Fiske's columns of heavy artillery, thundering in support of Herbert Spencer and religious change, still pleased Marble. If read, they spoke for causes in which he believed, and even if unread they gave a scholarly tone to his paper.

After six months in Middletown Fiske was heartily disgusted with the country and eagerly sought a way to return to Cambridge. He calculated that he had earned $498.50 by his writing since leaving Jamaica Plain, including in his total articles accepted that were to be paid for on publication (some of which he never was paid for). Fiske felt that he had in these six months demonstrated that he could earn $1,000 a year by writing and planned at the next quarter day to tell Mr. Stoughton that he needed no more of his money and so "deal a rude shock to his skepticism as to the feasibility of making literature a profession." [37]

To finance a move away from "this blasted, orthodox, unenlightened, denuded and deluded town," as he termed Middletown, Fiske agreed to join once more in a combined household with his in-laws. Abby and her mother would put up the money to buy a house at 123 Oxford Street, Cambridge; John would contribute what he earned by his writing towards the joint expenses, and his mother-in-law would pay the rest. Abby's unmarried sister, Martha Brooks, would naturally live with her mother. James Brooks, who

North American Review, 106:308–309 (January 1868). Reviews of Youmans in *Nation*, 5:45–46 (July 18, 1867), and *World*, July 23, 1867. JF, *Youmans*, 23, note. JF to G. L. Roberts, Aug. 12, 1866, HHL.

[36] Quotation from John Bigelow to W. H. Huntington, Dec. 6, 1867, in J. Bigelow, *Retrospections of an Active Life*, 5 vols. (New York, 1913), IV, 133–134.

[37] JF to James Brooks, Sept. 22, 1866, HHL.

was still a bachelor and had returned from the Paris mission to seek his fortune in western mining, would make his home there when in the East, and could be called on for help in case of financial emergency. Mr. Stoughton's money would not be asked for, nor would his advice be considered.[38]

IV

Late in March 1867 the Fiskes and Brookses moved into their Cambridge home. Although Marble took many of his articles, paying him nearly $100 a month, and further sums came in from the *Nation* and *North American Review,* Fiske's income proved inadequate. He soon found that he had greatly underestimated the cost of living in Cambridge. A second child, Fiske's first son, Harold, had come to increase his family obligations in May. "I was reading Buchner when the youngster arrived . . . ," he wrote Roberts. "But you see, I didn't expect him to come before the middle of the afternoon." He complained to his mother: "I am constantly receiving books to notice—& the $10s and $20s soon count up to a decent sum. [But] Everything is swallowed instantly by current expenses." Now, with his stepfather's money again desperately needed, Stoughton's advice was sought. In October Fiske wrote Abby from New York, "Mr. S. is going to send more money as soon as he gets back from the West. I have treated him very politely this time." Stoughton reluctantly resumed the subsidy which, except for short intervals, he would continue through most of his life.[39]

The *World* articles by Fiske that excited the most attention at the time were his answers to James Parton's *Smoking and Drinking.* Parton's book consisted of three essays previously printed in the *Atlantic Monthly.* "Does it Pay to Smoke?" argued that tobacco was a poison, dulled man's natural capacities, cost too much, and "by disturbing and impairing virility, tends to vitiate the relations between the sexes." In "Will the Coming Man Drink Wine?" Parton,

---

[38] Quotation from JF to Shepherd Gilbert, Nov. 7, 1866, HHL. JF to James Brooks, Dec. 8, 1866; JF to G. L. Roberts, Oct. 21, 1866, HHL.

[39] Quotations from JF to Roberts, May 15, 1867; JF to his mother, June 7, 1867; and JF to Abby, Oct. 22, 1867, HHL. JF to Spencer, Sept. 27, 1868, HHL (draft copy).

after listing all the evil effects of drink, decided in the negative. His "Inebriate Asylums and a Visit to One" described the pleasant nature of the cure of alcoholism and the wonderful results secured.[40]

Parton's attitude fell well within the American reform tradition, in which temperance played a major role. But Fiske had had little sympathy with this tradition even before he became a convert to evolution. Now drastic change seemed incompatible with the slow law of social progress he had worked out as a corollary of evolutionary science, and he welcomed the chance to attack a reformer.

The fact that Fiske himself enjoyed the use of both tobacco and alcohol added to his zest in attacking Parton. Publisher Henry Holt, long after Fiske's death, clearly remembered Fiske's "old black meerschaum pipe of the late sixties and early seventies. It was an equilateral triangle about two and a half inches on edge, cut from a slab of meerschaum a little over an inch thick. It had a cherry stem about a foot long." Fiske carried the parts of his pipe in separate pockets and would carefully assemble them, light up, "and then heave one of his immense sighs of contentment, and be ready for conversation." To the end of his life Fiske retained this deep enjoyment of tobacco. In 1884 he described his habits to an enquirer: "Very seldom taste coffee or wine, or smoke a cigar. But I drink beer freely (two or three quarts daily for the past twenty-four years) and smoke tobacco in a meerschaum pipe nearly all the time when at work." Both personally and intellectually, Fiske rejected Parton's ideas and attitudes. He was eager to use all his learning to support the practices and philosophic position he favored.

Fiske wrote to Marble in September 1868 on learning that Parton would bring out his articles as a book, to make sure that he would be the one to review it in the *World*. Marble published Fiske's two-part answer in his December 10 and 11 issues, and indicated his opinion of the articles by printing the second (on alcohol) in the top right-hand column of page one. In the five weeks Fiske worked on it, his reply grew into an enormous, two-part essay, running 163 pages in the expanded book version, in which he piled up citations from impressively titled volumes of physiology and pathology,

---

[40] Quotation from James Parton, *Smoking and Drinking* (Boston, 1868), p. 32.

written in seven languages, to prove that Parton was wrong in saying that nicotine and alcohol were always poisonous. Fiske massed evidence to show that, while large quantities of these drugs were poisonous, in normal quantities they were mild stimulants of great value to men living in the nervous tension of modern cities since they aided the restoration of nervous co-ordination and digestion.[41]

By 1868 Parton was already a well-known popular essayist and biographer; his book had attracted wide attention. Fiske's *World* articles drew readers since they were a vigorous attack on an established writer, and this interest seemed to offer him an excellent opportunity to reprint his articles as a book. Mr. Stoughton was persuaded to put up a financial guarantee, and in December, shortly after the *World* publication of the two essays, Leypoldt and Holt brought them out under the title *Tobacco and Alcohol*. By January, the first thousand had been sold and the expenses of publication paid off. Holt ran off a second thousand, but now sales slackened and by August only 1,551 copies of the 2,000 in print had been sold.[42]

While the book made little money, it did attract attention. Most observers thought Fiske had the better of the exchange. E. L. Godkin wrote to Norton that "John Fiske has written a reply utterly demolishing him [Parton], but think of a man like Fiske having to demolish such a creature! It is using siege artillery to quell a riot." The *Catholic World,* though sympathetic with Parton's aims, conceded that Fiske had the scientific advantage. "But whatever may be the scientific merits of Fiske's treatise, we can but feel that, morally, he is on the losing side." Charles W. Eliot, then professor of chemistry at the Massachusetts Institute of Technology, in reviewing the book for the *Nation,* praised the general soundness of Fiske's

[41] JF to Marble, Sept. 29, 1868, Nov. 23, 1868, LC. JF, *Tobacco and Alcohol,* (New York, 1868). Quotations from Henry Holt, *Garrulities of an Octogenarian Editor* (Boston, 1923), p. 343, and Massachusetts Historical Society, *Proceedings,* 46:173 (1912–1913).

[42] JF to Marble, Jan. 11, 1869, LC. JF to his mother, Apr. 3, 1869; JF to Lizzie Wilcox, Mar. 16, 1869; JF to Abby, Aug. 13, 1869; JF to Henry Holt, Feb. 2, 1879, HHL. JF to Holt, Dec. 27, 1888, in *Letters of John Fiske,* Ethel F. Fisk, ed. (New York, 1940), p. 558 [incorrectly identified as being to Henry Harper]. Fiske's total profits in 1869 were only $44.46. The book was still in print in 1879 and the plates were not finally destroyed until 1888.

JOHN FISKE

John Fiske.

John Fiske.

conclusions, but felt dubious about Fiske's boast that he had written the book in five weeks, "a fact which will hardly satisfy people who think that popular summaries on scientific subjects deserve the best thought and care of the most thorough students of science." [43]

V

Fiske's success as a writer brought him to the attention of Andrew Dickson White, who was searching for young talent to staff his newly founded Cornell University. Fiske had first been recommended to White in 1866, while he was still in Middletown, by James T. Fields, the publisher and editor of the *Atlantic Monthly*. White, who was trying to set up a nonsectarian university based upon scientific principles, one which would provide a close union of liberal and practical subjects, and devote much of its revenue to advanced instruction, found it difficult to hire men competent to teach the subjects he proposed to introduce into his expanded curriculum. For some subjects, like agriculture, there were no trained experts. For other subjects, the most competent men already had established positions, and White could not get them to shift to an insecure new institution. Although White could bring many of the great figures in American science and literature to Ithaca briefly as special lecturers, for his permanent staff he had to turn to promising young scholars. As he prepared for the formal opening of instruction at Cornell in September of 1868, White combed the country gathering the names of men who might be worth bringing to Ithaca. It was on such a hunting trip that White added Fiske's name to his list.[44]

Many aspects of Fiske's career and opinions probably attracted White, for the two men shared similar views of the value of Herbert Spencer's ideas, of the virtues of free trade, and of the dangers which religious orthodoxy presented to the advancement of science. The recommendations that Fiske received from Fields, and later from

[43] E. L. Godkin to C. E. Norton, Dec. 15, 1868, in Rollo Ogden, *Life and Letters of E. L. Godkin*, 2 vols. (New York, 1907), I, 304. *Catholic World*, 8:719 (January 1869). *Nation*, 8:14 (Jan. 7, 1869).

[44] JF to Abby, Nov. 17, 1866, HHL. A. D. White, *Autobiography*, 2 vols. (New York, 1905), I, 330–354.

Gurney, would make him a strong candidate for a position at Cornell, once White actually began to hire men.[45]

Fiske could not decide whether he wanted such a position. When he first heard of the possibility he was in process of moving back to Cambridge, expecting to support himself there by free-lance writing. The freedom of being his own master seemed more attractive to him then, especially as he still thought he would be able to continue scholarly studies along with his remunerative writing. When, after a time in Cambridge, he found that he had greatly underestimated the expense of supporting his family, he showed more interest in the financial security of a university position. In October 1867, just before Stoughton resumed his allowance, Fiske wrote to Marble asking him to intervene with White on his behalf.[46]

White was willing to oblige Marble, whose support had aided the passage of enabling legislation for the college by the New York legislature, and he promised to interview Fiske at the first opportunity. To impress White, Fiske had Marble send along cuttings of the semischolarly essays he contributed to the *World*. White met Fiske and spent a day talking with him in New York in February 1868. Fiske was certain that he had made a good impression and felt encouraged, although White made no offer at the interview. Fiske arranged with Norton to write a lengthy review of a book on liberal education for the *North American* "as, among other things, it might strike Mr. White just at the right moment." Several other articles by him on educational topics appeared in the *World* and *Nation* that year.[47]

When Cornell opened in September 1868 with no word from White, Fiske was bitterly disappointed, for by now his finances were in very bad shape. Free-lancing did not pay as well as he had hoped. With two children to care for and a third due early in 1869, his income did not suffice to keep him from running into debt. Marble permitted him to draw advances for articles he had not yet written,

---

[45] White, *Autobiography*, I, 363; II, 513–573.

[46] JF to James Brooks, Dec. 8, 1866, HHL. JF to Marble, Oct. 3, 1867, LC.

[47] Quotation from JF to C. E. Norton, Mar. 14, 1868, HUL. JF to Abby, Oct. 22, 1867, HHL. JF to Marble, Nov. 14, 1867, Dec. 13, 1867; A. D. White to Marble, Feb. 8, 1868, LC.

although the *World* normally paid only upon publication. To save Fiske from bankruptcy proceedings, Marble arranged a $2,000 loan in March 1869 from a wealthy friend of his, Mrs. Mary Elizabeth Richmond of Buffalo, New York, Fiske paid out the money in two days, settling up outstanding bills and smaller notes. Knowing Fiske's desperate financial condition and desiring to help him, Marble kept up his pressure on White but, in the course of doing so, irritated White and almost cost Fiske all chance of getting a teaching post at Cornell.[48]

In August of 1869 White assured Marble that he was impressed by Fiske's work and intended to hire him as soon as he could offer him a proper position. White explained that the course work at Cornell for the first two years consisted entirely of elementary required subjects, and that until the first class entered its Junior year there would not be sufficient demand for optional advanced courses to give Fiske "an audience and a position worthy of his work." When the expansion of Cornell made it possible, White promised to hire Fiske.[49]

Although this explanation encouraged Fiske, Marble was apparently not satisfied. On September 23, 1869, the *World* printed an editorial attacking "the University ring in this state." A million acres of land, as well as direct money grants, had been given to Cornell by the Republican governor and legislature, the *World* asserted. Since it was endowed with state property, it should be entirely nonpartisan, yet "recent elections to the faculty of the new university show that the concern is to be run mainly as a Radical [Republican] machine." White immediately fired back with an open letter to the editor, published in the *World* on September 29, putting the true facts before the newspaper's readers. He pointed out that Ezra Cornell had so skillfully managed the land grant that New York would get six to eight times as much as any other state had realized, that Cornell himself had made no profit from his management and had

[48] JF to James Brooks, Sept. 22, 1866; JF to his mother, Dec. 8, 1871, HHL. JF to Marble, May 30, 1868, Aug. 1, 1868, Sept. 29, 1868, Nov. 5, 1868, Nov. 23, 1868, Dec. 23, 1868, Jan. 17, 1869, Mar. 25, 1869, LC. JF to Henry A. Richmond, July 19, 1881, HHL.
[49] White to Marble, Aug. 30, 1869, LC.

instead given generously to the university out of his personal fortune. White listed the outstanding Democrats on the Board of Trustees and assured the *World* that the nonpartisan clause of the college's constitution was strictly obeyed. Of the last four appointments to the Faculty, he contended, two had gone to Democrats and two to Republicans. In a private letter written to Marble the same day as the published letter, White pointedly remarked that "if you suppose that the delay in Mr. Fiske's appointment arises from a political motive you do me great wrong." [50]

Faced with White's fury, Marble assumed an air of injured innocence. He claimed to have been out of town when the attack on Cornell was printed and said that had he seen it before publication it would not have appeared. Marble loftily deplore White's "insulting implication" that he had used the power of the *World* to advance the private interests of an individual—which was exactly what he had been doing persistently for the past year. "Now I chiefly regret the whole matter," he wrote, "for that it elicited what I wd [sic] prefer to be ignorant of—Mr. White's opinion that his doing or failing to do anything whatever concerning Mr. Fiske could determine an utterance in the *World* on a public question." [51]

By November the furor had been smoothed over, and White informed Marble that he intended to talk over the possibilities of an appointment with Fiske shortly. But not until the late summer of 1870 did he finally offer Fiske a position, that of instructor in American history. This Fiske rejected. The salary offered was not attractive, nor did Fiske then think of this as his field. "I am no more competent to lecture on the history of the United States than Mr. Bancroft or Mr. Parkman would be to lecture on positive philosophy," he wrote White. "There are only two subjects with which I profess to be sufficiently familiar to lecture upon them;— 'positive philosophy', which is, so to speak, my 'generality'; and 'comparative philology', which is my 'specialty'." Perhaps even more important was the fact that the new Eliot administration had already appointed him a University Lecturer at Harvard. This was only a

---

[50] JF to Mrs. M. F. B. Lewis [grandmother], Sept. 10, 1869, HHL. New York *World*, Sept. 23, 1869, Sept. 29, 1869. White to Marble, Sept. 24, 1869, LC.

[51] Marble to [E.?] Brooks, Oct. 2, 1869, LC.

temporary position. But Fiske hoped to attain a permanency, and even the possibility of a regular position at Harvard attracted him more than the new university far away from his beloved Cambridge.[52]

VI

When Charles W. Eliot became president of Harvard in 1869 he faced quite different problems from those which troubled White at Cornell, although both were pioneers in the development of the modern American university. White was trying to construct a university where none had existed, while Eliot's task was to guide a leading university into new paths despite the resistance of conservative elements strongly entrenched in the Faculty and governing boards.

By 1869 Harvard had already begun to depart from the pattern which had dominated its first two centuries, but the direction and speed of its development were unclear and heavily disputed. It would be Eliot's task to decide what changes to press for, when to introduce them, and how to muster the financial and intellectual resources necessary. His work was eased by the excellent quality of the Faculty he inherited and by the efforts of his predecessors, who had already begun the introduction of elective courses to make room for more science and modern languages in the curriculum.

An abortive attempt had even been made to begin a program of advanced instruction. In 1863, the first year of his administration, President Thomas Hill had set up a program of University Lectureships, open to mature men and women (undergraduates were barred) for nominal fees. But he had no funds to pay lecturers, making it impossible to secure the services of desirable instructors, nor did he make any provision for a continuous course of study. By 1869 the program was moribund.[53]

When President Hill resigned in September 1868 the alumni and

---

[52] White to Marble, Nov. 6, 1869, LC. JF to his mother, Feb. 24, 1870, HHL. JF to White, Sept. 6, 1870, Cornell University Archives.

[53] *Harvard University Catalogue*, 1860 through 1869. *Annual Report of the President of Harvard University*, 1862–63, pp. 8–9, 26; 1867–68, p. 16; 1869–70, pp. 19–20.

governing boards divided sharply over the choice of his successor. Two strong groups appeared. One, in which Louis Agassiz was active, desired to develop the advanced study program and secure a better position for sciences within the University; this group supported Fiske's friend Gurney as their candidate. Those who feared that the changes advocated by the first group would adversely affect the liberal arts program of the college desired a minister as president and rallied behind A. P. Peabody, professor of Christian morals and Preacher to the University. The dispute was so intense that for five months the Board of Overseers, suspicious of the consequences of a quick choice, delayed before giving its consent to the Corporation in February 1869 to proceed with the election of a new president.

Fiske enthusiastically enlisted among Gurney's supporters, contributing an editorial on the presidency of Harvard to the *Nation* in December 1868, in which he argued that the choice of a clergyman would inevitably involve the college in sectarianism. Even the choice of a Unitarian would not avoid this, since the Unitarians were themselves split and one faction was sure to take offence. He then went on to describe the ideal candidate as one with an interest in science, and alert to its significance, but not a specialist; rather a man of broad culture able to see science in perspective—terms designed to suggest the virtues of Gurney without naming him directly.[54]

Uneasy at the bitterness of the dispute, the Harvard Corporation decided to pass over the two men who had become symbols of the opposing parties. It first offered the post to the aged Charles Francis Adams, former Ambassador to England and Chairman of the Board of Overseers, a man acceptable to both parties. After Adams turned down the offer, the Corporation sent to the Overseers for confirmation the nomination of Charles W. Eliot, then professor of chemistry at Massachusetts Institute of Technology and a member of the Board of Overseers since the previous July. The choice satisfied neither party. To the conservatives any scientist was anathema, while to the "scientists" Eliot seemed more closely identified with technology than with science as they understood it. On March 21 the Overseers voted 11–10 to return the nomination to the Corporation,

[54] JF, "The Presidency of Harvard College," *Nation,* 7:547–548 (Dec. 31, 1868).

and not until that body put his name forward once more was he confirmed in the office on May 19.[55]

Eliot had clear ideas of the goals he would set for Harvard. If he was by no means so clear on the methods by which the goals could be achieved, he was young and would have forty years of active work in which to experiment and learn. In his inaugural address he outlined various reforms—expansion of the elective system, stricter entrance and course examinations, an increase in intellectual freedom for both students and teachers, and liberalization of the disciplinary procedures. But to one of the most puzzling problems he faced—how to provide instruction beyond the undergraduate level—he made no overt reference.[56]

Eliot did not know how to solve this problem. The most successful system of graduate education was that followed in Germany, which Eliot had studied during a trip to Europe. Its central core was a "Philosophical Faculty" of outstanding scholars and scientists who offered advanced courses to qualified students on a freely elective basis and guided the research efforts of selected students. But Eliot saw clearly that this model would fit Harvard "about as well as a barnyard would suit a whale." Harvard did not have the money to support research professors on a large scale; it was hard put to provide adequate salaries for the faculty needed for undergraduate instruction. Nor could it wisely permit as much freedom as the universities of Germany, where the necessity of University certification before entry into a profession insured that the students would do at least a minimum of work. America had no such threat of future consequences to encourage self-discipline among students.[57]

Unable to see any way of directly benefiting from the German example, Eliot turned to an extension of the already existing University Lecture system. To provide continuity of instruction, he organized the 1869–70 lectures into two courses, one in philosophy and the other in modern literature. A fee of $150 for each course permitted payment of a modest honorarium to the lecturer. Those who

[55] James, *Eliot*, I, 184–204.

[56] C. W. Eliot, "Inaugural Address," in *The Development of Harvard University*, S. E. Morison, ed. (Cambridge, Mass., 1930), pp. lix–lxxviii.

[57] James, *Eliot*, I, 136–138.

took the philosophy course heard Professor Francis Bowen on Locke and seventeenth-century philosophy, Fiske on positive philosophy, C. S. Peirce on the British logicians, Professor F. H. Hedge on theism, pantheism, and atheism, Ralph Waldo Emerson on the natural history of the intellect, J. E. Cabot on Kant, and Professor George W. Fisher of Yale on stoicism.[58]

Organizing these lectures was one of the first tasks Eliot undertook after assuming the presidency. Not only was it a first step toward providing graduate education, but it also signaled, even before his inaugural address, the direction the new administration would take. It encouraged the Faculty to use scholarly competence in the course offerings. Inviting Fisher, Cabot, and Peirce brought new talents and new topics to the service of Harvard. The use of Hedge and Bowen, both staunch Unitarians and members of the Faculty, assured the conservatives that the old traditions of Harvard would not be entirely overthrown. By inviting Emerson, Eliot not only gave the University's greatest living alumnus his first opportunity to teach a regular course there, but also symbolized the reconciliation of Harvard with the transcendentalist religious radicals of the past.

The choice of Fiske, who had been penalized for reading Comte in church as an undergraduate, to lecture on positivism, indicated Eliot's intention to open Harvard to those currently regarded as religious radicals. Fiske was a bright young man who might be put to use in building a modern university. Permitting him to lecture on a topic about which controversy still swirled would show in action the principles of intellectual freedom expressed in Eliot's inaugural address and also give Eliot a better idea of Fiske's promise as a future addition to the faculty.

To Fiske the offer was a dream come true. Although he would not be paid much for his lectures, a successful series would both give him a claim to a permanent position on the Faculty and establish his scholarly reputation. A professorship at Harvard seemed the ideal solution of his financial problems. Preparing the lectures would provide a first draft of a book in which he could display his knowledge and unique talents to advantage. Fiske entered upon his task with enthusiasm.

[58] *Harvard University Catalogue, 1869–70*, pp. 102–103. *Annual Report of the President of Harvard University, 1869–70*, pp. 19–20.

CHAPTER FOUR

BUILDING AN ACADEMIC REPUTATION

Fiske began his work eagerly, expecting that the lectures would immediately establish his academic reputation as well as lead to a major published work in philosophy.[1] But neither result came as easily as he optimistically anticipated in 1869.

Fiske rejoiced in this opportunity to spread his views before a wide audience under respectable sponsorship. He wrote exultingly to Spencer, telling him of the appointment and enclosing an outline of his proposed eighteen lectures. "Mr. Eliot is not a 'positivist,' nor a man of broad or deep culture; rather a scientific specialist, but nevertheless 'liberal' as regards theology," Fiske told Spencer. "That he began his official career by virtually inviting a man who is known to be neither a Christian nor a theist, to preach to the young men the views of Herbert Spencer, and to say whatever good word may be said for Auguste Comte,—is, I think, sufficient evidence that a new state of things has begun here." This was not quite the spirit in which Eliot hoped to have the course given. In his inaugural he had remarked that "philosophical subjects should never be taught with authority," and went on to object that "the notion that education consists in the authoritative inculcation of what the teacher deems true may be logical and appropriate in a convent, or a seminary for

[1] JF to Manton Marble, Nov. 2, 1869, LC.

priests, but it is intolerable in universities." Whatever Eliot might think of preaching the views of Herbert Spencer in a university, Spencer himself was pleased. He congratulated Fiske on his opportunity and approved the general outline.[2]

Although Fiske was eager to get to work on the lectures, financial problems made it difficult to set aside time. Not until September 13 could he afford to stop his other writing and begin preparing the lectures he had to give between October 26 and December 10.[3] In the six weeks remaining before his course began he wrote out the full text of eleven lectures, the other seven being written concurrently with delivery. He only completed the final address the day before it was delivered. "In all they make 654 pages, 4to letter paper," he boasted to his mother, "which I have written in 82 days, hardly looking at a book even to verify data." [4]

Fiske ran low on cash at the end of his first month of writing. To increase his income he suggested to Marble that the *World* reprint the lectures as they were given. After some hesitation, and the intervention of Youmans on Fiske's behalf, Marble agreed in November. In the issue of Saturday, November 13, he ran the first lecture in the top, right-hand column of his front page under the headline: "Introductory Lecture of Professor John Fiske at Harvard." An editorial in the same issue congratulated Harvard on being "the first of American colleges to give a chair to . . . the Positive Philosophy," and welcomed the prospect of an attempt to carry positivism "into the domain of theology and call upon the existing theologians to prove their positions or to fall, exactly as GALILEO demanded of the scientists of his time to prove the theory, upheld only by the senses of mankind, that the sun moved around the earth." [5]

This banner treatment (Marble ran three more lectures on page

[2] JF to Spencer, [Oct. 6.] 1869, HHL (draft copy). C. W. Eliot, "Inaugural Address," in *The Development of Harvard University,* S. E. Morison, ed. (Cambridge, Mass., 1930), p. lxii. Spencer to JF, Nov. 1, 1869, HHL.

[3] JF to his mother, July 5, 1869, LC; Sept. 6, 1869, HHL.

[4] Quotation from JF to his mother, Dec. 9, 1869, HHL. JF to his mother, Oct. 20, 1869, HHL.

[5] JF to Marble, Sept. 27, 1869, LC. New York *World,* Nov. 13, 1869, pp. 1 and 6. JF, "Preface," to *Outlines of Cosmic Philosophy,* 4 vols. (Boston, 1902), I, vii.

one before shifting the rest to inside pages) attracted public attention to Fiske's series and led to the whole affair being labeled "Harvard's raid on religion" by proponents of orthodoxy. It also gave Fiske a wider audience than the University provided, for Eliot's experiment in graduate education proved a failure. Only fifteen listeners turned out for Fiske's afternoon lectures, and not all of these paid. Complimentary letters poured in on Fiske from *World* readers, many asking when they would be able to buy the talks in book form.[6]

Eliot and Gurney were disturbed by the way the *World* publicized Fiske's lectures. Gurney objected to the by-line crediting the lectures to "Prof. John Fiske," which seemed "clearly done for his glorification." He requested Fiske to have this changed and after the fifth lecture the legend read "by Mr. John Fiske, at Harvard." The whole incident dismayed Gurney since "it will appear to an outsider, I fear, like a manifesto on the part of the new administration of the college that it has gone over, body & soul, to a 'Scientific Philosophy'." Although privately critical of Fiske's behavior, Eliot and Gurney characteristically reacted to the storm of public criticism the lectures evoked by reappointing Fiske to give thirty-five lectures on the same topic the next year.[7]

II

When Fiske completed his first series of lectures he had high hopes of attaining a permanent position at Harvard. There were several possibilities. If Eliot's plans for the University Lectureships succeeded, "the Corporation will have to appropriate money to carry it on. They will need regular post-graduate professors, such as they have in Europe, and then you see I will already have possession, which is 9 points of the law." In order to look properly professorial, he began to grow a beard, against the wishes of his wife. Fiske's dream faded when the University Lectures failed to attract students. His second opportunity came when Eliot created the post of Dean of Faculty, in order to reduce the administrative burdens on

[6] JF to his mother, Nov. 2, 1869, HHL. JF to Marble, Jan. 4, 1870, LC.

[7] Quotations from E. W. Gurney to C. W. Eliot, Nov. 17, 1869, HUA. JF to his mother, Nov. 11, 1869, HHL.

the president, and chose Gurney for the position. Eliot and Gurney asked Fiske to take over Gurney's history course during the spring semester of 1870. If the new arrangement proved satisfactory, and Gurney remained as dean, Fiske expected a permanent appointment.[8]

This plan ran into difficulties when the Board of Overseers balked at the first step. On January 6, 1870, Eliot presented to the Overseers two nominations involving Fiske, one reappointing him as University Lecturer for 1870–71, the other appointing him as instructor in history for the spring semester. The Overseers routinely confirmed the first nomination, but held up the second for several weeks of consideration before voting twelve to ten to accept it. The opposition stemmed from the religious controversy Fiske's lectures had aroused. He told his mother the Overseers were "more careful about who shall teach undergraduates than about who shall teach graduates." Permitting Fiske to express heterodox views before an audience of mature students was acceptable to the Overseers, whatever they thought personally of his propaganda for Spencer. But they were reluctant to let him do the same before the entire Senior class (as instructor, Fiske gave the course in medieval history required of all seniors).[9]

Thus, although the experiment of creating a dean to relieve the president of administrative routine satisfied both Eliot and Gurney, and they needed a permanent substitute to take over part of Gurney's teaching duties, Fiske did not get the post. Facing many hard fights with the Overseers on the various reforms the administration initiated, the president and dean did not want to stir up an unnecessary battle by nominating Fiske again. Instead, in September 1870, they selected Henry Adams, son of the chairman of the Overseers.

With the hope of a position teaching history at Harvard fading, Fiske turned back to his lectures and expanded them to thirty-five for the series he was scheduled to give in the spring of 1871. This

---

[8] Quotation from JF to his mother, Nov. 11, 1869, HHL. JF to his mother, Jan. 30, 1870, HHL. JF to Marble, Oct. 6, 1869, LC.

[9] JF to his mother, Feb. 17, 1870, LC. Harvard University, Manuscript Overseer Records, X, 385–386, 395–396, 399–400.

second series occurred in a quite different frame from the earlier. Eliot's first try at building a graduate school had failed badly. Only thirteen students had registered for the courses of University Lectures, though a handful more turned up as auditors.

Because of this lack of interest, Eliot retreated to a system closer to the original idea of University Lectures. In 1870–71 the program offered thirty-three separate lecture courses, twenty-two given by men connected with the University. Each of the series had a separate fee, and the lecturer was paid solely from fees paid to hear his course. Fiske's thirty-five lectures cost $10. Eliot abandoned all attempt to integrate the teaching and dropped the final examination. This was far closer to university extension or adult education than the start on a graduate school Eliot desired.[10]

Fiske gave his lectures in the spring of 1871, from February 15 to April 15. Despite some hesitation by Marble, who was now uncertain whether or not his full printing of the previous lectures had been journalistically justifiable, Fiske persuaded him to publish all new material in the *World*. Fiske argued that, if he could not have this source of income to supplement his Harvard fees, he could not afford to give them and would have to abandon his plan to expand his work into a comprehensive summary of Spencerian thought. Once again his lectures aroused the enthusiasm of *World* readers, one of whom wrote to Fiske in gratitude: "I pursue with joy the path of certainty." [11]

As a step toward building a graduate school this attempt proved no more successful than the earlier one, and Eliot permitted the University Lecture system to die out. In the spring of 1872 he turned, instead, to a system organized about the granting of advanced degrees. Previously, all holders of the A.B. could get an A.M., three years after the first degree, upon payment of a small fee. Now the A.M. would be awarded only after the successful completion of a year's study beyond the undergraduate level. At the same time, the

---

[10] *Annual Report of the President of Harvard University,* 1869–70, pp. 19–21; 1871–72, pp. 13–19. *Harvard University Catalogue, 1870–71,* pp. 108–110.

[11] Quotation from B. F. Stairley to JF, July 6, 1871, HHL. JF to Marble, Jan. 17, 1871, Jan. 24, 1871, Feb. 22, 1871, LC. Marble printed Fiske's nineteen new lectures in the *World* from May 1, to Sept. 1, 1871.

college instituted a Ph.D. degree, to be awarded after a minimum of two years of advanced study and the completion of a satisfactory thesis. With money still a problem, Eliot could offer no special courses to graduate students. Instead he opened all elective courses in the college to them and permitted them to undertake independent work in the libraries and laboratories under the direction of the college faculty.

Where the University Lectureships had proved to be a false step, this was indeed the germ of the Graduate School of today. As Eliot expanded the elective system, his most important single reform, the college could employ many scholars and scientists whose specialties could not have fitted the earlier pattern of required courses; this provided a wide range of instruction for both undergraduates and graduate students. Although this attempt to encourage a graduate school to grow out of the fertile soil of the college succeeded, it was not until Johns Hopkins had shown the way that progress became secure. Eliot learned, under the spur of competition from the newer school, that he would have to find funds to free his faculty for advanced research and teaching if he was to hold his best men. By the 1890's this system transformed Harvard into one of the leading graduate schools of the nation.[12]

III

Harvard did not occupy all Fiske's time during the years he worked on his lectures. In 1870 he turned to another of his favorite projects, the study of the early origins of Christianity, in two long articles entitled "The Jesus of History" and "The Christ of Dogma" which he sent to Marble in February. These essays drew heavily on Ernest Renan's thirteenth edition of his *Vie de Jésus,* as well as his recently published *Vie de St. Paul,* to portray Jesus as an attractive ethical teacher whose views were encrusted after his death with an aura of divinity and formalized into a dogmatic system. Fiske compared the process with the growth of myths about other historic figures. Marble refused to print this wholesale endorsement of the latest results of Biblical criticism, which was, in effect, a much more

---

[12] *Annual Report of the President of Harvard University,* 1871–72, pp. 13–19; 1883–84, pp. 46–47. Henry James, *C. W. Eliot,* 2 vols (Boston, 1930), II, 3–28, 132.

open attack on current concepts of Christianity than any Fiske had yet published. Marble's reaction surprised Fiske. "To tell the truth," he wrote Marble, "Christianity is so utterly a matter of history with me that I don't sufficiently realize how to many people it is a present and sacred reality." After some hesitation Fiske agreed to Marble's suggestion that David Goodman Croly, the managing editor of the *World* and one of the leading New York Comtists, print the articles in his radical review, the *Modern Thinker*. There they appeared under the title, "The Last Word about Jesus," a heading which claimed too much even for Fiske; he furiously repudiated the implication that this was a definitive study.[13]

Fiske did not give up his dream of making a reputation in philology. He squeezed out enough time to complete the lengthy essay on the origins of language that he had begun in Middletown. Published in the October 1869 *North American Review,* the sixty-three page article laid out an evolutionary scheme for the development of language and illustrated it with citations from obscure tongues. Fiske concluded that the remotest origins of nouns lay in vocal imitations of sounds made by objects, though in many cases the words had been so worn down over time that this was hard to prove. Most other parts of speech, he decided, were derived either from nouns or the gestures used to accompany them.[14]

Fiske took great pride in this essay. He boasted to his mother that it "deserves to be called an original and important contribution to Science, & I have no doubt will make my reputation as a philologist." Encouraged by John Spencer Clark, Fiske planned to expand it into a book early in 1870. He sent copies of the article to Michael Bréal in Paris, W. D. Whitney at Yale, and Max Müller at Oxford, requesting them to criticize it, and secured the consent of Max Müller to dedicate the projected volume to him. But Fiske never completed his revision. He apparently considered doing so as late as 1885, for he then dispiritedly noted that it "contains many philological errors and some of the side arguments . . . are of very doubtful value. The

[13] Quotation from JF to Marble, Apr. 6, 1870, LC. JF to Marble, Feb. 27, 1870, May 28, 1870, LC. JF, *Unseen World* (Boston, 1902), pp. 87–88.

[14] JF, "Genesis of Language," *North American Review,* 109:305–367 (October 1869).

whole essay needs thorough revision before it is fit to be republished among my works." [15]

More popular essays using philological materials appeared in other magazines. After his return to Cambridge, Fiske became friendly with William Dean Howells, sub-editor of the *Atlantic Monthly*. Howells commissioned five articles on myth and folklore for the *Atlantic*, in which Fiske summarized in a clear, easily comprehensible style the work that such philologists as Max Müller had done in elucidating mythology. In December 1872, J. R. Osgood & Co. of Boston, then the publishers of the *Atlantic* in succession to Ticknor & Fields, brought out the five articles (along with an essay that had first appeared in the *World*) in book form under the title *Myths and Myth-Makers*. In addition, Howells arranged for Fiske to proofread for the *Atlantic* and provide a regular column on new scientific books. [16]

Despite the help and money he received from Marble for publishing nineteen new Harvard lectures in the *World*, Fiske's financial problems intensified. His income dropped off sharply in 1871. "Having a wife, and little daughter, and three little sons, and wife's mother to take care of and having a strong *'gout de bien être'*, not to call it a taste for luxury, I find it rather hard to get along and keep out of debt," he told Spencer. As his income dropped, his indebtedness increased, and at times he grew rather pessimistic. "Sometimes I think I did very wrong when I married & incurred a responsibility which I am hardly able to shoulder," he told Marble. "But I was a blasted boy then, greener than grass." [17]

Such pessimism was uncharacteristic. More often Fiske went optimistically on, assuring himself that next year would be better, and then spending in advance what he expected to earn in the future. The result was an accelerating slide into debt. Nevertheless, in the fall of 1871 he began to plan a trip to England to consult

[15] Quotations from JF to his mother, Feb. 27, 1869, and Manuscript Critical Comments on Genesis of Language, Aug. 2, 1885, HHL. JF to Abby, Aug. 8, 1869; Max Müller to JF, Jan. 21, 1870, HHL.

[16] W. D. Howells, "John Fiske," *Harpers' Weekly*, 45:732 (July 20, 1901). JF to his mother, Aug. 11, 1867, Dec. 8, 1871, HHL. JF to Marble, Nov. 28, 1870, LC.

[17] JF to Spencer, Sept. 29, 1871, HHL (draft copy). JF to Marble, Mar. 7, 1871, LC. JF to his mother, Dec. 8, 1871, HHL.

Spencer, Darwin, and Huxley before revising his lectures into book form. He still hoped for an appointment to the Harvard faculty and speculated on the possibility of replacing Henry Adams if he moved on to another department in a few years, by which time opposition to Fiske among the Overseers might have eased off. But neither an incomplete book nor a faculty appointment in the future was of any help in meeting current bills.[18]

As a quick way of making money Fiske considered repeating his Harvard lectures before the public. In the fall of 1871 he planned a series for Boston, confidently expecting a hundred and fifty listeners to turn out, and also inquired about the possibility of delivering single talks before the lyceum circuit. Only twenty-five advance subscribers came forward in Boston. "No lyceum-association has invited me," he sadly reported to his mother, although he had carefully advertised his willingness to lecture. Eliot tried to secure him an appointment as lecturer in the public series supported by the Lowell endowment in Boston, but the trustees thought it unwise to select an openly proclaimed infidel.[19]

In December 1871 Fiske decided to risk the possibility of loss and announced a series of lectures in Boston over the fourteen-week period from December 19, 1871 to March 29, 1872. Although only twenty-five turned out to hear the opening lecture, by February his audience had risen to seventy or eighty. This was only half as many people as he had hoped for, but Fiske made the best of it and assured Marble that the audience was "made up of the cream of Boston." Julia Ward Howe, who attended Fiske's first lecture, was not impressed. She confided to her diary that she "did not think the lecture a very profitable one, yet we must be willing that our opposites should think and speak out their belief." Other auditors were more enthusiastic. Fiske reported that after the last lecture on science and religion, "several people told me that their lives would be brighter ever after for hearing these lectures, that they had never known any pleasure like it; etc., etc., and as these things were said

[18] JF to C. E. Norton, Oct. 23, 1871, HUL. JF to his mother, Dec. 8, 1871, HHL.
[19] Quotation from JF to his mother, Dec. 12, 1871, HHL. JF to his mother, Dec. 8, 1871, HHL. C. W. Eliot to JF, Mar. 27, 1872, printed in J. S. Clark, *Life and Letters of John Fiske*, 2 vols. (Boston, 1917), I, 395–396.

with moistened eyes, I have no doubt they came from the heart." Despite the slow start, Fiske cleared over $500 and drew invitations to repeat single lectures both in Boston and New York.[20]

In the spring of 1872 Fiske's finances took a turn for the better. James Brooks, who had returned with money earned in western mining and repurchased the family home in Petersham, bought a town house in Cambridge. In April he invited the Fiske family to move in with him. James offered to shoulder all house expenses, asking Fiske to contribute only what he now paid yearly on the mortgage on the 123 Oxford Street house. Fiske accepted his brother-in-law's proposal. Not only did it reduce his living expenses, but when he sold his present house he could use the money to reduce his debts. Since Fiske had paid his half-share of the house out of Abby's inheritance, this method of reducing indebtedness radically decreased the capital resources of the Fiske family, but he saw no alternative. Then in May Fiske received further help when Eliot and Gurney, who still desired to help him, appointed him assistant librarian at a salary of $2,500.[21]

This assured Fiske of a steady income greater than his free-lance earnings. He hoped to continue to devote at least six hours a day to his own writing and get time off for lecture tours as well. In September Fiske received permission to take a three-week leave and give nine lectures on evolution at the Milwaukee Unitarian church where his Middletown friend, Reverend J. L. Dudley, was now pastor. There he enjoyed a financial success and gloried in the admiration of the citizens, who treated him as an erudite and successful scholar from the East.[22]

In his first year of lecturing Fiske earned much less than he had hoped for and expected to get in the future. One of his major problems was the abstract nature of his subject matter. Not even Fiske's lucid style could make it easy to grasp Spencerian ideas of evolution

---

[20] Quotations from L. E. Richards and M. H. Elliott, *Julia Ward Howe,* 2 vols. (Boston, 1915), I, 312; JF to Marble, Feb. 14, 1872, LC; and JF to his mother, Mar. 31, 1872, HHL. JF to his mother, Dec. 8, 1871, Feb. 11, 1872, HHL.

[21] JF to his mother, Apr. 25, 1872, HHL. JF to Marble, June 24, 1872, July 29, 1872, LC.

[22] JF to his mother, Aug. 22, 1872, Sept. 6, 1872; JF to Abby, Sept. 15, 1872, Sept. 17, 1872, Sept. 24, 1872, HHL.

by ear. He drew primarily audiences attracted by his reputation as a religious radical. But the more lucrative offers were in control of lyceum managers and Lowell trustees who did not desire abstract subject matter or who feared that his heterodox religious position would offend their usual audiences.

IV

Fiske's work at the Harvard library, his writing of magazine articles, and his lecturing, left him little time to revise his lectures. Then in May of 1873 his great opportunity came. Mrs. M. A. Edwards, a Boston matron attracted by Fiske's religious views, offered him $1,000 to enable him to make his long-desired trip to Europe.

All his friends rallied about Fiske to help him take advantage of this offer. His wealthy brother-in-law, James Brooks, offered to pay all the expenses of Fiske's family during the year he would spend in Europe. Eliot approved of his project and arranged a year's leave of absence from the library, as well as having his appointment as assistant librarian made permanent. Fiske's debts had been substantially reduced the previous year, making it a financially opportune moment for the trip. To pay some small bills, Fiske persuaded the *North American Review* to print two of the Harvard lectures and rapidly wrote an article entitled "Agassiz and Darwinism" for E. L. Youmans' recently established *Popular Science Monthly*. Only Manton Marble failed to respond to a request for a loan.[23]

Fiske planned an ambitious itinerary. He would sail in mid-August, tour Ireland, Scotland, and England until early October, then settle down at Oxford or London until February 1874 to work on his book. He hoped to find an English publisher who would issue the book in England simultaneously with Osgood in Boston. In February he planned to leave for a six-month tour of the continent (which money problems later forced him to reduce to three months), visiting France, Italy, Switzerland, Germany, and Holland, before re-embarking for America.[24]

[23] JF to Abby, Aug. 1, 1873; JF to his mother, May 13, 1873, May 16, 1873, May 27, 1873, Aug. 1, 1873, HHL. JF to Marble, July 22, 1873, Sept. 14, 1873, LC.
[24] JF to his mother, May 16, 1873; JF to Spencer, June 8, 1873 (draft copy), HHL.

He sent home long and detailed letters from his trip, describing the scenery he passed and inserting cuttings from the greenery as souvenirs for Abby. He was delighted by the way his travels brought his previous reading in English history and literature to life. The dining room of an old hotel in Cork looked "just as if it had stepped out of 'Ivanhoe'." He went out of his way to stop off at the Great White Horse Inn at Ipswich, "the far-famed house where Mr. Pickwick had the romantic adventure with the middle-aged lady in yellow curl papers! I came here partly for that reason, and feel paid for my trouble, 'it is such a rum old place'." Though he raved about England he did not forget America. All along his route, in Ireland, in the Lake District of England, and in Scotland, he had his beloved Massachusetts in mind. "I still say, give me New England for scenery," he wrote Abby. "I still swear by Petersham." [25]

Fiske visited all the major libraries along his route, comparing them with Harvard, rarely to the disadvantage of his own domain. No matter how much the rarities and long history of a library he visited impressed him, he always found some aspect in which Harvard was superior. Nothing he saw seemed to him to equal the new card catalogue his predecessor, Ezra Abbot, had started at Harvard, the completion of which Fiske was supervising. [26]

He had no reservations in his admiration of the great cathedrals he saw. He examined carefully and described with awe every important cathedral on his route, especially Ely and York Minster. No comparison with America could satisfy him here. "This trip to Europe is a rich extension of experiences," he assured Abby. "I have learned a great deal about Gothic architecture since Sunday, compared to the little I knew before from books. There is nothing like seeing things." For the first time he took a critical attitude toward American buildings. "What a monstrosity is our Memorial Hall compared to the buildings of Christ Church in Oxford! I understand it now as I couldn't when at home." [27]

The aspect of England that pleased Fiske most was his reception by English writers and scientists. "I first saw our God the 9th Oct.,"

[25] JF to Abby, Aug. 24, 1873 (from Cork), Oct. 2, 1873, LC; Sept. 14, 1873, HHL.
[26] JF to Abby, Sept. 28, 1873, Oct. 6, 1873, Feb. 27, 1874, HHL, and Mar. 20, 1874, LC.
[27] JF to Abby, Oct. 2, 1873, LC, and Oct. 31, 1873, HHL.

he wrote to Marble after his meeting with Spencer, and the God proved as beneficent as any worshipper could desire. Spencer had John Tyndall see that Fiske received full guest privileges at the exclusive Athenaeum Club during his stay in London, introduced Fiske to leading authors and scholars, including Tyndall, Huxley, J. N. Lockyer, and Sir Joseph Hooker, gave dinner parties in his honor, and magisterially approved Fiske's revision and publishing plans. Fiske was already a major disciple; Youmans' reports on the American scene had made his value clear. Spencer felt attracted by Fiske's personality, and enjoyed the wide-eyed adoration with which his disciple listened to him. He did his best to make Fiske's stay both pleasurable and profitable.[28]

The warmest friendship Fiske formed in England was with Thomas Henry Huxley, whom Fiske met at a dinner party given by Spencer. At first Fiske was somewhat shy, thinking that Huxley might resent the polemic vigor with which Fiske had attacked him in his first series of Harvard lectures. But if Huxley had read the lectures he was prepared to be forgiving, and before the evening was over the two men were on friendly terms. The entire Huxley family found Fiske charming and invited him to have tea with them every Sunday while he remained in England.[29]

Darwin granted Fiske's request for an interview. On November 13 Fiske had lunch with him and wrote enthusiastically to Abby and his mother describing the event. "My lunch with Darwin [was] the climax of everything thus far," he assured his mother. Fiske used similar language to describe his meeting with Sir Charles Lyell the following month.[30]

Soon after arriving in London, Fiske met George H. Lewes, the leading English disciple of Comte, in Trübner's bookstore. Lewes invited Fiske to meet his wife, George Eliot, who had read Fiske's volume on *Myths and Myth-Makers*. Fiske found her fascinating, and greatly enjoyed their discussion of the Homeric problem. Fiske strongly defended the theory that the poems were the work of one

[28] JF to Marble, Nov. 29, 1873, LC. JF to Abby, Oct. 17, 1873, Oct. 23, 1873; JF to Spencer, Oct. 24, 1873, HHL.

[29] JF to Abby, Dec. 7, 1873, HHL. JF to Marble, Dec. 28, 1873; JF to his mother, Jan. 12, 1874, LC.

[30] JF to his mother, Nov. 13, 1873; JF to Darwin, Oct. 31, 1873; Darwin to JF, Nov. 3, 1873; JF to Abby, Nov. 13, 1873, Dec. 22, 1873, HHL.

man, rather than an accumulation of the efforts of many generations.
This surprised George Eliot, who remarked that she had thought
a Spencerian would support the theory that the Homeric epics
gradually evolved rather than were especially created. In one of her
letters she portrayed Fiske's reverent attitude in England when she
described him as "a large-headed man with rather a good-looking
face—what Milton might call a 'bush with frizzy hair implicit'—
staring at you as if in spell-bound silence when he put out his hand
to say goodbyes and altogether rather in the heavy style. Yet he is
not at all a heavy writer." [31]

Fiske's reputation as a religious radical, along with his friendship
with Spencer and the introduction which his writing gave him to
the Leweses and Darwin, aided his social success. Moncure Conway,
a Virginian who had become pastor of the Unitarian South Place
Chapel in London, was one of the first to welcome Fiske. He was
in process of transforming his church into a citadel of "free religion,"
discarding most trappings of Christianity and replacing Biblical
readings by selections from Conway's *Sacred Anthology,* drawn
from the holy books of all major religions. Fiske's views attracted
Conway, who did his best for his compatriot. At dinner parties in
Fiske's honor he introduced him to W. K. Clifford and James A.
Froude. He took Fiske with him on a visit to Lyell, Fiske's only
meeting with the aged geologist. Fiske found the radical religious
groups of London congenial and agreed to Conway's request that
he give two of his lectures on evolution as Sunday evening lay
sermons at South Place. Many of the Englishmen who welcomed
Fiske in London were unorthodox in religion. Fiske's open defiance
of the ruling religious ideas of his day, as well as the reverent
attitude he took in the presence of English thinkers, helped make
him an attractive figure for them.[32]

The only unpleasantness during Fiske's stay in London arose not

[31] Quotation from George Eliot to Mrs. Charles Bray, Jan. 14, 1875, in *The George Eliot Letters,* G. S. Haight, ed., 7 vols. (New Haven, 1954–1955), VI, 119; see also, V, 464, 453. JF to Abby, Oct. 23, 1873, Nov. 23, 1873, HHL. JF, *A Century of Science* (Boston, 1902), pp. 339–340.

[32] JF to Abby, Nov. 23, 1873, Dec. 7, 1873, Dec. 22, 1873, HHL. Moncure D. Conway, *Autobiography,* 2 vols. (Boston, 1904), I, 38–39, 328–332, 348–365. Moncure D. Conway, *Centenary History of the South Place Society* (London, 1894), pp. 110–115.

there but in America over his savagely polemic attack on Agassiz which Fiske himself referred to as "the diatribe on Agassiz." In it he called Agassiz "a sort of scientific pope," doubted whether Agassiz had any knowledge or understanding of the Darwinian theory, attacked Agassiz's reputation as "greater than his achievements—admirable as they are—would be able, on trial, to sustain," and attributed his rejection of Darwinism to a preference for theological rather than scientific reasoning. The article created an unfavorable impression in America, where most people, even those who disagreed with him on evolution, still revered the Swiss scientist who had cast in his lot with the young republic in days when it had few eminent scientists or scholars to boast about. Many came to Agassiz's defense against the ill-mannered attack, among them James Freeman Clarke, a moderate Unitarian minister who as a member of the Harvard Board of Overseers had supported Fiske's nomination as instructor in history. Resentment of Fiske's assault increased when Agassiz's death, two months after the publication of the article, made it seem not merely rude, but a positively malicious bludgeoning of a dying man who deserved gratitude for his past services to science and to the nation.

Fiske failed to realize the false position in which his article put him. Though he admitted that in writing hurriedly on the eve of his departure he had used expressions that would better have been deleted, he drafted a bitter thirteen-page reply to Clarke that he fortunately never published. The situation had many elements of a teapot tempest, but it was to have real and unfavorable consequences in the future. Agassiz had been one of the proudest names in Harvard's claim to intellectual leadership in America and many of his friends were influential in the University's governing boards. Fiske's article would be remembered against him when he made his next bid for a position on the Faculty.[33]

Fiske's relations with publishers were as gratifying as his social

---

[33] Quotations from JF to Abby, Aug. 1, 1873, HHL, and JF, "Agassiz and Darwinism," *Popular Science Monthly*, 3:693, 694 (October 1873). J. F. Clarke, "An Enraged Darwinian," *Christian Union*, Nov. 5, 1873 (clipping in HHL). Manuscript Draft of Reply to Clarke, entitled 'A Candid Theologian,' HHL. JF to his mother, Nov. 18, 1873; JF to Abby, Nov. 23, 1873, Dec. 7, 1873, Dec. 15, 1873, HHL. A. M. Davis, *Proceedings of the American Academy of Arts and Sciences*, 37:671 (August 1902).

success. He was soon on friendly terms with the heads of three publishing firms, Trübner, Williams & Norgate, and Macmillan, each of whom expressed interest in bringing out his *Cosmic Philosophy*. The best offer came from Macmillan, where the head of the house, Alexander Macmillan, had long shown an interest in contemporary religious speculation. Macmillan agreed to publish an English edition simultaneously with J. R. Osgood in Boston and offered Fiske a flat ten per cent royalty on all copies. This was better than Fiske had expected, for on his previous books he had received royalties only after all expenses of publication had been covered.[34]

He remained in London until he completed his revision and turned the full text over to Macmillan. On February 20 Fiske left England for France, determined to see as much as he could in the three months to which finances limited him. On the continent he found himself very homesick, with a curious combination of longings to be both at home with his family and also in his now-beloved London. Everything he saw seemed inferior to England. Paris disappointed him. No one spoke English, and he found that despite his linguistic studies a reading knowledge was not enough. No one understood his French, though a waiter managed to make enough sense of his attempts to speak German so that he could eat. Nothing he saw in the Louvre impressed him as much as had the South Kensington Museum. "The Seine is prettier than the Thames," he told Abby, "but I prefer the grand views, up and down, from Waterloo Bridge, to anything here." The Bibliothèque Nationale had much to learn from Ezra Abbot. Neither the people he met nor the sights he saw pleased him.[35]

The French and Italian countryside he passed as he proceeded south failed to arouse any enthusiasm. "It is all pretty to look at, but beastly uncomfortable, inhospitable, cold & dreary & gloomy." Language also proved a problem in Italy, but here he found that he could get by with his French, which he had been unable to use in Paris. He complained to Abby that "it seems very lonesome & dreary to be where you don't hear English spoken. I don't see how people can prefer the Continent to England." Only the antiquities he saw pleased him. Aside from this Italy was disgusting, the people all scoundrels. Not even the cathedrals impressed him. He rarely commented on the Gothic examples, and of Rome he wrote: "I don't see either the grandeur or the beauty of St. Peter's,—it isn't impressive—I think it hideous, and I would back York Minster against all the churches I've seen in Italy put together! and I've seen a heap." [36]

With a sense of relief he turned north to Switzerland, where he made a pilgrimage to "carry out the dream of my boyhood," visits to Rousseau's home at Les Charmettes and Voltaire's chateau at Ferney. From Switzerland Fiske traveled down the Rhine to Holland, happy to leave the uncongenial Latin lands behind, and happier still to be on his way back to England. Germany and the Low Countries were pleasant, but nothing could compare with England. The happiest letter of all records his return to London on May ninth. There he enjoyed two weeks of rapid sight-seeing trips to monuments he had missed earlier and a round of farewell parties. At the end of the month he left for America with his *magnum opus* complete and the memories of a year of social success in London to comfort him in Cambridge.[37]

[36] Quotations from JF to Abby, Mar. 20, 1874, LC; JF to his mother, Apr. 15, 1874, and JF to Abby, Apr. 14, 1874, HHL. JF to Abby, Apr. 2, 1874, Apr. 27, 1874, HHL.

[37] Quotation from JF to Abby, Apr. 27, 1874, HHL. JF to Abby, May 3, 1874, May 9, 1874, HHL; May 23, 1874, LC.

CHAPTER FIVE

AN OUTLINE
OF ALL KNOWLEDGE

In October 1874 Fiske published his *Outlines of Cosmic Philosophy,* the book on which he had been at work for so long. The invitation from Eliot in 1869 had given him his opportunity to try to write a large-scale philosophical investigation. From the first he wanted to do more than merely lecture on the ideas of one group of thinkers. He told Marble that the lectures themselves would be preliminary to a large volume which would "expound the philosophy of the sciences & give a general résumé of scientific doctrine and method."[1] It took Fiske five years to complete, and grew beyond even the goal he had outlined to Marble. He packed into his *Cosmic Philosophy* a summary of all knowledge he considered significant: all the recent scientific and philosophical ideas, the application of these to history, and the implications for religion.

Fiske prepared his survey of all knowledge in three distinct stages. In 1869 he wrote a series of eighteen lectures for Harvard. In 1871 he expanded the series to thirty-five and, although he needed only seventeen additional talks, he discarded two early lectures and provided nineteen new ones for this presentation. In 1873 and 1874, while in England, Fiske revised and expanded these lectures into the thirty-nine chapters of his *Outlines of Cosmic Philosophy.* The

[1] JF to Manton Marble, Nov. 2, 1869, LC.

evolution of Fiske's ideas and attitudes becomes apparent when the three versions are considered chronologically.

The eighteen lectures of 1869 break down into three divisions. The first eleven presented the basic principles of what Fiske then termed the positive philosophy, sketched the historical development of this school of thought, and contrasted its views with the ideas of other philosophers. Then followed five lectures on the laws of history and progress. The seventeenth lecture briefly summarized what Fiske meant by positivism and explained why he considered Comte and Spencer to be properly described by the same label.[2]

The first eleven consisted of a mélange of the ideas of Comte, Spencer, Lewes, and J. S. Mill, with Spencer predominating. When these men disagreed, Fiske usually took Spencer's side as in his third and fourth lectures, where Fiske expounded and affirmed Spencer's test for absolute truth—that "a belief of which the negation is inconceivable is necessarily true." Fiske illustrated the operation of this principle by remarking that while one could state the proposition that "the Whole is equal to its Part," no one could think the thought which the proposition expressed. Thus, since the negation was inconceivable, the proposition that "the Whole is always greater than its Part" was absolute truth. This was an unfortunate illustration for, as Royce later pointed out, the development of the mathematics of infinity would result in "the exact definition and clear conception of infinite assemblages of objects in which the Whole is equal to the Part." Fiske devoted much space to refuting Mill's criticism of Spencer. Mill had contended that what could be conceived depended on past experiences and altered with the advance of knowledge. Fiske wanted a test of truth which he could carry out in his armchair without undertaking any investigations and which yielded absolute certainty. He did not heed Mill's warning that it opened the way to treating beliefs as certainties on subjective grounds that could, on the same basis, be denied by someone else.[3]

[2] The eighteen lectures appeared in the New York *World* from Nov. 13, 1869 to Jan. 10, 1870.

[3] New York *World,* Nov. 16, 1869. J. S. Mill, *Auguste Comte* (London, 1865), pp. 72–73. Josiah Royce's comment is quoted from his footnote to JF's *Cosmic Philosophy,* 4 vols. (Boston, 1902), I, 217.

Fiske attempted little originality in these lectures. The only significant deviation from his masters came in his sympathetic treatment of Berkeleian idealism, an unusual attitude for a positivist and an early example of Fiske's tendency to interpret ultimate reality in what he later called "psychical" rather than material terms.

These eleven lectures closely parallel Part I of the *Outlines of Cosmic Philosophy*, which covers much the same material in a similar sequence, with some minor alterations in wording and choice of illustrative examples. The major difference between the earlier and later treatments is in the attitude to Comte. In 1869 Fiske praised most of Comte's ideas, while rejecting his views on religion and modifying some details of Comte's concepts in the philosophy of science in the light of Spencer's work. In later versions Fiske reversed this favorable estimate and savagely criticized Comte's ideas. As early as 1872, while preparing his second series of Harvard lectures, he told Marble he was revising the earlier talks "so as to stand them on non-Comtean legs." [4]

Lectures twelve to sixteen showed more originality. Here Fiske developed the ideas he had first expressed in his essay on Buckle into a law of progress that would explain social evolution. Most of the conclusions derived from Spencer, and the final definition paraphrased Spencer's famous law of evolution. Fiske's law read: "The progress of society is a continuous establishment of psychical relations within the community, in conformity to physical and psychical relations arising in the environment, during which both the community and the environment pass from a state of incoherent homogeneity to a state of coherent heterogeneity, and during which the constituent units of the community become ever more distinctly individuated." Although borrowing his approach and language from Herbert Spencer, Fiske covered ground which Spencer had not yet reached—the first volume of the *Principles of Sociology* was not published until 1876. When he saw copies of the lectures, Spencer wrote to Fiske that "in several of the sociological propositions you set forth, you have to some extent forestalled me in the elaboration of the doctrine of Evolution under its sociological aspects." It is

[4] JF to Marble, Jan. 24, 1872, LC.

proof of how thoroughly Fiske had assimilated the ideas of his master that he could draw out the implications of Spencer's thought and reach conclusions satisfactory to the originator of the system.[5]

Three major themes dominated the five lectures on the "laws of progress and history." First, Fiske tried to show that history had regularity and causation (a position he had taken in his first published work, the essay on Buckle). Second, Fiske attempted to refute the religious interpretation of history that explained events in terms of final cause and God's will. Third, he presented his own view, which treated Comte's law of the three stages of progress as incomplete and true only insofar as it was a corollary to the law Fiske himself developed in Spencerian terminology.

In his seventeenth lecture, Fiske turned briefly to religion. He made it clear he did not follow Comte's hierarchical religious views; he drew rather on the unified vision of the universe, described in the earlier lectures, for an object to worship. Fiske argued that the Christian concept of God, while not necessarily in conflict with a concept of God derived from science, needed to be stripped of elements incompatible with science, especially the concept of God as a person. Deanthropomorphization was the barbarous-sounding treatment Fiske prescribed to adapt the Christian concept of God to the modern world. This would produce a deity approaching the Spencerian concept of the "Unknowable," and Fiske thrilled at the prospect.

"What is this wondrous Dynamis which manifests itself to our consciousness in harmonious activity throughout the length and breadth of the universe, which guides the stars for countless ages in paths that never err, and which animates the molecules of the dew-drop that gleams for a brief hour on the shaven lawn?" Fiske asked his hearers. "Shall we call it gravitation, or heat, or life, or thought, or, summing up all in one most comprehensive epithet, shall we call it Force?" But these, though suggestive, were "but scientific terms, expressing affections of our consciousness; they are powerless to express the unknowable and ineffable reality." Before

[5] New York *World*, Jan. 1, 1870. Spencer to JF, Feb. 2, 1870, HHL. The final version of Fiske's law of progress in *Cosmic Philosophy*, III, 328, is modified only to bring it into accord with Spencer's later revision of his law of evolution.

his ultimate reality "science must ever reverently pause; acknowledging the presence of the mystery of mysteries. Here religion must ever hold sway, reminding us that from birth until death we are dependent upon a Power to whose eternal decrees we must submit, to whose dispensations we must be resigned, and upon whose consistency we may implicitly rely." [6]

The final lecture summarized Fiske's conclusions. He listed the five main points of the positive philosophy as he understood it. Two were held also by thinkers who could not be called positivists in the strict sense: these were the principles that all knowledge is relative, and that unverifiable propositions should not be made a part of philosophy. The final three were specific to positivism: that the evolution of philosophy was a continuous process of deanthropomorphization, that philosophy must synthesize the ideas and methods of science, and that critical philosophy should be constructive and not destructive, positive and not negative. Whoever accepted all five was a positivist; whoever denied any one of them was not a positivist. Fiske told his listeners that "thus we obtain a complete conception of positive philosophy. And, as we have seen, that conception of philosophy is due to Comte. In his elaborate attempt to prove the contrary, Mr. Spencer correctly interprets the positive philosophy, but he does not correctly interpret Comte. The foregoing discussion has shown that on all points of supreme importance Comte and Spencer agree." [7]

Religion, while only directly treated in one lecture, formed a running undercurrent to the whole endeavor. Fiske revealed the spirit of his approach in his boast to Manton Marble, shortly after the series began, that "a perverse and iniquitous Deity was ungrateful enough to reward my assiduous efforts in the cause of truth with a severe cold & neuralgia just as I began the business of spouting. In revenge I shall insert, later in the course, a portion of my Fortnightly article, which demolishes Him." This contemptuous attitude, along with praise of such suspect men as Comte in terms which seemed to a member of the Harvard audience to be "delivered with

[6] New York *World*, Jan. 8, 1870.
[7] *Ibid.*, Jan. 10, 1870.

the positiveness of an ardent disciple," alienated religiously oriented readers and listeners.[8]

II

The second year of Harvard lectures provided Fiske with an opportunity to expand his brief survey of recent philosophy of science into an outline of knowledge. His thirty-five lectures began with a survey of the history of philosophy and the rise of scientific philosophers, proceeded to an explanation of the development of the universe, then elucidated the origin of life and the growth of society and morality, and concluded with an exposition of a system of religion based on "scientific" principles.

Nineteen of these lectures were new.[9] The first eleven of the new lectures published in the *World* covered approximately the same material as the first sixteen chapters of Part II of *Cosmic Philosophy*. Four of the eleven were a concise and remarkably clear summary of Part II of Spencer's *First Principles*. Lectures five and six described the origin of the universe, the formation of planets, and the geological evolution of the earth. Lectures seven and eight briefly presented Darwin's theory of the origin of species, the only significant use of Darwin in the entire series. The next three lectures approximated a highly selective summary of Spencer's *Principles of Biology*. In none of these did Fiske attempt originality, other than in arrangement of ideas and clarity of expression.

Lectures twelve to fifteen of the new group revised his earlier discussion of the law of progress, which Fiske now presented as a wide-ranging law governing all of social evolution.

The sixteenth lecture drew on the ideas of Alfred Russell Wallace, co-propounder with Darwin of the new views of biological evolution, to describe how the mind of man evolved. In the seventeenth Fiske advanced an idea he later called his major contribution to the

[8] Quotations from JF to Marble, Nov. 2, 1869, LC, and F. G. Peabody, "The Germ of the Graduate School," *Harvard Graduates' Magazine,* 27:179 (December 1918). See also, Peabody's Manuscript Notebook of Philosophy Lectures, 1869–70, HUA.

[9] The nineteen new lectures appeared in the New York *World* from May 1, to Sept. 1, 1871.

theory of evolution—a consideration of the role played by the prolongation of infancy in the evolution of man.

Fiske built on Wallace's suggestion that, once the brain of man appeared on the biological scene, natural selection ceased to operate upon bodily factors and instead concentrated on selecting for intelligence. The major method of producing a more flexible mind, said Fiske, was by prolonging the infancy of humans. This provided sufficient time for the organization of the brain to be perfected before the individual had to fend for himself. A long period of plasticity made man capable of progress, for nonorganic improvements, including the whole of human culture and skills, could be passed on to the young in this time. The prolongation of infancy made necessary the development of the permanent family to protect the young during their state of helplessness, and holding the family together on a permanent basis, began the evolution of society. Because family relations call for the subordination of personal desires in order to help others, the prolongation of infancy produced the idea of morality, which progressed by the steady substitution of altruism for egoism. And morality was the most important part of religion. Thus Fiske thought that his theory of the effects of the prolongation of infancy on mankind explained the origin of the family, society, culture, progress, morals, and religion.[10]

Fiske's idea of the role of infancy in the production of civilization and morality proved convincing mostly to readers already attracted by the Spencerian concept of evolution as a law explaining all phenomena. Although cited with approval in an 1876 address by the vice-president of the American Association for the Advancement of Science, it appealed even more to popularizers like John M. Tyler, who used it in his exposition of the origin of man, and Henry Drummond, who used it in his works on the relation of science to religion.

The theory had little attraction for scientists since, in the form in which Fiske expounded it, it is impossible to verify. Fiske, indeed, felt that verification was not needed; never, in his many later references to the theory, did he bother to answer the basic question

[10] New York *World*, Aug. 11, 1871.

raised by a critic whether the period of infancy was actually a greater part of the life span of humans than of the other higher primates. Spencer himself was puzzled over what use to make of the theory. When he reached the appropriate place in his *Principles of Sociology* in 1876, he contented himself with referring to it in a footnote as "an important suggestion made by an American adherent of mine . . . . [regarding] a co-operating factor in social evolution." Spencer's American disciple, F. H. Giddings, thought that Fiske had reversed the true order of evolution; he argued that social and family life gave rise to the prolongation of infancy, rather than the converse. Few except convinced Spencerians paid much attention to the theory after the first flurry of interest, and although histories of sociology mention it, they give it little space.[11]

The last two new lectures of the 1871 series Fiske devoted to an extended treatment of the religious implications of science. Fiske continued to argue that the idea of a personal God could not be reconciled with modern knowledge, but he now went on to assure his audience that atheism was not the alternative, since a concept of God in harmony with recent science was possible. This was again Spencer's "Unknowable," but Fiske now felt more reluctant to use the words "force" or "energy" in describing his deity. Since it was not a person, this deity could not be held responsible for evil as the personal God of theology could. Thus Fiske argued, it provided a better support for morality. One had only to remove "illegitimate formulas" from the idea of God and the reconciliation of science and religion would be simple.[12]

III

Fiske carried out the final revision of his *Outlines of Cosmic*

[11] *What American Scientists Have Done for Evolution; An Address by E. S. Morse before the American Association for the Advancement of Science* (Salem, Mass., 1876), pp. 39–41. John M. Tyler, *The Whence and Whither of Man* (New York, 1896), pp. 146–147, 178–179. Henry Drummond, *The Ascent of Man* (New York, 1894), pp. 267–291. Herbert Spencer, *Principles of Sociology* (New York, 1877), I, 630n. F. H. Giddings, *Principles of Sociology* (New York, 1896), p. 229. J. F. Leuchtenberg, *The Development of Social Theory* (New York, 1925), pp. 286–287. C. S. Peirce, *Nation*, 70:18 (Jan. 4, 1900).

[12] New York *World*, Aug. 25, 1871, Sept. 1, 1871.

Philosophy during his 1873 stay in London. His active social life there gave him little time for research and he seems to have consulted no books, not even the works of the philosophers he criticized. He drew many of the quotations he used from G. H. Lewes's popular history of philosophy. He did discuss his problems with the men he met socially, consulting Huxley on the biological chapters, and heavily modifying the section on astronomy under the criticism of William K. Clifford.[13]

Fiske listened attentively and humbly to his advisers, but he showed independence in the use he made of their advice. He sometimes disagreed even with Spencer. The occasions of disagreement were minor, but they help illustrate the different points of view from which the two men approached philosophy. Spencer had begun as a liberal in the early nineteenth-century sense and turned to philosophy to find both a rational explanation of the failure of revolutionary action and a substitute for it. For these purposes the idea of an inevitable process of slow change seemed attractive. It is a measure of the difference between England and America that a social philosophy designed to validate change should become the mainstay of American conservative thought in the latter part of the nineteenth century. Spencer's interest in science grew partly out of his engineering background; he thought of it as a way to manipulate the world as well as a means of large-scale generalization. Fiske, on the other hand, had little interest in fostering social change, nor did his interest in science at all relate to technique. The center of his concern was religious. Above all he wanted an explanation of the universe that would be both emotionally and logically compelling. The three areas in which the divergent aims of the men showed itself in Fiske's *Cosmic Philosophy* were in Fiske's disagreement with Spencer over the name of their philosophy, in his modification of Spencer's view of the relation of the physical to the mental world, and in the greater prominence he gave to religious implications.[14]

The controversy over the name for Spencer's philosophy clearly

[13] JF to Abby, Dec. 7, 1873, Dec. 8, 1873, HHL.
[14] Herbert Spencer, *Autobiography,* 2 vols. (New York, 1904), I, 237–264, 438–439. Hugh Elliot, *Herbert Spencer* (London, 1917), especially ch. IV.

illustrated the differing angles of vision of the two men, one intent on producing a philosophy that would appeal to practical men, the other trying to raise his power of comprehension to embrace the entire universe. Spencer had, since 1867, desired to use the term "synthetic philosophy" to describe his system of thought, but had permitted the objections of Huxley and Lewes to overrule him. Fiske used "positive philosophy" in the title of his 1869 lectures despite Spencer's objections. Even after becoming convinced that Spencer rightly differentiated himself from Comte, Fiske preferred the phrase "cosmic philosophy," suggested by Manton Marble, to Spencer's more neutral term. Fiske's use of the word "cosmic" in his circulars for the public lectures of December 1871 finally stimulated Spencer to order that "synthetic philosophy" be printed as the running title on all his volumes. However, Youmans told him that this would not control American usage; "nothing short of the Cosmic will satisfy the American spread-eaglism." [15]

When Fiske showed Spencer his proofs and title page in December 1873, Spencer immediately objected that "giving to the Philosophy of Evolution a name which I am known to disapprove, and which I finally gave my own name for the purpose of excluding, is a somewhat strange step." He urged Fiske to abandon the word "cosmic." Fiske objected that "synthetic" described the method used by many philosophers other than Spencer, and thus was not fully distinctive, while "cosmic" described the results achieved, in which no one else approached Spencer. This philosophy, Fiske argued, "is not merely a Synthesis, but it is a 'Cosmic Synthesis'; that is, it is a system which, without making appeal to data that are ontological or to agencies that are extra-cosmic, brings all known truths concerning the coexistence and succession of phenomena into relation with one another as the corollaries of a single primordial truth." When his philosophical reasoning failed to convince Spencer, Fiske added a practical objection, pointing out that he could not alter his title without also revising the sections where he had contrasted "cosmic

[15] Quotations from *Life and Letters of Herbert Spencer*, David Duncan, ed., 2 vols. (New York, 1908), I, 209. Spencer to JF, Nov. 1, 1869, Feb. 2, 1870, Nov. 27, 1871; JF to Spencer, Sept. 29, 1871 (draft copy), HHL. JF to Marble, Apr. 10, 1871, LC.

theism" with "anthropomorphic theism." This would be difficult and costly since much of the first volume was already in print. Faced with this problem, Spencer reluctantly agreed that Fiske might go ahead if he would make it clear in his preface that Spencer himself did not think the adjective "cosmic" properly described his system.[16]

The other differences provoked less asperity from Spencer. Fiske's religious inclinations led him to conceive of the ultimate reality of the universe in spiritual and mental, rather than physical, terms. Spencer was uninterested in ontological speculation and his statements bearing on problems of ultimate reality were vague and often contradictory. Fiske wanted to quote a passage from Spencer's *Principles of Psychology* in which Spencer used nerve and psyche as interchangeable terms. To avoid the implication that the two were identical, a favorite maxim of materalists, Fiske desired to revise the passage so that the distinction would be clear. Spencer casually consented to the emendation when Fiske asked him about it. Although verbally authorizing Fiske to modify the passage, he did not himself change the passage in later editions of his book. For Spencer the matter was minor; for Fiske, Spencer's willingness to accept this alteration made it possible for him to develop his religious thought and still claim that he had not deviated from Spencerian principles.[17]

Spencer had no strong objection to the heavily religious interpretation which Fiske gave his thought. He had probably become accustomed to this tendency among his American admirers and contented himself with telling Fiske that the religious suggestions of the first part of *First Principles* were a minor part of his thought. While Spencer did not think of himself as primarily a religious philosopher, he had no quarrel with anyone who admired his views on these matters. Indeed, in later years he showed some tendency to increase the religiosity of his own writings as his American

[16] Quotations from Spencer to JF, Dec. 22, 1873, HHL, and JF, "Introduction" to *Cosmic Philosophy*, I, p. xii (see also, pp. x–xiv). JF to Abby, Dec. 22, 1873; Spencer to JF, Dec. 24, 1873; JF to Spencer, Dec. 24, 1873; Spencer to JF, Dec. 27, 1873; JF to Abby, Dec. 31, 1873, HHL. See also, letters printed in JF, *E. L. Youmans* (New York, 1894), pp. 233–234, 236, 254, 290–292; and in *Life and Letters of Herbert Spencer*, I, 206–209.

[17] JF to Abby, Feb. 2, 1874, HHL. JF, *Cosmic Philosophy*, IV, 280n. Compare Spencer, *Principles of Psychology*, I (2nd ed., 1872), pp. 158, and later editions.

followers began to convince him that he was a major religious thinker.[18]

The greatest difference between *Cosmic Philosophy* and the lectures on which it was based lay in the increased attention given to religion in the book. Part I of the *Cosmic Philosophy,* in which Fiske rapidly surveyed the philosophical background of modern scientific thought, giving a brief history of philosophy, needed little change. He completed the elimination of praise of Comte, begun between the first and second series of lectures. Fiske added a contrast between his cosmic theism, with its view of the universe as orderly and regular, and what he called anthropomorphic theism, by which he meant the view of the universe in which modifications of regularity by miracle and special providence could occur. Part II, where Fiske surveyed Spencerian and Darwinian ideas and capped them with his own view of social evolution and the origin of morals, required only the addition of information garnered from Huxley and Clifford in London.[19]

Part III of *Cosmic Philosophy* showed the greatest change. In his first series of lectures, religion had been covered in one lecture of the seventeen; two of thirty-five lectures sufficed in the 1871 version. Now Fiske devoted six of his thirty-nine chapters to the religious implications of his thought. This change derived in part from Fiske's own increasing interest in religious consolation as his personal difficulties increased. It also reflected his sensitivity to the desires of his audience, for this part of his lectures drew most comment from listeners. Fiske reduced polemic attacks upon orthodoxy and placed greater stress on how his ideas agreed with general religious concepts. "As for the comfort which 'my science' has for aching hearts, the form of your question shows how little you understand what 'my science' is," Fiske wrote vigorously to his mother, while at work on his book in London. "If I were to say that my chief comfort in affliction would be the recognition that there is a Supreme Power manifested in the totality of phenomena, the workings of which are

---

[18] Spencer, *Autobiography,* II, 544–549. Elliot, *Spencer,* pp. 217–232. *The Nature and Reality of Religion; a Controversy between Frederic Harrison and Herbert Spencer* [E. L. Youmans, ed.], (New York, 1885).

[19] Compare New York *World* reprint of lectures with *Cosmic Philosophy.*

not like the workings of intelligence but far beyond & above them, and which are obviously tending to some grand and worthy result, even though my individual happiness gets crushed in the process, so that the only proper mental attitude for me is that which says 'Not my will but thine be done,'—If I were to say this you would probably reply, 'Why this is Christianity!' Well, so it is, I think." [20]

Fiske still rejected the idea that God might be a person, whether the orthodox concept of an intervening deity or the Deistic notion of a person outside the universe who set the process into motion. Both these views he termed anthropomorphic, and objected that by putting God outside the universe they unnecessarily split God from nature. From this split resulted the apparent conflict of religion and science, which he called a conflict based upon misunderstanding rather than real antagonism.

He tried to refute charges that his ideas were atheistic, materialistic, or pantheistic. They were not pantheistic because he did not identify deity with the universe, but by stressing that deity was unknowable refused to place any limits on it. They were not materialistic because, though his deity was mysterious and unknowable, Fiske felt sure it was spiritual rather than physical in nature. Nor were his views atheistic, for his system presented an object for worship which Fiske claimed had all the vital attributes of the central concept of all religions. By this Fiske meant that his deity fitted Matthew Arnold's definition of "a Power, not ourselves, that makes for righteousness."

Fiske followed Spencer in considering aspects common to all systems of belief as the essence of religion. These consisted primarily in a sense of a mysterious power outside the self, which Part I of *First Principles* had argued was essentially unknowable, yet of which Spencer was able to state definitely that it was infinite and the source of all phenomena. Fiske was even more certain than his master of the attributes of unknowability, being sure that it was also spiritual and moral.

Fiske's stress upon moral aspects of religion involved him in a struggle with the problem of evil. If God and the universe were

---

[20] JF to his mother, Nov. 13, 1873, HHL.

indivisible, then God must be responsible for all evil in the universe. But this conflicted with the benevolence which Fiske optimistically posited of the universe and also seemed to separate deity from morality. Since Fiske thought religion consisted primarily of a belief in God and the practice of morality, he had to solve this dilemma. He found his solution in the Spencerian view of the function of struggle in evolution as the means to insure the survival of the "fittest." He concluded that since pain and death were the necessary accessories of progress, they could not in themselves be evil. He argued that so long as God was viewed as a Person and not as the source of order in the universe, pain and death appeared to be deliberately inflicted by this Person upon his creatures. Therefore, he concluded, his concept of God was a better source of morality than Christian theology. He told his readers that, "though we may, and do, throw overboard the whole of the semi-barbaric mythology in which Christianity has hitherto been symbolized, we shall find, nevertheless, that we have kept firmly in our possession the ethical kernel for which Christianity is chiefly valued even by those who retain the whole of this mythology." [21]

In his concluding chapter Fiske stressed the social conservatism of his ideas. Spencer had desired to develop a philosophical position for radicalism, one which would explain the failure of revolutionary action and also provide a guide to those changes which were beneficial and possible. Fiske used these ideas to prove the entire futility of any attempt to guide or force change. He emphasized this in the religious context. No sharp alterations in religion would follow the adoption of his philosophy, no radical attacks on existing churches or institutions were needed. The slow processes of inevitable change would eliminate the dross and transform all institutions into expressions of the pure religion Fiske advocated. Meanwhile the essential continuity of this religion of the future with the best of current beliefs should be emphasized, to insure that the process of change would not involve even temporary loss of valuable elements.

During the five years that Fiske had been at work on his book, his ideas had altered. He began his task calling himself a positivist, and boasting that he was "neither a Christian nor a theist." [22] He ended advocating a "cosmic theism" which he assured his readers was fully compatible with essential Christianity. As he himself came to feel more need for religious consolation, as well as for religion as an explanation of the world, he tended to stress what his religious system retained, rather than what it replaced. Elements of both approaches remained in the finished work; the alteration had been too gradual for Fiske to feel it significant. Thus he retained in the final version the praise of Dynamis from his 1869 lectures, and still called for the deanthropomorphization of God, although Christians found such concepts offensive.

Fiske was very proud of his book. It had grown from a survey of positivism to a survey of all knowledge. He felt sure it would establish his reputation as a philosopher of science and religion, and win him both wealth and glory.

IV

Published on October 31, 1874, Fiske's *Outlines of Cosmic Philosophy* won respectful attention from the nation's reviewers. All praised the clarity of the writing and the skill with which Fiske had summarized the thought of Herbert Spencer. J. B. Warner in the *Atlantic Monthly*, indeed, claimed that "the book contains an outline of the Spencerian theories, so clearly stated and so vividly illustrated that most readers will prefer the disciple to the master." [23] The range of knowledge displayed in the survey of the universe of nature and man impressed almost all.

Yet when reviewers directly discussed the book's ideas, they showed that Spencer's doctrines still had some way to go before being fully accepted by Americans. *Popular Science Monthly,* edited by E. L. Youmans, the dedicated propagandist of Spencerian views, hailed "this long-expected work" and especially praised Fiske's original contributions, like the chapters on sociology, the theory of the significance of infancy, and the treatment of religion. But less convinced Spencerians were more dubious. Warner in the *Atlantic,* and also J. E. Cabot in the *North American Review,* objected to the

[22] JF to Spencer, [Oct. 6] 1869, HHL (draft copy).
[23] *Atlantic Monthly,* 35:616 (May 1875).

test for truth via inconceivability and pointed out that it permitted Fiske both to hold the idea that all knowledge was relative and to make absolute statements about the nature of the universe. They doubted that Fiske had found "a single *formula* expressing all truth concerning the whole world of phenomena," for such a level of abstraction simplified to the point where the formula said nothing about the actual world. Fiske's law of social evolution was so comprehensive, in its attempt to cover all the known facts of history, that it had been emptied of all definite content.[24]

General circulation magazines tended to brush lightly over the controversial religious aspects of Fiske's thought and dealt mostly with its philosophical implications. Warner noted that a bald statement of Fiske's position seemed almost a scientific parody on religion, but felt that in the full context of his ideas, it was redeemed by "the strength of Mr. Fiske's religious feeling, and the simplicity of his fervor." H. W. Holland in the *Nation,* after respectfully considering the philosophy, briefly rejected the theology: "The vague awe with which we turn to this impersonal, unchangeable, unknowable Essence of Cosmism, seems but ill-fitted to replace the martyr-zeal of Christianity."[25]

In the denominational press, Fiske's remarks received less respectful treatment. Many printed lengthy analyses of the book as a full-scale exposition of the implications of Spencer's philosophy. But Fiske was much too polemic for their taste. The liberal Congregationalist, John Bascom, himself engaged in working out a reconciliation of modern science and religion, objected to the reference by Fiske to "the semi-barbaric mythology of Christianity" as something which could "hardly receive a milder epithet than offensive." The *Congregationalist* fastened on Fiske's panegyric to the Wondrous Dynamis, entitling its review "Great is Dynamis, and John Fiske is Its Prophet," a choice of heading which sufficiently indicated their opinion. M. Stuart Phelps, in the *New Englander,* resorted to parody. "In the continuous redistribution of Matter and Motion, there has at last been evolved, by integration of the homogeneous, the American Apostle of the Truth hitherto hidden from the eyes of men. A series of states of consciousness (plus a Something?), resident in Cambridge, has worked over a certain amount of sunshine, and has communicated it to the other possibly existing series of states of consciousness, in the shape of a book entitled *'Outlines of Cosmic Philosophy.'* " [26]

All religious journals, regardless of whether they supported orthodox or liberal positions within their denominational lines, found Fiske's ideas unsatisfactory. Catholics, Methodists, and even moderate Unitarians, along with the Congregationalists, rejected Fiske's elimination of any degree of personality in deity. Fiske's austere concept was too remote from the God to whom the worshipper could turn directly for assurance and comfort. Fiske's intellectual desire to use his religion as a support and sanction for morals seemed to many of his contemporaries to have resulted in a sacrifice of the emotionally significant rewards of religion. In his zeal for stripping off "illegitimate formulations" Fiske had scrapped some of the most cherished and valued aspects of religion. [27]

Interest in Fiske's book was heightened by the controversy touched off by the appearance in 1871 of Charles Darwin's *Descent of Man*. Religiously oriented writers had, for the most part, been able to reject the *Origin of Species* on scientific grounds. But in the intervening decade scholarly acceptance of Darwin had grown. Continuing to use the scientific arguments which had once seemed effective, and even adding to them a request to be shown the "missing link," did not adequately meet the new challenge; religious writers needed new grounds on which to defend the rejection of Darwin. Charles Hodge, the professor of theology in Princeton Theological Seminary who boasted at the celebration of his semicentenary that in his tenure "a new idea never originated in this Seminary," posed the problem they faced when he bitterly contrasted the reception of *Vestiges of Creation* in 1844 with the enthusiasm

[26] J. Bascom, *Bibliotheca Sacra*, 33:619 (October 1876). *Congregationalist and Boston Recorder*, Dec. 3, 1874, p. 390. *New Englander*, 34:530–531 (July 1875).

[27] *Methodist Quarterly Review*, 58:655–678 (October 1876). *Unitarian Review*, 3:576–587 (June 1875), and 5:482–496 (May 1876). *Catholic World*, 14:633–645 (February 1872), especially pp. 642–643.

for Darwin. "The facts are now what they were then. They were as
well known then as they are now. The theory, so far as evolution
is concerned, was then just what it is now. How then is it, that what
was scientifically false in 1844 is scientifically true in 1864?" Unable
to understand the scientific value of Darwin's work, yet seeing its
wide acceptance, Hodge fell back on the explanation that it was the
result of a conspiracy of infidels. "There is only one cause for the
fact referred to, that we can think of. The 'Vestiges of Creation' did
not expressly or effectually exclude design. Darwin does."

As acceptance of Darwinian ideas grew, the tone of the discussion
became bitter. Hodge organized his widely read and influential book
about an examination of the question "What is Darwinism?" and
concluded bluntly, "It is Atheism." Even the *Unitarian Review,*
which a year earlier had lamented the possibility that "these dreams
of evolution in which our young men, intoxicated as it were by the
opium smoke of Buddhistic speculation, so rapturously indulge, may
possibly prove . . . true," took heart. When Hodge's volume appeared, it cheerily predicted that "Mr. Darwin's hypothesis will soon
take its place among the exploded things." [28]

The main reason for religious discomfort was the apparent in-
compatibility of Darwin's views with the cherished proof of the
existence of God through the argument from design. Most religious
people refused to follow the few farsighted theologians like President James McCosh of Princeton, who took the view earlier expressed by Asa Gray that any method shown by science was
compatible with the idea of God. The concept of design, viewing the
adaptation of life to environment the result of God's forethought,
made it possible to accept the scientific postulate of an orderly
universe without abandoning the idea of a benevolent deity respon-
sive to the needs of his creatures. But when Darwin explained the
multiform adaptations displayed by life through the operation of

[28] Quotations from A. A. Hodge, *The Life of Charles Hodge* (New York, 1880),
p. 521; Charles Hodge, *What is Darwinism?* (New York, 1874), pp. 145–146, 177;
Unitarian Review, 2:339 (November 1874) and 3:249 (March 1875). Attacks on
Darwin can be sampled in *Monthly Religious Magazine,* 45:501–507 (May 1871);
Catholic World, 17:143–157 (May 1873) and 17:641–655 (August 1873); *Bibliotheca
Sacra,* 29:240–289 (April 1874); *Methodist Quarterly Review,* 56:129–146 (April
1872); *American Church Review,* 24:15–25 (January 1872).

simple natural causes over infinite stretches of time, he seemingly left no place for any direct relation between God and the existing universe. The only concept of God that appeared plausible was one which put him at the beginnings of things, but in which he refrained from intervention as the relentless play of fixed laws worked itself out. This sort of God was of little use to believers.[29]

This problem, rather than the apparent conflict between Darwin and Genesis, lay at the root of the difficulty. Scripture had been re-interpreted before to eliminate apparent contradictions with science, and could be again, but to do so was of no use if the God that remained was beyond the reach of the believer. Fiske did not adequately deal with this problem in his *Cosmic Philosophy*. Indeed, his lack of sympathy for orthodox patterns of thought prevented him from fully appreciating that it was an emotional difficulty, though expressed in theological terms. To accept Spencer's Unknowable as a substitute for God seemed to many readers a mere refusal to consider the dilemma on the ground that it was impossible to solve. By failing to face the real problem of how to adapt to Darwinism without losing all the meaning that religion had held in the past, and by treating all theological ideas as outworn superstitions, Fiske rendered his attempted reconciliation of religion and science unusable to many who ardently desired such an outcome. Not until his own experience modified his approach to religion further would he arrive at a version of his ideas that would win wide attention.

The greatest enthusiasm for Fiske's views came from the extreme radical wing of American religion. It was marked among members of the Free Religious Association. This organization had been founded in 1867 by a group of radicals who thought that the newly established National Conference of Unitarian Churches retained too much Christianity. Under the leadership of Octavius Brooks Frothingham and Francis Ellingwood Abbot, the F.R.A. drew into its membership transcendentalists, disciples of Theodore Parker, Reformed Jews, Hindus, Spencerians, and even proclaimed materialists like B. F. Underwood. It vigorously attacked Christianity, as

---

[29] James McCosh, *Christianity and Positivism* (New York, 1871). *The Life of James McCosh, a Record Chiefly Autobiographical*, W. M. Sloane, ed. (New York, 1896).

Fiske had in his Middletown days. "In the name, therefore, of Human Intelligence, of Human Virtue, of the Human Heart, of Human Freedom, of Humanitarian Religion, I seriously and earnestly impeach Christianity before the tribunal of the Humanity it still continues to outrage and enslave," Abbot grandiloquently proclaimed.[30]

Fiske's ideas and nomenclature appealed to people unable to find emotional and intellectual satisfaction in the usual theological concepts, who sought in science a clear confirmation of their religious desires. Many of the independent churches affiliated with the F.R.A. began to call themselves "Cosmists," to symbolize their claim that their religion was founded upon the latest science. Their enthusiasm was at least potentially embarrassing to Fiske, for they were often more extreme than he. Fiske had been steadily becoming less antagonistic to Christianity and now disapproved of the idea of vocally attacking it. Indeed, he had assured his mother that his book would prove that Christianity modified would endure forever. In addition, Fiske distrusted the political and social radicalism that for many of the free religionists was a logical counterpart of their religious position. The same demand for change and improvement that motivated their search for a new religion led to an interest in social reform for which Fiske felt no concern. He often tried to disassociate himself from these extremists and only with reluctance could he be persuaded to speak to such groups as Mrs. John T. Sargent's Radical Club in Boston or permit the F.R.A. to print one of his religious essays in their series of tracts.[31]

If radical theists found Fiske attractive, extreme agnostics tended to reject his views. In England, George John Romanes devoted a twenty-two-page appendix of his *Candid Examination of Theism* to a refutation. Romanes argued that in divesting deity of all elements

---

[30] F. E. Abbot, "The Impeachment of Christianity," *Index*, 3:5 (Jan. 6, 1872). O. B. Frothingham, *The Assailants of Christianity* (New York, 1879), *Recollections and Impressions* (New York, 1891). William J. Potter, *The Free Religious Association* (Boston, 1892). [F.R.A.], *Freedom and Fellowship in Religion* (Boston, 1875). Stow Persons, *Free Religion* (New Haven, 1947).

[31] Count Eugene Goblet d'Alviella, *The Contemporary Evolution of Religious Thought* (London, 1885), pp. 214–215. Mrs. John T. Sargent, *Sketches and Reminiscences of the Radical Club* (Boston, 1880), pp. 132, 346–349. JF to Martha Brooks, Feb. 23, 1873, LC. JF to his mother, Apr. 11, 1871, HHL.

of personality, Fiske ended up with a concept of God that was too remote and abstract to support theistic conclusions. "In the theory which Mr. Fiske calls Cosmic Theism, while I am able to discern the elements I think may properly be regarded as common to Theism and to Atheism, I am not able to discern any single element that is specifically distinctive of Theism." On strict logic, Fiske's only legitimate conclusion was that he could neither prove nor disprove the existence of God. Romanes accused Fiske of teaching "mistaken views concerning the ontological tendencies of recent thought, and this with no other apparent motive than that of unworthily retaining in the new philosophy a religious term [God] the distinctive connotations of which are considered by that philosophy to have become obsolete." Few in America reacted to Fiske this way. There were hardly any austere agnostics of this sort in the New World.[32]

To the general public Fiske seemed a thoughtful expositor of modern science. His reputation grew, especially after he began to use in his publicity a letter in which Darwin remarked that he had never really understood Spencer until he read Fiske's summary.[33] To the religious press and its readers, Fiske was a purveyor of false ideas. To the radical fringe he seemed a valuable thinker. To everyone Fiske now appeared to be primarily a philosopher, from whom further contributions to philosophy were expected.

[32] G. J. Romanes, *A Candid Examination of Theism* (London, 1878), pp. 129–151, quotations from pp. 145 and 151.
[33] C. Darwin to JF, Dec. 8, 1874, HHL.

CHAPTER SIX

END OF AN
ACADEMIC CAREER

Fiske's survey won him a reputation as a leading American philosopher, but did not bring much monetary reward. Sales were small and Fiske found it difficult to turn his fame to direct advantage. The same monetary problems that had plagued him before his European trip recurred between 1875 and 1879.

Soon after his return from England he anxiously asked his mother whether Stoughton would continue to send his quarterly checks, for he had already begun to fall behind. Accumulated debts totally swallowed the small inheritance that came to him upon the death of his grandmother. When in December 1875 President Eliot increased his Harvard salary, Fiske solemnly promised his mother to use the money in reducing debts, but in the course of the next year he fell so far behind that his mother took over the payments on his life insurance. To keep up the flow of income Fiske stayed home each morning to write book reviews and articles, only going to his post in the Harvard library after lunch. He arranged to contribute regular book reviews to the *Nation* and also tried unsuccessfully to resume the monthly scientific column in the *Atlantic* that he had discontinued while in Europe.[1]

[1] JF to his mother, Sept. 12, 1874, Oct. 3, 1874, Dec. 31, 1874, Nov. 15, 1875, Jan. 1, 1876; JF to Abby, July 9, 1875, HHL.

In February of 1876 Fiske gathered together several long essays written for the New York *World* and the *Atlantic,* headed them with his most recent article on religious themes, and published them under the title *The Unseen World and Other Essays.* These, considering their slight nature, sold well. By May his publisher reported that the first thousand copies were gone, while only nine hundred copies of *Cosmic Philosophy* had been bought in its eighteen months on the market.[2]

The most consequential article in the book was the title essay, a seventy-six-page review of a book by two British scientists, Balfour Stewart and P. G. Tait, who had speculated on the possibility of immortality in another universe, with psychical though not physical links to this one. After a long survey of the nature of the universe and a consideration of various ideas on immortality, Fiske regretfully concluded that modern science offered no support for Stewart's and Tait's ideas.

Yet, he went on, this did not settle the matter. Since no experimental test of immortality was possible, science could not disprove the idea. Fiske warned his readers that "to hesitate to adopt a well-supported theory because of some vague preference for a different view is in scientific matters the one unpardonable sin. . . . Even in matters which lie beyond the reach of experience, where evidence is inaccessible, desire is not to be regarded as by itself an adequate basis for belief." But Fiske felt that these considerations did not apply to the problem of immortality. "The hypothesis of a purely spiritual unseen world, as above described, is entirely removed from the jurisdiction of physical inquiry, and can only be judged on general considerations of what has been called 'moral probability'; and considerations of this sort are likely in the future as in the past to possess different values for different minds." He therefore called for tolerance of those who favored this view, for "he who, on such considerations, entertains a belief in a future life may not demand that his skeptical neighbour shall be convinced by the same considerations; but his neighbour is at the same time estopped from stigmatizing his belief as unphilosophical."[3]

[2] JF to his mother, May 10, 1876, HHL.
[3] JF, *Unseen World* (Boston, 1902), pp. 72–73.

This was as positive a conclusion as Fiske felt able to support intellectually, though his own desires came through clearly in the concluding sentence: "Believing, however, though as a simple act of trust, that the end will crown the work, we may rise superior to the question which has here concerned us, and exclaim, in the supreme language of faith, 'Though He slay me, yet will I trust in Him!' " [4]

Most reviewers of *Unseen World* concentrated on the title essay. The *Unitarian Review,* praised its spirit of candor, but found its negative conclusions unconvincing. The best the *Atlantic* reviewer could say was that "certainly, scientific denial of religious belief could not be less offensive." Few noticed that in the struggle of Fiske's religious desires with his intellect, in which this essay marks a stage of progress, the balance had begun to tip in favor of the desires. Fiske, however, was not yet sure how to provide a more adequate intellectual scaffolding for his faith, and, until he did, his position would remain somewhat ambiguous.[5]

Fiske also made several attempts at lecturing, though with little success, while he remained at the Harvard library. In September 1876 he projected a tour of the West with speaking engagements in Chicago, Milwaukee, St. Louis, and Cincinnati as a prelude to a visit to Philadelphia, where he joined the conference of librarians at the Centennial Exhibition grounds that gave birth to the American Library Association. Unfortunately the Chicago and Cincinnati proposals failed to materialize. In 1877 he accepted invitations to address radical churches in New Canaan, Connecticut, and Florence, Massachusetts, for nominal fees.[6]

The only significant speaking engagement in these years was an invitation from the Peabody Institute of Baltimore to give four lectures in February and March 1877 on "Our Aryan Ancestors; Their Culture, Myths, and Folklore." The lectures offered a welcome opportunity to renew his interest in philology. Fiske tried for little originality, contenting himself with summarizing the results of Indo-European philology and of the attempts to reconstruct prehistoric

[4] *Ibid.,* p. 76.

[5] *Unitarian Review,* 7:572–573 (May 1877). *Nation,* 23:214 (Oct. 5, 1876). *Atlantic Monthly,* 37:750 (June 1876).

[6] JF to his mother, Sept. 8, 1876, Dec. 11, 1877, Dec. 18, 1877; JF to Abby, Sept. 19, 1876, HHL. *Library Journal,* 1:95 (November 1876).

ways of life from linguistic clues. He pleased his audiences by including many amusing examples of the derivation of current clichés and
slang expressions.[7]

II

Fiske's steady writing schedule did not prevent an active social
life. In Cambridge his close friends included leading writers like
William Dean Howells and Thomas Sergeant Perry, and rising
young members of the Harvard faculty like William James and
Charles Eliot Norton. Chauncey Wright was a special friend with
whom Fiske enjoyed discussing their differing philosophical positions. Fiske described how Wright sometimes escorted him home
after an evening of talk, "by way of finishing the subject, but on
reaching my gate a new suggestion would turn us back,—and so we
would alternately escort each other home perhaps a dozen times." In
Boston Fiske could turn to the *Atlantic* circle of writers, and in New
York the *Nation* group befriended and encouraged him. It was of
the Cambridge circle that Howells later remarked that they were
united not only by common intellectual activities, but also "got on
admirably in the common interest of our growing families and the
constant question of the butcher's bills. . . . The cost of living then . . .
so nicely adjusted itself to one's income in Cambridge, that we nearly
all had to count the cost; but nobody dreamt it was not worth it."
When possible, they tried to help one another. Perry and Howells
and Norton, in their editorial capacities, gave Fiske many chances
to get his work into print. In turn, when he could, Fiske aided them.
It was at Fiske's suggestion, after he had himself decided that he
could not do the job, that his New York friend, Henry Holt, commissioned the survey of psychology by William James that securely
established James's early reputation.[8]

The Cambridge group had no formal social structure, but it did

---

[7] JF to Abby, Feb. 25, 1877, HHL. The lectures, after being given in other places,
were printed in the *Atlantic Monthly* in 1881 and in JF's *Excursions of an Evolutionist* in 1885.

[8] Quotations from JF, *Darwinism,* p. 101, and W. D. Howells, "John Fiske,"
Harpers' Weekly, 45:732 (July 20, 1901). JF to Abby, Feb. 12, 1876; JF to his
mother, Nov. 21, 1877; JF to Henry Holt, May 30, 1878, HHL. Henry Holt,
Garrulities of an Octogenarian Editor (Boston, 1923), pp. 54, 56, 108–109.

develop institutional expressions, primarily the dinner club at which members gathered for a good meal followed by a paper read by one of the initiates which served as the start for a symposium on the topic of the evening. Fiske was a member of at least two famous clubs, the Metaphysical Club where C. S. Peirce, Chauncey Wright, and William James first developed the germs of pragmatism, and The Club, which never took any other name and still survives. The original fourteen members of The Club included Henry and William James, Howells, Fiske, J. C. Ropes, Henry Adams, O. W. Holmes, Jr., John T. Morse, Jr., and T. S. Perry. In later years Henry Lee Higginson, Alexander Agassiz, James Ford Rhodes, and Bliss Perry joined. It was at such a dinner that the incident took place, which William James remembered long after with amusement, when Fiske fell asleep in the midst of a meeting whose main purpose was a critical examination of his *Cosmic Philosophy*.[9]

Fiske spent his summers in Petersham, his wife's old home in the Massachusetts hill country. His brother-in-law had repurchased the family homestead and other Petersham property after his return from the West where he had made a fortune in mining. Each year he invited his sister's family to spend the summer there. While vacationing in Petersham in 1876, Fiske introduced his American friends to T. H. Huxley when the Englishman and his wife stopped over with the Fiskes for several days while touring America.

Fiske's physical appearance altered greatly during these years. No longer was he the "youth, with fresh ruddy face, tall and not broad, a rather slender pillar of a man, corniced with an abundant pompadour of brown hair," that J. K. Hosmer had met in the mid-sixties. To look more academic, he had grown an impressive beard. Advancing years and worries thinned his once abundant hair. Fiske's sedentary life—he spent much of his time at his desk, "his only exercise being to cross the room for a book or a pipe"—and his undiminished appetite for food and drink soon led to a great increase in bulk. Fiske himself began to joke about his "undistributed

⁹ C. S. Peirce, *Collected Papers*, C. Hartshorne and P. Weiss, eds., 6 vols. (Cambridge, Mass., 1931–1935), V, par. 12–13. William James, *Letters*, H. James, ed., 2 vols. (Boston, 1920), II, 10, 231. J. T. Morse, Jr., *Thomas Sargeant Perry* (Boston, 1929), pp. 47–49.

middle" or "university extension" as his weight advanced well
beyond the two hundred pound mark.[10]

A quarrel between the Fiskes and their Brooks in-laws, who lived
in a joint household at 4 Berkeley Street, Cambridge, disturbed
Fiske's home in 1877. The dispute was quite awkward for Fiske,
since bachelor uncle James Brooks paid the major costs of the house
where he, his wife, and five children—soon to become six—lived. In
May 1877 Mr. Stoughton reluctantly came to the rescue. Stoughton
advanced $13,000 to buy a lot and erect a large three-story mansard-
roofed house at 22 Berkeley Street for his stepson.[11]

Shortly after construction of the new house began in August 1877,
Fiske's sixth and last child was born. "Abby's favorite name was
Hugh and mine was Herbert, and we compromised on Hubert,"
John told his mother. "But nobody liked Hubert, and so we have
finally altered it to Herbert." They added Huxley as a middle name
and thus named their last child after Fiske's two English friends.[12]

The Stoughtons did not remain in America to see the house
completed. Mr. Stoughton, who had served as attorney for Rutherford B. Hayes before the Electoral Commission investigating the
disputed presidential election of 1876, was appointed United States
Minister to Russia, and departed in December 1877.[13]

The architect included many special features requested by Fiske
in the design of the house. Separate bedrooms for himself and his
wife, sufficient space for the children, and a library that was the
largest room in the house, taking up half the ground floor, were his
primary requirements. Fiske assured his mother that in Cambridge
society it was quite permissible to receive guests in a library and
thus he could add to it the space usually allotted to a drawing room.

[10] JF to his mother, Aug. 6, 1870, Aug. 16, 1870, Sept. 18, 1878; Henrietta Huxley
to Abby, Oct. 18, 1876, HHL. Quotations from J. K. Hosmer, *The Last Leaf* (New
York, 1912), pp. 168–169; T. S. Perry, "John Fiske," *Atlantic Monthly*, 89:637
(May 1902); and W. R. Spaulding, *Music at Harvard* (New York, 1935), p. 194.

[11] JF to E. W. Stoughton, May 21, 1877; JF to his mother, May 31, 1877, Aug. 22,
1877, June 18, 1878, HHL.

[12] Quotation from JF to his mother, Aug. 28, 1877, HHL. JF to his mother, Aug.
22, 1877, May 2, 1878, HHL.

[13] JF to his mother, Oct. 17, 1877, Apr. 15, 1878, May 21, 1878, June 18, 1878,
Sept. 18, 1878, HHL. *Dictionary of American Biography*, s.v. Edwin Wallace
Stoughton.

A dining room and music room shared the floor with the library; the kitchen was in the cellar. Eventually Fiske accumulated some 12,000 books, and even this library was not big enough, but in 1878 Fiske felt very proud of it. The children's playroom he strategically located on the third floor, just over the guest room. In his bedroom, Fiske installed a large bell, with a cord running down to the kitchen, so that the cook could pull it at 6:30 each morning. This did not awaken Fiske, but did arouse the rest of the household, whose combined efforts, when successful, brought him downstairs for breakfast about 8:00 o'clock.[14]

III

Many at Harvard shared the popular impression, engendered by the critical success of his *Cosmic Philosophy*, that Fiske's main field of competence was now philosophy. President Eliot, as late as 1895, suggested to William James that Fiske be invited to fill a temporary vacancy in the Philosophy Department.[15] But in the late seventies, Fiske had difficulty using this reputation since the opportunities that opened up at Harvard came in the field of history.

In May 1877 Henry Adams resigned his professorship and Fiske became an active candidate for the post. Fiske told his mother that Gurney had assured him, after the dispute among Overseers in 1870 over his temporary appointment as an instructor in history, of Eliot's intention to give him a permanent position in the History Department when it became feasible for him to be confirmed by the Overseers. Fiske thought that time had now arrived and wrote confidently to his mother of his chances. Meanwhile he would stay on in the library until Eliot was ready.[16]

But Fiske never got the position. Since the only record of the alleged promise appears in Fiske's correspondence, it is difficult to be sure of its precise terms. In any case, although Fiske had fitted well with Eliot's plans in 1870, seven years later this was no longer true. Not only was Fiske's area of professional competence

---

[14] JF to his mother, May 24, 1877, June 18, 1878, Sept. 18, 1878, HHL.

[15] Ralph Barton Perry, *The Thought and Character of William James*, 2 vols. (Boston, 1935), II, 416–417.

[16] JF to his mother, Dec. 8, 1871, July 6, 1877, HHL.

in philosophy, but Eliot had begun to develop standards for selecting professors that Fiske's previous work in history failed to meet. Stimulated by the challenge of a newly established graduate department at Johns Hopkins, Eliot sought to provide for Harvard a group of scholars equal to those gathered by D. C. Gilman at Baltimore. To do so he wanted to add to the faculty men with established reputations or professionally trained young men who gave promise of developing into renowned scholars. Since Eliot had limited funds, he more frequently hired young men and gave them a chance to develop. This he now proceeded to do in the History Department; Henry Adams's courses were divided among three bright young Ph.D.'s—Henry Cabot Lodge, Ephraim Emerton, and Ernest Young. Fiske felt confident that he would get the position after a year's experiment with the young men. But Eliot found them satisfactory, whereas Fiske fitted into neither of the two groups attractive to Eliot.[17]

Changes in the library further weakened Fiske's position at Harvard. John Langdon Sibley, whose eyesight had begun to fail, resigned in July 1877. Fiske's work as his assistant had not been satisfactory. He had continued, with the consent of the administration, to take leaves for his wide-ranging lecture tours, and had also devoted as much time as possible to his own writing. Exaggerated rumors asserted that Fiske devoted the regular work-week to his own affairs and appeared in the library only during week-ends, when it was closed to the public and he could finish undisturbed the tasks that had accumulated during his absence.[18]

To replace Sibley as librarian, Eliot chose Justin Winsor, who had earned a national reputation through his ground-breaking work at the Boston Public Library in developing educational and service functions for a mass public. Winsor was then quarreling with the Boston City Council, which had cut salaries at the library during the 1873–79 depression in ways that Winsor considered offensive,

---

[17] JF to Holt, May 30, 1878, HHL. *Harvard University Catalogue,* 1876–77, through 1885–86.

[18] JF to his mother, July 6, 1877, HHL. This apocryphal anecdote about Fiske was told me by a Harvard graduate student and credited to an unidentified retired professor.

and he was willing to leave his Boston post for Harvard. Winsor fitted well with Eliot's plans for building Harvard. He was a pioneer professional librarian, a founding member and first president of the American Library Association, and, in addition, had a reputation as a scholar for his work in compiling historical bibliographies to make it easier for unsophisticated readers to use the resources of the Boston Public Library. His acceptance of the position represented a definite gain for the University.[19]

These changes left Fiske without a future at Harvard. With Winsor in the library, Fiske's position became superfluous. His salary had been raised until it equalled Sibley's, because with Sibley old and half-blind, Fiske had to take over many of his responsibilities. After 1877 Winsor carried out most of the independent duties. As Fiske put it in a letter to his mother two years later: "I resigned because, after the appointment of a real librarian, I felt my position to be anomalous. . . . I ought to have resigned a year ago, and should have done so, but for the house-building & sickness & consequent interference with literary work. By sticking on, simply to extort a salary from the courtesy of the College, my prospects would not be improved but deteriorated." This Fiske saw in 1879, but in the earlier years he had not felt this way. Instead he used the permanent tenure in the library which Eliot had granted him in 1873 as an easy source of income, while bringing pressure on Eliot to give him the history professorship. Fiske had influential alumni intercede with Eliot and Gurney, and tried to build up his reputation as a scholar by continuing to write and lecture. When his resignation became public, Sibley noted in his private journal: "John Fiske quits the library on the first of April. My astonishment is that he was allowed, after one year's experience, to be continued there; his heart is not in it and never was. 'During the last eighteen months he has not done three months solid work.' "[20]

Once it became clear that Fiske would not get a position at

---

[19] *Dictionary of American Biography,* s.v. Justin Winsor.

[20] Quotations from JF to his mother, Feb. 25, 1879, HHL, and J. L. Sibley, Manuscript Private Journal, entry of Mar. 12, 1879, HUA. JF to his mother, Nov. 21, 1877, June 13, 1878, HHL. Sibley did not identify the Harvard Library official whose remarks he quoted in his last sentence.

Harvard, his wrath turned on Eliot, whom he blamed as the cause of all his misfortunes. Abby expressed the opinion that the creator of all the difficulty was "Pres. Eliot whose course toward John if made known to the public would ruin his reputation with a very large number of influential people connected with the College." She complained that "the sudden manner in which he withdrew the salary without giving him the professorship (which was *promised as the cause* of the withdrawal of the librarianship), . . . [was] unpardonable let the interpretation be what it may *it was* a *criminal* breach of faith." There is no evidence in the Eliot-Gurney correspondence of any such promise, nor did Fiske, at the time, claim that this was the cause of his resignation. Then he spoke of it as a way to clear more time for lecturing and writing which would convince Eliot of his qualifications for a professorship, rather than as part of an understanding.[21]

It is not necessary to postulate a conspiracy to cheat Fiske out of his just deserts in order to explain Eliot's failure to appoint him to the faculty. Fiske plainly did not fit into the new Harvard. His reputation as a scholar declined as he continued to work in many fields. Philosophy, science, linguistics, anthropology, and history were too much for any man to master, and Fiske was a master in no field, though a connoisseur in all. In an age in which professionalization and specialization were becoming the keys to academic success, Fiske's wide-ranging amateurism detracted from rather than added to his attractiveness. Furthermore, Fiske's personality was not well suited to an academic career. As in his thinking he showed a desire for short cuts, for large generalizations, without having the patience to go through the slow process of detailed proof, and so in his life Fiske showed impatience and an inability to cope with the host of petty details and regulations in which academic life abounded. In the library, he had shown how difficult and uncongenial it was for him to keep up with academic routine. Fiske's talents and personality were far better suited to the career of free-lance popularizer that he later followed, where he could alternate heavy bouts of work with long periods of idleness in the manner he enjoyed,

[21] Quotation from Abby to JF's mother (Mrs. M. F. B. Stoughton), Oct. 26, 1879, HHL (italics in source). JF to Eliot, Dec. 31, 1878, HUA. JF to his mother, Feb. 25, 1879; JF to E. E. Hale, Apr. 8, 1879, Apr. 16, 1879, HHL.

and where his outstanding talent for lucid statement was more important than original thought or research.[22]

But Fiske did not feel himself unsuited to academic life. He still hoped to get on to the Harvard faculty and seriously considered two other opportunities for a teaching position. While Fiske was in Baltimore in February and March of 1877, President D. C. Gilman of Johns Hopkins came to his lectures at the Peabody Institute, and Fiske visited the site of the new university. There is no evidence that Gilman ever made an offer to Fiske, but the careful consideration which Fiske gave to the pros and cons of a move to Baltimore indicate he expected one. Had Gilman invited him, Fiske would have refused, for he felt that on balance the disadvantages of a move away from his favorite city outweighed the advantages. Fiske then preferred to wait in Cambridge and bring pressure on Eliot to appoint him.[23]

In January 1879, the College of the City of New York offered him a position, but, after talking over the job with President Alexander Stewart Webb, Fiske refused. By then he had begun the preparation of his lectures on American history and thought the prospects of financial independence they presented more attractive than anything the New York institution could offer.[24]

IV

In the spring of 1878, while his future at Harvard remained unclear and Fiske continued halfheartedly at his library duties, he received an offer which proved a turning point in his life. Mrs. Mary Hemenway, a Boston matron attracted by Fiske's writing and lectures and currently engaged in raising money to save the Old South Meeting House from destruction, offered him $1,000 for six lectures on American history to be given the following year.

Fiske welcomed the lectures since they aided his continued quest

[22] See S. E. Morison's remarks to L. C. Powell, based on information from Edward (not Ellery, as Powell states) Channing in Powell's "John Fiske—Bookman," *Papers of the Bibliographic Society of America*, 35:231 (1941), for faculty opinion of Fiske. "Fiske Anecdotes," *Bookman*, 14:10–11 (September 1901).

[23] JF to Abby, Feb. 25, 1877; JF to his mother, Mar. 28, 1877; JF to Holt, [March 1877], HHL. Nothing in Fiske's letters or in the Johns Hopkins University Archives indicates that any offer was made.

[24] JF to Abby, Jan. 20, 1879; JF to Holt, Feb. 2, 1879, HHL.

for a Harvard position. Henry Adams had added work in American history to the curriculum, which Henry Cabot Lodge now offered; by demonstrating competence in American history Fiske would show his ability fully to replace Adams. Moreover, since many of the sponsors of the movement to save the Old South were influential in Harvard affairs, he would make valuable friends by aiding a cause dear to them. Fiske consulted Charles Eliot Norton and Francis Parkman, both of whom advised him to accept the offer.[25]

In November 1872 the Old South Meeting House had been badly damaged in a great fire which leveled much of downtown Boston. Until then the eighteenth-century building, famous for the patriotic meetings that had taken place in it during the early phases of the American Revolution, had been in continuous use as a place of worship. The Congregational church that owned the building did not have the funds to repair it, nor did the Massachusetts Historical Society, to which it was offered. The church had already purchased the property on the corner of Boylston and Dartmouth streets where its second building now stands, and in the spring of 1876, having failed to get anyone to take responsibility for the historic monument, put it up for auction, with the expectation that the purchaser would raze the meeting house and replace it with an office building. This aroused a public outcry and patriotic New Englanders rallied to save the monument from destruction. A public meeting on June 14 appointed a committee to raise the $400,000 that the church had been offered for the land and so save the building from destruction. The bulk of the money was raised by the women of Boston, especially Mrs. Hemenway, who herself contributed half the $200,000 down payment needed to complete the transaction, the other $100,000 coming from small donations.[26]

The outburst of interest in the American past aroused by celebrations of the centennial of American independence greatly aided the Old South drive. In addition, it served as a vehicle for the filiopietistic pride of many whose chief claim to present fame was their ancestry. An admirer said of Mrs. Hemenway: "She had a deep

[25] JF to his mother, June 13, 1878, HHL.
[26] H. A. Hill, *History of the Old South Church,* 2 vols. (Boston, 1890), II, 528–547. E. D. Mead, *The Old South Work* (Boston, 1899). *Freedom and the Old South Meeting House* (Old South Leaflet, no. 202).

feeling of personal gratitude to the founders of New England and the fathers of the Republic. . . . Boston, the Puritan city,—how proud she was of its great line of heroic men!" She may be taken as an exemplar of the women who founded many patriotic organizations in the ensuing decades.[27]

Sparked by Mrs. Hemenway's enthusiasm, the committee succeeded in raising the money to complete the purchase and repair the building. She then organized a further fund drive to endow special series of lectures for adults, children, and schoolteachers, and to sponsor prize competitions on patriotic themes among the youth of Boston. Fiske's lectures would aid this second fund drive.

As Fiske worked along with the preparation of his lectures he became more and more enthusiastic over the prospects they opened up for him. He sensed a wide interest which would permit him to repeat them throughout the country. He concentrated on approaches that would render his lectures interesting to a wide popular audience, still feeling certain that popular success would also aid him toward his desired scholarly career. Viewing the lectures as his best chance for success, Fiske resigned as assistant librarian on December 31, 1878, to take effect the following April first. His lectures would be given once each week from March 10 to April 14, 1879. Thus he could continue to receive his college salary until the lectures were well launched, and then be free to tour the country with them once he had finished his talks at the Old South. He tried to arrange a repetition in New York for late April or May, and hoped to tour the west the following winter. He opened negotiations with lecture managers in Cincinnati, Dayton, St. Paul, Madison, Milwaukee, Racine, Kenosha, Chicago, Davenport, and St. Louis. Prospects were promising and he confidently assured his mother he would easily surpass his $3,000 Harvard salary.[28]

Fiske chose as his theme for the lectures "America's Place in World History." The first of the six talks dealt with the discovery of America, the second with Spanish and French exploration, the third with the expulsion of the French and triumph of the English empire, the fourth described life in the thirteen colonies, the fifth

[27] Mead, *The Old South Work*, pp. 1–2.
[28] JF to his mother, Feb. 25, 1879, HHL. JF to Laurence Hutton, Feb. 18, 1879, PUL.

the causes of the American Revolution, and the final lecture dealt with the future of "what is loosely called the 'Anglo-Saxon' race." [29]

In each lecture Fiske tried to show how the details of American history fitted into an over-all philosophical scheme. From the opening sentence of the first lecture, "The voyage of Columbus in 1492 was in many respects the greatest event which had occurred in the world since the birth of Christ," Fiske expounded his vision of the true meaning of American history. He drew a picture of the United States as the peak of an evolutionary process which operated through history to produce the free democratic republic that emerged from the Revolution and which in the future would produce a world republic led by "Anglo-Saxons" bringing peace and prosperity to the entire globe. This view was precisely calculated to please his audience—if calculated is the right word for an effort in which much of the effect stemmed from the luminous sincerity with which he presented information and ideas. Fiske fully shared the filiopietistic pride which animated the sponsors of the Old South movement and brought his audience together. To keep their attention while the grand sweep of his evolutionary reading of American history unfolded, Fiske included much interesting social detail on life in the colonies, sparkling character sketches of the heroes of exploration and Revolution, and dramatic descriptions of gory incidents like "the Huguenot colony in Florida, & its horrible destruction by the Spaniards in 1565." [30]

Given the nature of the task he set himself, Fiske had little need for research in original sources. He drew almost all his material

[29] Quotation from JF to E. E. Hale, Apr. 8, 1879, HHL. Three lectures, in revised form, appeared in *Harpers' Monthly:* "How America Came to be Discovered," 64:111–119 (December 1881); "Romance of the Spanish and French Explorers," 64:438–448 (February 1882); "Overthrow of French Power in America," 65:99–112 (June 1882). The three other articles printed in *Harpers* ["Virginia in the Colonial Period," 65:895–907 (October 1882); "New England in the Colonial Period," 66:111–124 (December 1882); and "Maryland and the Far South in the Colonial Period," 66:414–425 (February 1883)], are chapters from Fiske's unfinished "Short History of the American People," and represent an expansion of the fourth lecture. The fifth appeared as "Why the American Colonies Separated from Great Britain," *Fortnightly Review,* 34:147–163 (August 1880). The sixth was printed in *Harpers' Monthly,* 70:578–590 (March 1885), under the title of "Manifest Destiny," and forms chapter three of *American Political Ideas* (New York, 1885).

[30] Quotations from *Harpers' Monthly,* 64:111 (December 1881), and JF to his mother, Mar. 17, 1879, HHL.

from secondary accounts. Parkman's work on the conflict of France and England provided much of the material for two lectures, while Washington Irving's *Life of George Washington* seems to have been Fiske's major source for the lecture on the Revolution. The concluding lecture, by far the most popular Fiske ever delivered (in a revised form and entitled "Manifest Destiny," Fiske gave it more frequently than any other single talk), needed no research at all since it primarily expressed Fiske's optimistic vision of a future millennium.

The audience, gathered in the newly repaired Old South Meeting House to hear Fiske, responded with an eagerness that lived up to his most ardent expectations. For the first time he experienced a full rapport with his listeners. "I felt the sense of having the people drinking in every word and tone with hushed breath & keen relish. Half unconsciously I deepened and intensified my voice & began to lose myself in the theme with which I was greatly fascinated myself." The experience exhilarated Fiske. "I had a sort of sense that I was fascinating the people,—and it was delicious beyond expression." These lectures differed from his earlier ones in their greater immediacy, achieved by the use of concrete detail and ideas which were not too abstract to be understood and seemed directly meaningful to the listeners. This made it easier to grasp these lectures by ear than had been the case with those on Spencer and evolution. Although the audience was not too large (Fiske did not give the numbers but merely called it "the very cream of Boston," his characteristic expression for a small house), the enthusiasm with which they received his work promised well for the future. "This thing takes the people, you see: they understand & feel it all, as they can't when I lecture on abstruse things. The fame of it is going about briskly, and I believe I shall get full houses all over the country. The Centennial has started it, & I have dropped in at the right time. Glory, hallelujah!"[31]

V

But full houses all over the country did not come as quickly as

[31] Quotations from JF to his mother, Mar. 17, 1879, HHL. JF to his mother, Mar. 11, 1879, HHL.

Fiske hoped. His plans for a spring tour fell through. Too few people were willing to buy tickets in New York to warrant hiring a hall for the series. In other parts of the country, also, he had little luck. It would take much more careful preparation before people thought of Fiske as a lecturer whom they should pay money to hear. Another factor was the difficulty in fitting Fiske's lectures into the ordinary lyceum circuit, which preferred well-known speakers who toured the country with a single carefully prepared address stressing either entertainment or uplift. Although Fiske would willingly give single lectures that combined both, his subject matter still seemed esoteric to most lecture managers. They were not eager to undertake the task of selling him to their usual clientele.[32]

Disappointed in his immediate expectations, Fiske turned to a scheme designed to increase as quickly as possible his reputation as a lecturer. England was still the final arbiter in cultural and intellectual matters to many Americans. Fiske therefore decided to use his London connections to arrange a series of lectures there. He could take advantage of a London success in his publicity and advertising to interest the American audience of the hinterland in hearing the man who had taught the English how great the United States was. On May 1, 1879, Fiske was still considering whether or not he should go. On May 24 he boarded the Cunard liner *Samaria,* having requested his English friends to get him a hall in London. He arrived in Liverpool on June 4, writing Abby that he felt "perfectly mad [underlined five times] with joy at setting foot on the shores of old England again: It seems like Paradise." On June 11 he began his six lectures; by August first he had completed his brief visit and returned home.[33]

In London his friends rallied around him. Huxley greeted him warmly. Sime and Conway took him to dinners and made much of him. When Fiske arrived uninvited at a party in the home of his English publisher, Alexander Macmillan, his host welcomed him

[32] JF to Laurence Hutton, Apr. 3, 1879, PUL. JF to his mother, May 24, 1879; JF to E. E. Hale, Apr. 8, 1879, HHL.

[33] Quotation from JF to Abby, June 5, 1879, HHL. JF to Laurence Hutton, May 1, 1879, PUL. JF to his mother, May 24, 1879; JF to Abby, June 1, 1879, June 23, 1879, HHL.

back to England and took him around introducing him to the various guests. Many of those present had read his *Cosmic Philosophy*, among them the star of the evening, William E. Gladstone, then out of office between his first and second ministries. Macmillan agreed to bring out a volume of Fiske's occasional pieces under the title *Darwinism and Other Essays* (not until 1884 did Fiske find an American publisher for this book). Darwin invited Fiske to his country home. Spencer again extended all the courtesies he could to him, and joined him on excursions into the country. Soon Fiske had again settled into the rooming house and club routine he had so much enjoyed in 1873.[34]

While Fiske was still on his way, Huxley and Sime had consulted together on how best to aid Fiske's lecture plans. On Huxley's application, University College, London, reserved a room for the six talks. They were given in three weeks on Wednesdays and Fridays at 3 p.m., beginning on June 11. For these Fiske received no money, but neither was he asked for any rent.[35]

Fiske's intoxication with England affected the manner of his delivery, and the resulting emphasis on aspects of American history that flattered English pride pleased the audience. He probably did little revising, for the text of the Boston lectures undoubtedly already expressed his high regard for England and the English; indeed he noted that his listeners responded to many "remarks which we shouldn't notice in America, but which seemed to hit them here most forcibly."[36]

While he received no pay, he did achieve the success he desired. Fiske drew "the very élite of London"; his friends and acquaintances were a good share of the élite of intellectual London, and they did their best to bring him listeners through their word-of-mouth advertising. By the end of the series he was speaking to a packed hall. His final lecture, with its prediction of a future in which the entire world would be one peaceful commonwealth led by Britain and America, was especially well received. While Fiske's description of

[34] JF to Abby, June 23, 1879, July 12, 1879; Darwin to JF, June 10, 1879, June 14, 1879, HHL.
[35] J. Sime to JF, May 31, 1879; JF to his mother, June 15, 1879, HHL.
[36] JF to Abby, June 23, 1879, HHL.

the closing scene is best read as an attempt to impress his mother and Abby and Mrs. Hemenway, he does seem to have stirred his British listeners to unwonted expressions of enthusiasm with his picture of imperialism as the high point of the evolutionary processes of world history. "At the end of the lecture, they fairly *howled* applause. Gentlemen stood up on the benches and waved their hats; ladies stood up on the benches & fluttered their handkerchiefs; and they kept it up until I had to make a pretty little speech. Then they clamoured again; and one old white-haired man made a speech of thanks; and then another gentleman got up and seconded the other with another pretty little speech, winding up by proposing three cheers." [37]

Whether or not the scene took place quite like this other than in Fiske's imagination, he did leave London well satisfied. Huxley had agreed to arrange three paid lectures the following year on the evolution of American political ideas, to be given at the Royal Institution; in addition, he had invited Fiske to bring Abby along and stay at Huxley's house while in London. His American supporters had not been idle and in June the alumni elected Fiske to the Harvard Board of Overseers, putting him in a strategic position to exert pressure on Eliot. He returned to America determined to use his success in London to build a lecturing career which would earn enough money to wipe out all his debts and give him an income sufficient to satisfy his needs and desires.[38]

[37] JF to Abby, June 23, 1879, HHL (quotation from section dated June 27, 1879).
[38] JF to Abby, July 12, 1879; JF to his mother, June 15, 1879, Oct. 9, 1879; E. L. Osgood to Abby, June 26, 1879; Abby to JF's mother [July? 1879]; Mrs. Henrietta Huxley to Abby, Mar. 15, 1880, HHL.

CHAPTER SEVEN

STRUGGLE FOR SURVIVAL

In 1880 Fiske still had a long way to go before achieving the success he anticipated. He faced many years of struggle and the most severe financial problems of his career while learning to attract an audience and developing effective methods of handling his lectures.

Fiske's first American tour with his history lectures contrasted sharply with his English success and testified more to difficulties still to be overcome than to the eventual triumph. He appealed to all his friends for help. He requested Harvard classmates in New York and Brooklyn to arrange lectures. He asked Edward Everett Hale, active in moves to aid the Old South, for assistance in getting on New England lecture circuits. E. L. Youmans vigorously recommended Fiske in the pages of *Popular Science Monthly,* assuring the many Spencerians among his readership that "these are the sort of lectures that deserve encouragement and are worth working for." Fiske eagerly explored opportunities in the West. Immediate success seemed vital to Fiske, for six months had passed without income, his debts had increased, and his creditors had become clamorous.[1]

The first tangible result was a three-week engagement in Maine during October and early November, with lectures two days each week in Portland, Brunswick, and Lewiston, shuttling between the

---

[1] JF to his mother, Sept. 20, 1879; JF to E. E. Hale, Oct. 2, 1879; JF to Abby, Nov. 12, 1879, HHL. *Popular Science Monthly,* 15:560 (October 1879).

three cities to give each of them the full course of six. These he hoped to follow with lectures in Brooklyn later in November and in Boston during December.

The first omens were unfavorable. Only eighteen people turned out for the opening lecture at Lewiston, and Fiske despairingly decided to cancel the rest of the course, since he had not even met expenses. Brunswick did somewhat better, for there Bowdoin College students increased his audience to sixty-five. Portland, too, showed a slight profit. Only a clever stroke by the Lewiston lecture manager saved the tour from disaster. He convinced Baptist-endowed Bates College to offer free use of the college chapel and then sold $35 worth of tickets to the students. "Those who *do* go are delighted extremely," Fiske assured Abby, "and the newspapers puff loudly & without any urging, but somehow the rabble are terribly hard to stir." For his three weeks' discomfort he had earned $200, far less than he had confidently predicted, and out of this all expenses had to come.[2]

In addition to difficulties in attracting an audience, this first tour had turned up another severe problem—the effect on his family life. Fiske had been away on lecture tours before, but they had been few and relatively brief. Now the prospects were that he would be away from home for long stretches of time for an indefinite number of years ahead. Abby wrote dispiritedly, "What a fearfully lonely two weeks! . . . Is the whole winter going to be like this pray? Tis so dreary I haven't seen anybody since you went away nor *cared* to for that matter & that fact makes it all the harder sparing my precious old boy. My whole world goes with him wherever he goes & I only brood my chickens till he comes home to me."[3]

Fiske's wife and children paid a significant part of the cost of his success. Nor was Fiske himself immune to the strains of separation. He frequently bemoaned his inability to spend more time with his family. Later, when separated by a lengthy lecture tour, he objected vigorously when Abby wanted to cancel a visit to New

[2] Quotation from JF to Abby, Oct. 25, 1879, HHL (italics in source). JF to Abby, Oct. 23, 1879, HHL.

[3] Abby to JF, Nov. 1, 1879, HHL (italics in source).

York. "I don't want you to say one word about not coming to see me. You don't want to break . . . [my] heart."[4]

Fiske felt confident he could learn from the Maine fiasco and do better in the future. His Portland agent had "relied too much on newspapers & not enough on subterranean wire-pulling." This would be rectified in the future. The following year Fiske planned to double the price and use the voluntary services of some twenty or so residents who were enthusiastic about the lectures. These would be asked to "take a certain number of tickets each & work them off at their own risk, on their friends & acquaintances," thus providing both a financial guarantee and valuable word-of-mouth advertising.[5]

His optimism increased when his Brooklyn and Boston friends succeeded in arranging lectures. In Brooklyn, three Harvard classmates, Benjamin Frothingham, Augustus White, and Frederick Cromwell, took over responsibility for organizing the lectures, hired a hall, and sold $250 in series tickets among their friends. After the Maine disappointment this was a much-needed boost. "Don't you love my dear old Ben & Gus & Fred?—three of the dearest boys that ever were!" Fiske exulted to his wife. "These are some of the sweet things in this world, these college brotherhoods. We don't see or hear of each other for years, but the moment a little favor is desired, you have only to suggest it, and its 'Come on, my dear old fellow, we'll do what we can for you.' That's why, I say, let all my boys go to Harvard College. It pays." Although he did not earn as much as he he had hoped for in Brooklyn, since expenses proved higher than he had anticipated, the lectures were successful enough to take away much of the sting of the earlier failures.[6]

In Boston, Mrs. M. A. Edwards, whose gift had permitted Fiske to make the trip to England to revise his *Cosmic Philosophy,* organized two presentations of his lectures, one in Hawthorne Hall on Park Street, and another in the parlors of her Boston friends, where Fiske would have no overhead for either rent or advertising.

---

[4] JF to Abby, Mar. 4, 1885, HHL.

[5] JF to Abby, Nov. 2, 1879, HHL.

[6] Quotation from JF to Abby, Nov. 2, 1879, HHL. JF to his mother, Dec. 1, 1879, HHL.

As a result, he cleared more in Boston than from the better-attended Brooklyn lectures.[7]

While Fiske lectured in Brooklyn his mother, who had returned to New York with her husband after he resigned his Russian ministry, combined with Mrs. Hemenway to pay off Fiske's debts. With some difficulty she raised $4,500, while Mrs. Hemenway contributed $2,000. This relieved him of interest payments; whatever he earned from his lecturing would now be available for living expenses. However, Mr. Stoughton thereafter discontinued his annual subsidy to the Fiske household.[8]

Fiske's Harvard friends kept up pressure on Eliot to get Fiske on to the Faculty. Not only had they elected Fiske to the Board of Overseers, but he was also appointed a member of a committee to study the History Department. The committee urged Eliot to appoint a new professor in place of the young instructors and suggested that he choose someone qualified to teach the philosophy of history. But Eliot proved unreceptive to this broad hint.[9]

In the spring of 1880 Fiske tried to storm the major cities of the country—New York, Philadelphia, and Washington—before taking off on a tour of the West. In New York, Youmans organized a course of four lectures at Chickering Hall and arranged a public invitation by eminent residents. In Philadelphia, Unitarian minister Joseph May sponsored Fiske and introduced him to the first night's audience. For Washington the preparations were even more impressive. Fiske's agent (possibly with the aid of Stoughton's political connections) secured an invitation signed by President Rutherford B. Hayes, members of his Cabinet, and other leading citizens.[10]

Socially, the tour was a great success. In New York the Century Club, and in Philadelphia the Penn Club, gave dinners in Fiske's honor. More invitations to private dinners and parties than he could accept poured in on him. In Washington, Carl Schurz entertained Fiske in his home and President Hayes received him at the White House, taking him in to a Cabinet meeting where Fiske chatted

[7] JF to his mother, Dec. 1, 1879, HHL.

[8] JF to Abby, Nov. 12, 1879; Abby to JF's mother, Oct. 28, 1879; JF to his mother, Dec. 13, 1880, HHL.

[9] JF to his mother, Oct. 9, 1879, HHL.

[10] JF to Hutton, Jan. 6, 1880, PUL. JF to Abby, Jan. 15, 1880; printed program of Washington lectures, HHL.

with the ministers for fifteen minutes before they settled down to business.

Financially, the trip was a miserable failure. In Washington, despite the official and social sponsorship, Fiske barely covered expenses, and only managed to do that when his landlord, the Congregational Church at 10th and G Street, reduced the rent of the hall. Only the generosity of some private citizens prevented a deficit in Philadelphia. New York proved a moderate success, but, while seven hundred people turned out, high rent and publicity expenditures kept the total profits down to a few hundred dollars.[11]

Nor was the tour of the West, on which Fiske lectured at Buffalo, Cleveland, Cincinnati and Dayton, any more successful. In December of 1880, replying to his mother's reproaches at his falling into debt again, he listed his net earnings from lecturing since October 1879 at $1,179.24. In addition, he had received $1,200 from Mrs. Hemenway for preparing two new lectures for her Old South campaign. "Therefore," he complained bitterly to his mother, "$2,379.24 was to cover all the expenses of this great family for *more than a year.*" [12]

Fiske found it difficult to explain his failure. He had expected his sponsorship by society and official Washington to bring out crowds of listeners, but he sadly reported to Abby that "the big 'invitation' by the President &c. produced *no effect* whatever. I probably didn't gain *one hearer* by it." While he reaped social and intellectual glory, he had not achieved the financial results he needed. "Fact is, I have got all the brains of Washington to hear me, & they are wild with delight. But *brains* won't pay, you must rake in the pu[trid?] rabble, and the rabble won't come to hear me, no matter how loud the gong is sounded." He complained to Abby, "This business is futile. I care nothing for their praise. *All* I want is *money,* and money I cannot get. I might much better stay at home with my darlings." [13]

[11] JF to Abby, Jan. 18, 1880, Jan. 21, 1880, Jan. 25, 1880, Feb. 15, 1880, Feb. 19, 1880, HHL.

[12] Quotation from JF to his mother, Dec. 13, 1880, HHL (italics in source). JF to Abby, Mar. 3, 1880, HHL, and Mar. 9, 1880, LC. JF to his mother, Mar. 11, 1880, HHL.

[13] JF to Abby, Feb. 15, 1880, HHL (italics in source).

II

To gather more European laurels for use in his advertising, Fiske departed on a second lecture tour to England in the summer of 1880. With adequate advance warning his friends were more successful in locating sponsors than in the previous year. Huxley arranged for three paid lectures on American political ideas at the Royal Institution. In addition, Conway agreed to have Fiske give the same lectures in the South Place Chapel in the evenings, and the Philosophical Institute of Edinburgh contracted for four historical lectures. An attempt to get Ernest Renan and Hippolyte Taine to sponsor lectures in Paris fell through, but otherwise the trip was a gratifying success.[14]

At the invitation of the Huxleys, he took Abby with him and introduced her to his friends and to the English people and countryside he so much admired. In London, the couple stayed with the Huxleys, who gave receptions and dinner parties in their honor. Darwin invited them to his country home for a week-end. Spencer, Conway, and others of Fiske's friends showered attentions on them. Abby proudly witnessed the successful delivery of Fiske's three lectures. But the emotional high point of the visit came during their tour of England on the way to Edinburgh, when the couple spent a day ancestor-hunting in the Suffolk countryside not far from Ipswich. There, at Stadhaugh Manor, Laxfield, Fiske discovered that a house once occupied by his ancestors still remained. "This morning I didn't even know that the old Fiske place had survived. Now I have actually drunk a glass of wine in the dining room; and know beyond peradventure that my forefathers ate in that very room; and a lovely old room, too!" he wrote back in joy to his mother. "And to have had Abby with me, to see it all!!! . . . Abby has been very happy today. I think it one of the most romantic days of my life." [15]

Their projected tour of the Continent had to be abbreviated, due to a shortage of funds, and included only Paris and the northern

[14] JF to his mother, Apr. 12, 1880, Apr. 26, 1880, HHL, and May 27, 1880, July 5, 1880, LC.

[15] Quotation from JF to his mother, June 4, 1880, LC. Mrs. Henrietta Huxley to Abby, Mar. 15, 1880, HHL. JF to his mother, May 27, 1880, LC.

part of France. Neither was greatly impressed. "We should like Paris better if it didn't smell so strong," Fiske wrote his mother. "We like Massachusetts the best of all. We Yankees lick the tarnal earth for general bang-up niceness, *selon moi*. We are très homesick." Late in July, after a three-month stay in Europe, the two returned home.[16]

The most consequential result of Fiske's trip was the preparation of three fresh lectures. Of these only the first two were entirely new. Fiske took his highly successful final lecture on the future of the Anglo-Saxons and, after revising it, used it as the last of the three under the title "Manifest Destiny." He prefaced it by two entirely new talks, "The Town Meeting" and "The Federal Union," in which he traced out the course of development of American political institutions.

In his first two lectures Fiske drew heavily on the work he had previously done on the "Aryans," following most closely the ideas of that school of English historians who may be termed "Anglo-Teutonists," especially E. A. Freeman, William Stubbs, and Sir Henry Maine. These writers traced back the origin of English self-government to the Teutonic mark, or independent village community, whose development they thought they could see in all the lands of western Europe. To them the purest form of this development took place in England, where the institution could adapt itself to changing times undisturbed by continental wars and invasions. While accepting the work of German scholars who saw in Tacitus' description of the German tribes the germ of future European political growth, it was only in their own England, and especially in its local self-government, that they found the true descendent of the independent and freedom-loving Teutonic spirit.

Fiske, in his first lecture, proceeded to cap the work of these English scholars by adding that it was in the New England Town Meeting, even further removed from the disturbances of the continent of Europe, that these tendencies reached full flower. Although the development of local self-government took place in all Teutonic

---

[16] Quotation from JF to his mother, July 5, 1880, LC (italics in source). JF to his mother, June 11, 1880, LC.

nations, only in an atmosphere where pressure for central govern-ment was least strong could the trend reach maturity.[17]

In his second essay Fiske turned to what his sources regarded as the great contribution of England to modern political ideas, the principle of parliamentary representation. Again Fiske argued that the United States had carried the development to its highest peak, this time in the American federal union. The germs of the principle of representation had been present among the ancient Germans. These ideas had died out on the Continent, but had been carried to new heights in the English Parliament. The articulated development of representative government made an efficient central power in the state possible, without destroying local or individual freedom. This principle permitted the formation of large-sized free states, while avoiding the dilemma of the ancient world, where the only way to form extensive states was for one locality to tyrannize the rest. Fiske added the claim that the American Union had success-fully extended this principle to a continental land mass and thus proved that there was no limit to the area a free state could occupy.[18]

From this point Fiske projected his vision of the future. England having solved the problem of combining a powerful central govern-ment with local and individual freedom, and the United States having demonstrated that this form of government could rule large geographic areas with full freedom for all, nothing now limited the expansion of the Anglo-American political ideas. On this basis Fiske predicted a great extension of the area of the earth ruled by English-speaking peoples. "The day is at hand when four-fifths of the human race will trace its pedigree to English forefathers, as four-fifths of the white people in the United States trace their pedigree today." [19]

Fiske expected this development to produce a peaceful and pros-perous future for the entire world, as other races accepted the leadership of the gifted Anglo-Americans. "Thus we may foresee in general outline how, through the gradual concentration of the

---

[17] Fiske freely acknowledged his debt to Freeman, Stubbs, and Maine in his preface and in the footnotes to *American Political Ideas* (New York, 1885).

[18] *American Political Ideas,* ch. II.

[19] *Ibid.,* p. 143.

preponderance of physical power into the hands of the most pacific communities, the wretched business of warfare must finally become obsolete all over the globe." In the long reaches of time it seemed clear that the final outcome must be a world federation led by Anglo-Americans. This would indeed take evolutionary ages to come about, but "meanwhile it is pleasant to feel that the dispassionate contemplation of great masses of historical facts goes far towards confirming our faith in this ultimate triumph of good over evil. Our survey began with pictures of horrid slaughter and desolation: it ends with the picture of a world covered with cheerful homesteads, blessed with a sabbath of perpetual peace." [20]

This glowing portrait of the magnificent future in store for England and America pleased audiences as well as critics who, reviewing it in book form, highly recommended it to their readers. One termed it "a careful and a faithful study of history." Fiske repeated the lecture fifty times in Britain and America, seven times in Boston alone. The Pennsylvania Institution for the Blind published it in a Braille edition. The vision of the meaning of America and of its historical experience expressed in this essay remained the basis of Fiske's historical writing to the end of his career and was an important factor in his great popularity.[21]

Fiske did not claim that his ideas were original. The view he took of the roots of Anglo-American political development had already been worked out by Freeman and Stubbs and Maine. The picture of the future of the world as a massive federation in which peaceful, industrial tendencies would replace and eliminate warlike trends he drew directly from Spencer's ideas of political and social evolution. Fiske carried these views to a wider audience and made their flattering connotations clearer and more precise than his mentors had done. Not only did he show to American listeners how the United States had accomplished these goals on a continental scale, but he drew for his English auditors a picture of the British Empire doing for the world what the United States had done for itself. By insisting

---

[20] *Ibid.*, pp. 151, 152.

[21] Quotation from the *Critic*, 6:159 (Apr. 4, 1885). See also, Chicago *Dial*, 6:16–17 (May 1885); *Methodist Review*, 67:487 (May 1885); *American Church Review*, 48:198–199 (August 1886); *Harpers' Monthly*, 70:972 (May 1885). "Introduction" to *American Political Ideas*, pp. 9–10.

that the inevitable end-product of imperialism was the spread of peace and freedom over the globe, he tried to transform imperialism into a liberal and liberating idea.

The running undercurrent of this thought is racist, but Fiske, like Freeman, was aware of the biological ambiguity of the term "Anglo-Saxon," and realized that there was no such thing in the modern world as a pure race, or any identity between national groups and biological or anthropological classifications. Indeed, when defining race he tried to restrict his use of the term to language groups, following Freeman in preferring the term "English race" to "Anglo-Saxon." In practice, however, Fiske was not too careful in his usage; he frequently used "race" in contexts where there were definite biological connotations. Although Fiske said the characteristics of his "English race" were transmitted by descent, he did not think these traits were indelible, for Fiske fully accepted Spencer's ideas on the inheritance of acquired characteristics. If what was deliberate adaptation in early generations would in time become part of the biological inheritance of descendents, then rapid assimilation of individuals with different cultural and biological characteristics was possible. Since Fiske felt absolutely certain that the English strain was the best, he was sure it would dominate in any situation and succeed in assimilating all other groups to it. This he claimed the American experience demonstrated, for non-English groups had adapted themselves to the English language and spoke, thought, and acted in a manner which made them the heirs of the great English political and cultural traditions. So long as he felt convinced that the English traditions remained dominant in America, Fiske's racism was little more than pride in a distinguished ancestry. It would, however, create problems later, especially in the 1890's, when Fiske came to the conclusion that groups he thought of as inherently inferior were no longer willing to follow "English" political and social leadership. But in the relatively calm situation of the early eighties, with the peaks of mass immigration still in the future, and while challenges to the dominant position of the "English" by other ethnic groups seemed unlikely, Fiske's racist view of the Anglo-American future created no problems and won wide approval.[22]

[22] See, especially, *American Political Ideas*, pp. 103, 105, 143–144.

III

In his lecture tours of 1880–1881 Fiske effectively used his three new lectures to increase the financial returns. The steady growth of his reputation aided him. Admirers assured the country that here was a chance to learn the true philosophical import of the American experience by listening to a man who had captivated the critical audiences of the world's cultural center, London. The intellectual success of the previous year had attracted the attention of lecture managers, one of whom undertook to guide Fiske's season. The agreement provided that the agent would receive a commission on all engagements he secured, while Fiske retained the percentage if he or his friends arranged the lecture date. Although the tour succeeded, the manager did not bring in enough lucrative contracts to satisfy Fiske, who severed the connection at the end of the season. For the most part the agent secured only short engagements for one or two lectures, on which travel expenses took away much of the profit. The most profitable arrangement made by the manager was for a series of six lectures at Haverford College. But Fiske's connections, through his growing body of admirers, were more effective in securing college dates than those of any commercial manager.[23]

Fiske earned larger amounts in 1881 than in 1879 or 1880 because he had reduced the risks he undertook. Most of his engagements were for fixed fees, with any profits going to the church or college which sponsored the lectures. He made more effective use of his friends than before, and stayed away from the largest centers. In Milwaukee, the Unitarian church that had organized his evolution lectures in the seventies, guaranteed him $500 for seven lectures. Cornell, where President A. D. White had long shown an interest in Fiske, presented his series of three lectures to the students. A third such sponsor was Washington University of St. Louis. Its president, William Greenleaf Eliot, a Unitarian minister and transplanted New Englander, had drawn on New England models and New England funds in building his young institution, then in its third decade. One of his most valued contributors was Mrs. Hemenway,

[23] JF to his mother, June 4, 1880, LC, and Aug. 24, 1880, Nov. 12, 1880, HHL. JF to Holt, Oct. 19, 1880; JF to Abby, Feb. 13, 1881, HHL.

at whose summer home he and Fiske had met the previous year. From this meeting came an invitation to speak to the students in St. Louis. Other lectures, either to the public or to students, at the Peabody Institute in Baltimore, in Poughkeepsie, Newburgh, Brooklyn, Indianapolis, and Madison, Wisconsin, rounded out the tour.[24]

Although Fiske himself was unaware of it, and it would still take some years before his success became secure, he had already laid the basis for his eventual triumphs on the lecture platform. He had put together the leading ideas which, elaborated in his later volumes of history, would win much applause. Although he had not attracted the lucrative mass audience he wanted, he had begun to draw the specific body of listeners who became his major supporters.

Fiske desired a mass audience that would flock to his lectures and bring him substantial monetary rewards. To achieve this he felt that he had to broaden his appeal and attract what, in his moments of depression, he termed the "rabble." But this he never succeeded in doing. No amount of advertising by the social and intellectual leadership of the communities he visited, not even the widely publicized invitation from President Hayes in 1880, brought out the crowds; nor did his attempts to stress colorful incidents and use the magic lantern achieve success on the lyceum circuit. Fiske proved incapable of appealing to a mass audience. He could adapt only to listeners whom he respected intellectually or socially. He tried to attract crowds by advertising his lectures as something all should attend if they desired to attain true culture; this appeal remained his major reliance all through his career. Never did he consciously or unconsciously adapt his lectures to make them relevant to the actual situation of the masses of Americans in the latter part of the nineteenth century. The "rabble" were to be told what was good for them, not what they wanted to hear. Consequently they never turned out to listen to Fiske. He drew only those to whom what he felt was good for them did seem relevant to their own lives, and with this audience he developed an almost automatic rapport.[25]

---

[24] JF to his mother, Aug. 24, 1880; JF to Abby, Feb. 2, 1881, Feb. 7, 1881, Feb. 13, 1881, HHL. JF to Abby, Feb. 18, 1881, LC. *Dictionary of American Biography,* s.v., William Greenleaf Eliot.

[25] The above, and the following six paragraphs, are based primarily on indications

Fiske achieved financial success by an intensified exploitation of the audiences he had already begun to attract in the early 1880's. In his years of struggle he developed highly successful methods of organizing lectures to provide the maximum possible monetary gain. In one type of engagement Fiske himself hired a hall for four to twelve lectures on a given topic, and assumed all financial risks. He then called on Harvard classmates and other acquaintances who were successful community leaders to aid him. They did not depend on posters and newspapers alone. Each drew in friends to help out who would take part of the tickets and sell them to their acquaintances. Word-of-mouth advertising and personal sales campaigns proved very effective in bringing Fiske's lectures to the attention of élite community leaders and those who admired and desired to imitate their patterns of social and cultural behavior. In this manner sufficient series tickets could be sold to pay all expenses in advance, while single admissions or series tickets sold after Fiske arrived on the scene would be all profit. During his first years of lecturing not enough people turned out, and the physical arrangements were frequently mismanaged so that expenses were disproportionately high. He cured both these defects in time, as his reputation grew and brought in more of those striving for culture, and as his grasp of the correct way to handle a lecture series improved. This pattern, with a socially prominent group of sponsors, many of them Harvard graduates or expatriate New Englanders, selling by personal recommendation enough series tickets to pay all expenses in advance, produced some of Fiske's most lucrative engagements.

In Fiske's second important type of arrangement he spoke for a fixed fee, and an institutional sponsor took all risk, as well as all profit above the speaker's fee. These lecture series were usually sponsored by colleges or churches. Never did Fiske succeed in breaking into the lyceum circuit which provided other successful lecturers with their most profitable engagements.

Two minor types of activity rounded out the list of Fiske's successful engagements. While in a city for a lecture series, which might stretch over an entire month, he frequently arranged to speak

---

scattered through Fiske's letters, especially those to his wife and mother in the Henry L. Huntington Library and the Library of Congress.

at private schools in the neighborhood, giving either an entire series or single talks. Similarly, he would often give "parlor lectures" to select groups in the homes of his socially prominent sponsors. While both these activities brought lower fees than his more profitable arrangements, they did serve to increase his monetary returns in a given period without greatly increasing expenses.

The geographic areas in which Fiske achieved his greatest success were New England, the Middle Atlantic States, and the region of New England migration across the country—cities where New Englanders or their descendants held substantial social and cultural leadership. When he penetrated into areas in which at first glance this does not appear to be true, as in Wisconsin and St. Louis, or in his two tours to the Pacific Coast, his main support came from New England elements in the community. In Wisconsin and St. Louis he was sponsored by Unitarian clergymen who had been born and educated in New England. He first went to California at the invitation of Mrs. Augustus Hemenway of Boston, who paid his railroad fare and introduced him to her influential friends there. In Oregon he was sponsored by the Unitarian minister at Portland, Thomas Lamb Eliot, son of President Eliot of the Washington University at St. Louis. In New York and other Middle Atlantic states, many, though by no means all, of his ardent supporters shared with Fiske his New England heritage.[26]

The audience which Fiske drew to his lectures were not the masses, but rather those who desired to follow the social leaders of their community in the quest for culture. A large proportion of them, as well as of the sponsors, felt that their intellectual homeland was in New or Old England. Since they were for the most part an educated group, Fiske's articles in the *Atlantic* and *North American Review,* as well as his books, helped make him a celebrity in their eyes. Fiske called them, with some truth, "the cream of society." If they were not all community leaders, they were people who aspired to that position and imitated the cultural behavior of the New Englanders among them who acted as if they were the top of society.

As a group they were interested in the filio-pietistic ideas which

[26] See, especially, JF to Abby, Feb. 18, 1881, Apr. 6, 1884, June 25, 1887, LC, and June 16, 1887, HHL.

Fiske eloquently expressed. Although he had little to say that appealed to a mass audience, Fiske's version of the meaning of American history agreed with the view of themselves held by this aspiring élite. These people also had a great interest in new religious ideas. If the majority were undoubtedly as staunchly conservative in their religion as in their political and economic ideas, they were educated and aware of the new science and philosophy of the century. Believing themselves to be modern and acquainted with the latest word on all subjects, they were most open to the religious questioning and disturbance that grew out of the penetration of new ideas. The churches attended by this social group were those most affected by the religious changes of the century. Fiske's later religious writing attracted these people. They were not the mass audience for which Fiske had hoped. But they were potentially numerous enough, since they had both a desire for culture and the money to invest in series tickets, to provide lucrative rewards for a lecturer who attracted them.[27]

IV

In the early 1880's, Fiske had not yet succeeded in drawing such listeners upon a regular basis. He turned back to writing as his best hope of expanding his income. In the fall of 1881 Fiske negotiated with Ginn & Company and with Harpers about the possibility of writing a two-volume history of the American people modeled on the popular short history of the English people which his friend Richard Green had published in 1874. He consulted Francis Parkman, who encouraged him, writing, "I believe that you could do the work better than anybody else!" Fiske finally accepted Harpers' offer of $5,000 in advance royalties on delivery of the finished manu-

[27] Fiske's manipulation of social and political leaders can be sampled in his correspondence with Mrs. Anne Lynch Botta (HUL) and Henry A. Richmond (HHL); his use of schools in the letters to Marshall Snow (WUA) and Sherrard Billings (HUL). See also, *Critic*, 12:74 (Feb. 11, 1888), and 23:418–419 (Dec. 23, 1893). The reaction of his audiences is indicated in the reminiscences of S. M. Crothers, in *Later Years of the Saturday Club*, M. A. DeWolfe Howe, ed. (Boston, 1927), pp. 273–278; F. H. Head, *John Fiske* (Chicago, [1902?]); T. S. Perry, "John Fiske: an Appreciation," *Atlantic Monthly*, 89:627–637 (May 1902); and W. R. Thayer "A Sketch of John Fiske's Life," *Harvard Graduates' Magazine*, 10:33–38 (September 1901).

script. On the strength of this contract, John Codman Ropes, the
military historian and fellow member of Fiske's Cambridge clubs,
arranged a substantial loan. Other friends also helped out. Benjamin
Frothingham of Brooklyn, one of his classmates there who had
helped his lectures; Henry A. Richmond of Buffalo, whose mother
had lent Fiske money at the request of Manton Marble while he was
at work on his *Cosmic Philosophy;* and Samuel J. Tilden, a close
political friend of Marble, all advanced money. After the death of
her husband on January 7, 1882, Fiske's mother again came to his
assistance.[28]

With these substantial sums on hand, Fiske settled down to write
his book. He had been able to consolidate all his debts and felt sure
that the cash remaining would provide him two clear years in which
to work. The only lectures he gave in 1882 were at St. Louis in
March, where he read several chapters from his new volume to the
students at Washington University, and two in November for Mrs.
Hemenway in Boston. The remainder of his time he enthusiastically
devoted to his writing. Not only had the book solved his immediate
financial problems, but it fitted well with his future plans. When he
achieved the success he confidently anticipated from its publication,
the publicity would greatly increase his reputation as a historian and
his attractiveness as a lecturer. Green's model for a history, with its
emphasis on social development, intrigued him; Fiske hoped to
turn out a volume that would use social history in such a manner as
to be both philosophical in the Spencerian sense and scientific on the
order of Freeman's historical works.[29]

When he began his task Fiske expected to finish easily in two
years. To Fiske the function of the historian was to shape a narrative
that would make clear the underlying philosophical principles which
explained the events of history. These principles he knew in advance; he drew them from his previous study of Spencer and the
Anglo-Teutonic school of historians. He saw no need for research

[28] JF to Abby, Apr. 25, 1881, Dec. 7, 1881, LC. JF to Henry A. Richmond, July
19, 1881, Oct. 31, 1881; JF to his mother, Mar. 6, 1882, Sept. 10, 1885; Estate of
S. J. Tilden to JF, Sept. 17, 1887, HHL. F. Parkman to JF [undated], John Fiske
Papers, Department of Special Collections, The Library, University of California,
Los Angeles.
[29] JF to Abby, Mar. 3, 1882; JF to Mrs. Hemenway, Jan. 11, 1883, HHL.

and depended on previous histories of the nation for details. After a year's work, in the summer of 1882, he had most of the first volume done and hoped to complete the rest by the following May. He had already sent some of his opening chapters to the publisher to be printed in *Harpers' Monthly,* in order to arouse the interest of the reading public, when he decided that he needed to increase his knowledge of American history. He wrote from Petersham to Justin Winsor at the Harvard Library, asking him to "send me by express *one* good history of N.Y. & Penn. each," as well as one on New Jersey. He told Winsor, "My scheme is clear in my mind; & of illustrations from general U. S. histories I have plenty; but it occurs to me that some of these local histories will give me still more." Winsor sent the books. With these and the fifty or sixty volumes from his own library that he had brought to his summer home with him, Fiske continued on schedule until his return to Cambridge in October. There he found, however, that the bustle and turmoil of a household of six children made work difficult. He soon fell behind schedule.[30]

To find more peaceful working conditions. Fiske thought of the manner in which he had completed his two-volume treatise on philosophy, and planned a fourth, and last, trip to England. There he hoped to work rapidly and complete his book by the deadline. Following his stay in England he proposed a tour of the Continent to see if the German, French, and Italian publishers who were cooperating with E. L. Youmans and Appleton in the International Scientific Series would be interested in bringing out translations of his history. He raised more money from his mother and two of his friends and, on January 31, 1883, sailed from New York, intending to spend nine months in Europe.[31]

In England Fiske received the warm welcome he had come to expect from his friends. The director of the British Museum reading-room arranged for him to have full stack privileges. Macmillan praised the book. Huxley welcomed him back to his Sunday teas.

---

[30] Quotation from JF to Winsor, Aug. 4, 1882, HUL (italics in source; MS bears notation in corner, "Books sent"). JF to his mother, Aug. 9, 1882, Oct. 4, 1882, HHL.

[31] JF to his mother, Oct. 4, 1882; JF to Mrs. Hemenway, Jan. 11, 1883; JF to Abby, Jan. 30, 1883, HHL.

Spencer again extended to him the courtesies of his clubs. At first Fiske settled down to his work with vigor, moving ahead rapidly on the narrative of the American Revolution on which he had been engaged in Cambridge.[32]

But for the first time in his experience England did not satisfy him. Everything he saw reminded him of the last trip when Abby had accompanied him. He despondently wrote to her that "now for the first time London seemed a great lonely place, and it seemed as if Hezzy must take the first steamer back for America." He made little use of the club privileges Spencer had arranged and kept much to himself. When his homesickness grew severe he went for long walks searching out literary landmarks, but even this favorite occupation failed to take his mind off his loneliness. Nor was company any improvement. After an evening spent with Frederick Macmillan and his wife, Fiske gloomily returned to his room "and had a hard cry for home. I cried so hard that I fell asleep from sheer exhaustion and felt weak and mean Saturday when I got up at 10.30." His resolve to stay on and work was badly weakened when he suffered a severe chill and had to be nursed for several days by his friends, the Trübners. For the first time he complained of the damp London climate and found it hard to shake off the effects of his illness. The continued feeling of depression led him to consider consulting a mental specialist. Before he had spent two months in London he wrote urgently to Abby demanding that she find some way to come to him, assuring her that if only she raised the passage money, they would both be able to live on the funds he had brought with him. But Abby could not come. After struggling along despondently until he could stand it no longer, Fiske booked passage home in April. "I shall *never* be *restless* for England any more," he assured Abby. "I am going to stay in my *home,* work in it, & stick to it. It is where I *belong.*" [33]

That summer he was back in Petersham again, at work on the

[32] JF to Abby, Feb. 16, 1883; JF to Lizzie Wilcox, Mar. 1, 1883; Spencer to JF, Feb. 23, 1883, HHL. JF to his mother, Mar. 2, 1883, LC.

[33] Quotations from JF to Abby, Feb. 20, 1883, LC, and Apr. 12, 1883, HHL (italics in source). JF to Abby, Mar. 24, 1883, Mar. 29, 1883; JF to his mother, Feb. 22, 1883, Apr. 4, 1883, LC. Spencer to JF, Mar. 29, 1883, HHL.

history and, although he had now passed his original deadline, felt quite optimistic about finishing before the end of the year. He looked forward to his next two books, one to cover the history of the early Aryans, and the other the life of Jesus and the growth of the early Christian church. At the same time he considered issuing a new and revised edition of his *Cosmic Philosophy*. But to his great surprise he discovered that the project had got out of hand, and had expanded to a size beyond the two volumes of 100,000 words each that he had originally planned. As he worked away in London and Massachusetts, the section on the military history of the Revolution had grown to thirteen chapters, and other parts of the narrative showed a similar tendency to enlarge under his hands. The increase in size made it impossible for him to finish the book on time.[34]

But this delay meant more than just postponing a book, for now the flimsiness of his financing entangled him in the most severe monetary problems he ever encountered. Since his work was not complete by November 1883 as specified in the Harper contract, he received none of the $5,000 he had expected and could not repay the loan negotiated by Ropes. The other loans also came due about the same time, but Fiske could pay none of them. In August of 1883, still unaware that a storm was in the offing, he had borrowed $100 from his Harvard classmate, Shepherd Gilbert, promising to repay in a month or so; it was March 1887 before Fiske repaid the money, and even then he protested that he was still penniless.[35]

When this prolonged financial crisis caught him, Fiske's resources were lower and his needs greater than at any time before. Previously he had always been able to draw on his mother and her husband. But, with Mr. Stoughton dead, his mother's income decreased. In the period immediately following her husband's death, his mother had generously advanced to Fiske part of the money left to her. Now she could do little for him without reducing her own scale of living, for the elaborate house she had had built at 90 Brattle Street, Cambridge, and the luxuries to which life with a wealthy lawyer had accustomed her consumed all the income from her inheritance.

[34] JF to Holt, June 8, 1883, Dec. 14, 1883; JF to Richmond, June 11, 1884, HHL.
[35] JF to Shepherd Gilbert, Aug. 9, 1883, Aug. 17, 1883, Dec. 15, 1884, Mar. 17, 1887, HHL.

While his mother's ability to help lessened, Fiske's expenses rose. As the children grew older their expenses increased. Illness caused further drains on his income, a need for money which reached a tragic peak when his eldest son and daughter suffered what Fiske later termed a "nervous prostration." After several relapses Maud recovered sufficiently to marry and lead a normal life. But Harold, though recovering partially and entering Harvard in 1887, suffered a severe relapse the next year and needed treatment in a sanitarium and the attention of male nurses for some time thereafter. He did not fully recover during Fiske's lifetime.[36]

With the pressure severe to raise money to stave off the demands of his creditors and provide medical attention for his children, Fiske turned to his friends, and to the chapters of the history that he had completed. Mrs. Hemenway sponsored twelve lectures on the American Revolution for the Old South Association. To increase his income he also gave the same talks twice in private parlors in the afternoon, and offered them a third time in an evening course open to the public. Although these were chapters of his history that he had never intended to have stand alone, his simple, highly colorful narrative of the military campaigns of the Revolution proved the most popular series of lectures he had yet given.[37]

As never before, Fiske called on his admirers for help. He persuaded Washington University, which had desired only five lectures, to sponsor thirteen, give him a hall rent free, guarantee $500, and promise all surplus profits over that figure. In return, Fiske permitted students to attend the lectures free. So great was the charm which these lectures exerted that, after listening to the series, President Eliot of Washington University spoke of raising money to endow a professorship that would make yearly visits by Fiske possible. When the $500 loan made by Richmond came due in October 1883, Fiske persuaded him to extend it until the following January. When Richmond then presented it for payment through his bank, Fiske had to let the note go to protest. This annoyed Fiske.

[36] JF to Abby, Apr. 14, 1886; JF to William Wilcox, July 30, 1884; JF to J. G. Wilson, May 7, 1888, June 6, 1888; JF to Henry Holt, Aug. 26, 1888; JF to T. H. Huxley, Aug. 5, 1893, HHL. Harvard Class of 1891, *Secretary's Report*, 11:140 (1941), has a brief sketch of Harold's life.

[37] JF to M. S. Snow, Feb. 4, 1884, WUA.

"It is the first instance in my experience in which I have had any difficulty in getting a note extended, as I have always paid things sooner or later," he ingenuously informed Richmond. Fiske's solution of the problem of repaying the note was for Richmond to sponsor a lecture series in Buffalo: Fiske would give twelve lectures if Richmond would guarantee $1,000. He went on to praise their value in such glowing terms that he embarrassed himself. "Excuse me for blowing my own trumpet," he concluded. "It is business you know." Richmond did not take offence. Although he did not immediately comply with Fiske's request, in future years he arranged several lecture series for Fiske, both before and after Fiske repaid the money, and usually invited Fiske to stay at his home while in Buffalo.[38]

Not all attempts at increasing income worked out. Since Fiske's church sponsor in Milwaukee would not turn over all profits, he hired a hall himself and offered his lectures to the public, confidently expecting to earn much more than the church had previously paid him. But he badly mistimed his series, arriving just as the 1884 election campaign of Cleveland and Blaine reached its climax. Wisconsin turned out to be more interested in current than Revolutionary history and few auditors appeared.[39]

At the nadir of his financial trouble, Fiske was practically bankrupt, and creditors seeking payment for household bills legally attached his assets. At one point he had so little cash that he appealed to his mother for five dollars to pay the fare from New York to Washington, where a lecture engagement would provide funds to meet travel expenses for the rest of his tour. Only the fact that the title of the house at 22 Berkeley Street was in Mrs. Stoughton's name kept a roof over his family's heads. To prevent creditors from attaching the copyrights of his books, he assigned them to his mother.[40]

The severe problems he faced, and his inability to turn to anyone to rescue him, as he had done in the past, shook Fiske's normal

<hr>

[38] Quotations from JF to Richmond, Jan. 15, 1884 and Jan. 18, 1884, HHL. JF to M. S. Snow, Feb. 4, 1884, Feb. 20, 1884, WUA. JF to Abby, Apr. 6, 1884, LC.

[39] JF to Abby, Oct. 13, 1884; JF to H. A. Richmond, Oct. 21, 1884, HHL.

[40] JF to his mother, Feb. 15, 1885, Sept. 1, 1885, Sept. 10, 1885, HHL.

optimism. "Several times I have wished I could shuffle off this mortal coil," he told Richmond. "Life is a coil—just that—and I am disgusted with it." Yet such cries of despair were only temporary aberrations. More characteristically Fiske treated all hopeful signs as if they were predictions of future glory and ease. He rejoiced when President Eliot of Washington University praised his lectures and arranged to have him appointed a nonresident professor of history, thus assuring that he would lecture there each year. He wrote Abby, "If Harvard's nastiness ends by making me a teacher loved and honoured in all the great cities of America, perhaps I shall be the more useful, & grow thereby in breadth, myself. Dr. Eliot thinks ten years more will make me *the* honoured man of all America." When Grover Cleveland's election as President seemed imminent, Fiske wrote to Richmond, a political associate of Cleveland in Buffalo, reminding him that he, Fiske, had been a loyal Democrat for some time and suggesting that the new administration consider him for a diplomatic appointment. "I am hardly so wild as to think of *England,*" he assured Richmond, but he would accept any ministry to a nation in Western Europe. Richmond's reply does not survive, but a few months later Fiske sadly renounced this dream.[41]

Fiske had difficulty writing amid the manifold distractions of a household of six children afflicted with recurrent and often serious illnesses, where he was constantly reminded of the load of debt that hung over him. Only the need for material to use in St. Louis, where the repeated presence of the same students made it necessary to provide fresh lectures, kept him working on the chapters of his history. The rush in which he worked made it difficult for him to revise or seek out new material; for the most part he contented himself with what he could remember and checked only in the reference books on his shelves at home or in those he carried with him on his tours.[42]

But the steady expansion in size that his project underwent, as

[41] Quotations from JF to Richmond, Aug. 10, 1884, July 10, 1885, HHL; and JF to Abby, Apr. 6, 1884, LC (italics in sources). JF to Richmond, May 2, 1885, HHL. JF to W. G. Eliot, Jan. 20, 1885, WUA.

[42] JF to M. S. Snow, Oct. 8, 1884, Mar. 27, 1885, Mar. 2, 1887, Mar. 23, 1888, WUA. JF to Abby, May 24, 1887, HHL, and June 25, 1887, LC.

Fiske turned more and more of the chapters of his history into lectures, finally caused a rupture in his relations with Harpers. In 1881 he had set out to write a survey running some 200,000 words and filling two volumes, expecting to complete it in two years. By 1884 he was talking of a four-volume work, with each volume longer than the original set, to accommodate a history that would run to 820,000 words. As the scale of his writing increased, he began to consider further expansion. But this was too much for Harpers. They had agreed to carry chapters of the history in *Harpers' Monthly* in order to advertise the book (as well as increase Fiske's income) and did carry seven such installments in 1882 and 1883. But they found the new chapters Fiske sent them in the fall of 1885 much more than they had bargained for and declined to print them.[43]

Despite all his disappointments, Fiske kept on hoping that somehow he would be able to raise enough money to clear away the enormous load of debt he had accumulated. Even more than in earlier years, his letters grasp eagerly at each sign of success and report them back to Abby and his mother. Every word of praise was carefully recorded, and perhaps somewhat exaggerated, as if he felt it necessary continually to reassure himself and his family that he really was a great man, or soon would be.

V

The expedients to which Fiske turned in the years from 1883 to 1885 were mostly an intensification of the methods he had used in the seventies to increase his income. Along with these came a last desperate attempt to attract mass audiences. He now put less stress on free-lance writing, for lecturing was clearly more profitable. Most of the articles he published were derived from his lectures or his book. In 1884, however, he brought together a scattering of miscellaneous items, under the title of *Excursions of an Evolutionist,* consisting of the lectures on the early Aryans that Fiske had hoped to expand into a full-scale book, some religious lectures, book

---

[43] JF to Abby, Mar. 30, 1884; JF to Richmond, June 11, 1884; JF to his mother, Sept. 1, 1885, HHL.

reviews, and occasional magazine pieces like the memorial essay on the death of Darwin.

While his new lectures brought increased returns, they did not solve his financial problems. In the 1884–1885 season he added to his available talks the chapters from his history covering events from 1783 to 1789, later published as *The Critical Period,* and spent six months touring the country with these as well as his series on the American Revolution. Financially, this was the most successful tour to date. Despite the fiasco in Wisconsin with which he began, he would earn five to six thousand dollars. Although this income far exceeded his previous earnings, it came nowhere near meeting his needs for money to reduce his debts and cover current expenditures. Fiske felt despondent until Henry Ward Beecher suggested a way in which Fiske could again try to attract the mass audience that had so far eluded him.[44]

Beecher interested his lecture manager, Major James B. Pond, in the possibilities Fiske's talents presented. Pond was the leading lecture manager of the country and had guided the tours that had established Beecher and Mark Twain as the two leading attractions of the American lecture platform. Pond told Fiske that his lectures were too intellectual for the bulk of the country's audiences. They did well in college towns, but he would have to come up with more concrete and graphic talks if he wanted to broaden his appeal. If he would write some lectures on this order, Pond offered to manage his tour for the following season and inspired Fiske to dream of earning $10,000 a year.[45]

Spurred by this ambition, Fiske planned four lectures on the Civil War campaigns in the Mississippi Valley stressing graphic and colorful narration. He would omit his customary attempt to attain a philosophical level by pointing to the significance of the events he described. They would be similar to the successful Revolutionary War lectures, but more immediately meaningful to a mass audience since they dealt with matters which either listeners themselves had

[44] JF to Abby, Mar. 4, 1885, Mar. 27, 1885, HHL. JF to M. S. Snow, Oct. 8, 1884, WUA.

[45] JF to Abby, Mar. 4, 1885, Mar. 9, 1885, HHL. J. B. Pond, *Eccentricities of Genius* (New York, 1900).

experienced or their fathers had told them about. Pond approved of Fiske's plan and through the summer of 1885 Fiske worked on his lectures, seeking colorful incidents and asking his friends to hunt out maps and pictures so that he could use the appeal of the magic lantern to draw in paying customers.[46]

On November 12 Fiske set out confidently with Pond to make his fortune, but by December 16 he could cite chapter and verse to support Mark Twain's remark to William Dean Howells on the profits of lecturing: "If you got half as much as Pond prophesied, be content and praise God—it has not happened to another." In thirty-four days Fiske gave forty-three lectures while following an itinerary that crisscrossed the northeastern section of the country; but, after deducting travel expenses, he found himself no better off financially than when he had begun his arduous tour.[47]

The audience response had been disappointing. These lectures were not the most attractive he could present to his old audience. In such series as the *Century Magazine's* "Battles and Leaders of the Civil War" they could read memoirs of actual participants that had a far greater aura of authenticity than Fiske could produce. Where he had been educational on the Revolutionary War, he was now repetitious on the Civil War. To attract a new audience would take time. Pond routed Fiske to many localities where he had never been before, where he was unknown, or at best only vaguely familiar. In time his talents might have made him a star of the lyceum circuit, but Fiske could not afford the time. He needed an immediate success and this Pond had not been able to produce.

The broken itinerary Pond laid out for him increased Fiske's discontent. Previously he had given lengthy series of lectures that permitted him to use one city as a base and commute from it to nearby sites as demand for the series or individual lectures developed. But Pond secured mostly one-night stands, since lyceum managers hesitated to take more than one lecture from a man new to the circuit, whom they could not be sure would please their regular

---

[46] JF to Laurence Hutton, Oct. 13, 1885, PUL. JF to M. S. Snow, Oct. 27, 1885, WUA. JF to Abby, Oct. 28, 1885, HHL.

[47] Twain to Howells letter printed in *The Portable Mark Twain*, Bernard de Voto, ed. (New York, 1946), p. 780. JF to M. S. Snow, Jan. 23, 1886.

customers. But this necessitated almost continuous traveling, increasing the cost of transportation and intensifying the physical strain of giving so many lectures in so short a time.[48]

This combination of physical and mental tension combined to produce a severe case of laryngitis in December; on the sixteenth Fiske cancelled the rest of his engagements and took to his bed while negotiations went on to end the agreement with Pond. An itemized statement of debts drawn up by Fiske on December 22 showed the desperate state of his finances. He listed $11,000 in overdue debts, much of it owed to merchants who had sold him goods on credit and the rest represented by notes he had been unable to pay at maturity. The total did not include long-term notes which had not yet matured, nor did he mention the substantial sums he had been given by his mother and his brother-in-law. Since he had left the Harvard library he had put in six years of hard work and at the end found himself deeper in debt than ever before in his life. The final attempt to capture a mass audience had failed. He saw no alternative except to struggle along on the same line he had already been trying, hoping desperately that in the future the results would justify his optimistic expectation of an income far higher than Harvard could pay.[49]

[48] JF to M. S. Snow, Jan. 23, 1886, WUA. JF to Richmond, Jan. 22, 1886; JF to Courtlandt Palmer, Jan. 26, 1886, HHL.
[49] Itemized Statement and Summary of Debts, Dec. 22, 1885, HHL.

CHAPTER EIGHT

THE DESTINY
OF MAN AND GOD

Changes in Fiske's way of life affected his religious orientation. As his personal problems increased during the 1880's, he turned to religion for its emotional rather than its philosophical values and, in his years of greatest personal difficulty, wrote his most widely hailed essays on religious themes.

Had he not met the severe personal difficulties described in the preceding chapter, he would probably not have changed sufficiently to win the wide attention he received in the last fifteen years of his life. Even in the 1870's he had been interested in finding a way to accommodate science and religion. But a simple logical development of his ideas would not have made them attractive to a broad audience. His argument in the seventies that his views were the best possible way to reconcile religion and science impressed only radicals. Fiske's earlier view valued religion as a way of looking at the universe and as a philosophical system that supported a useful set of morals. Originally he had only a secondary interest in its emotional aspects and he frequently resorted to polemic when orthodox writers questioned his views. Only after he had modified his approach so that what he had to say seemed less radical and controversial, and after he had begun to stress nonlogical values in religion, did his work become meaningful to a wide audience.

While the impetus towards this shift in attitude stemmed from Fiske's personal development, his widened experience also encouraged it. His historical lectures brought him into contact with moderate religious groups; not only Unitarians and Free Religionists, as had been the case with his evolution lectures, but Congregationalists, Presbyterians, Episcopalians, and even some Baptists now welcomed him as a speaker in their colleges and churches. His view of American history had a broader appeal than his earlier comments on religion and science. Fiske found these contacts rewarding, both financially and psychologically, and the tone of his references to orthodoxy altered. He ceased attacking those who disagreed with him. His assumption of intellectual superiority continued, but he modified his expression of it to avoid unnecessarily irritating his new friends.

The first signs of the change appeared in the series of articles on religion Fiske contributed to the *North American Review* in the early eighties, even before his perplexing financial problems descended on him. Only one of these articles—an assault upon the Reverend Joseph Cook, who had devoted a series of his Boston Monday Lectures to attacking Darwin and Huxley—was still polemic, and it was, interestingly, the only one of the essays of these years that Fiske felt reluctant to reprint. Under the title "Theological Charlatanism" Fiske vigorously condemned Cook for setting up straw men and refuting arguments his opponents never advanced. But Fiske did not in any way cast aspersions on the religious position Cook defended.[1]

Even more symptomatic were the two essays "The Historic Genesis of Protestantism" and "The True Meaning of Protestantism." The first essay surveyed primitive religion and the early Christian church, identifying all valuable aspects with developments that seemed to forecast later Protestantism. The second, originally given as an address to a conference of Unitarian ministers, assured them that Protestantism was an immediate deduction from his, and Spencer's, favorite doctrine of laissez faire. "The true lesson of

---

[1] JF, "Theological Charlatanism," *North American Review*, 132:287–295 (March 1881). The essay was not reprinted until 1899, when Fiske used it to fill out his *A Century of Science*, retitling it, "Guessing at Half and Multiplying by Two."

Protestantism . . . is simply this: That religious belief is something which in no way concerns society, but which concerns only the individual." Even those listeners who did not care for his secularistic method of deducing religious principles from nonreligious studies could not but be pleased by the respectful manner in which Fiske spoke of their religion and the way in which he used his reputation as a scientist and a philosopher to bring these studies to the defense of their faith.[2]

Only a hint of these changes can be found in Fiske's address at the dinner held in New York in honor of Herbert Spencer during his visit to America in 1882. There Fiske showed the same secularism that had dominated his views a decade earlier, though with minor shifts in tone. Speaking in reply to a toast, "The Doctrine of Evolution and Religion," Fiske devoted himself to a lengthy demonstration of the emotional and moral values of a religious system based on Spencer's philosophy of evolution. To Fiske, Spencer provided a scientific proof of the existence of an eternal Power Who guaranteed that all would work out for the best in the end. As Fiske experienced the pressures of an extremely difficult personal situation, he turned to his religious beliefs for assurance that the evil he knew was transitory, while the good he could imagine was permanent and real. In 1882 Fiske still used the religious terminology of Spencer to express himself. As his own problems worsened he began to use wording more akin to the traditional symbols of Christian religion.[3]

II

Fiske's opportunity to express his new attitude came in 1884 and 1885 when the managers of the Concord School of Philosophy asked Fiske to address their sessions. Bronson Alcott had organized the Concord School as a summer meeting at which philosophical

[2] JF, "Historic Genesis of Protestantism," *North American Review*, 132:356–368 (April 1881); "The True Lesson of Protestantism," *ibid.*, 134:259–271 (March 1882), quotation from p. 271. These essays were included in the 1884 *Excursions of an Evolutionist*.

[3] JF, "Evolution and Religion," in *Excursions of an Evolutionist* (Boston, 1902), pp. 268–278. *Herbert Spencer on the Americans and the Americans on Herbert Spencer*, E. L. Youmans, ed. (New York, 1883), has a full report on the Spencer dinner. Spencer to JF, Nov. 24, 1882, HHL.

issues could be discussed before interested audiences. Gathering at first in his home, and later in a small auditorium built by a Boston woman who admired the purposes of the institution, the sessions drew a small but intent group of listeners, attracted by the idea of studying in a rural setting made famous by the New England sages who had lived and worked nearby. Most of the auditors were female, with schoolteachers from across the land and a scattering of Boston society matrons evident among them. Emerson spoke at the first year's course, and the sponsorship of Alcott assured the continuance of a strong Transcendentalist influence. A second major sponsor, William Torrey Harris of St. Louis, who joined in the activity of the school from the start, brought with him his favorite Hegelian ideas. Thus organized, the school had a strong bias in favor of philosophical idealism, and all varieties of naturalism came under attack. One observer said the sessions presented "the spectacle of Herbert Spencer falling in ruins regularly, every forty-eight hours." When the management of the school chose immortality as the topic for discussion in 1884, they invited Fiske to address them as a spokesman for a naturalistic, scientific approach. Despite a heavy rain on the evening of July 31, a large crowd turned out to hear him, and were pleasantly surprised at the religious tone adopted by this disciple of Spencer.[4]

Although invited to speak on immortality, Fiske did not turn to this topic until the very end of his paper. His own title, "The Destiny of Man Viewed in the Light of His Origin," far better described what he had to say. Fiske briefly surveyed the evolutionary view of man's origins and interpreted this to mean that man was the "end" of evolution in all possible senses of the word—as the latest in time, the inevitable product, the final stage, the highest possible point, and the intended goal of the process. Where in his earlier work Fiske had scornfully rejected teleological argument as useless, he now proclaimed that evolution itself demonstrated a

[4] Quotation from G. P. Lathrop, "Philosophy and Apples," *Atlantic Monthly*, 46:655 (November 1880). *Index*, 16:74–75 (Aug. 14, 1884). Boston *Evening Transcript*, Aug. 1, 1884, Aug. 2, 1884. J. H. Ward, "The Concord School of Philosophy," *International Review*, 9:459–467 (October 1880). Austin Warren, "The Concord School of Philosophy," *New England Quarterly*, 2:199–233 (April 1929).

dramatic tendency which proved man to be the goal of the entire process. Thus Fiske tried to rehabilitate the argument from design in a more sophisticated form. He told his listeners that once man appeared upon the scene evolution worked no longer in physical but in mental terms, so that no higher creature than man could possibly evolve. Man as the end of evolution was its final stage, beyond which there could be no progress, as well as the latest stage and the intended goal toward which the entire universe had been working for countless ages.[5]

Fiske then recapitulated for his audience the theory of the significance of infancy which he had used in his *Cosmic Philosophy* to demonstrate the naturalistic roots of society and morality, and thus also of religion. Now he used it to argue that religion was the final goal of social evolution, and that the exalted position religion occupied in the evolutionary scheme proved its importance and truth. "He who has mastered the Darwinian theory, he who recognizes the slow and subtle process of evolution as the way in which God makes things come to pass, . . . sees that in the deadly struggle for existence which has raged throughout countless aeons of time, the whole creation has been groaning and travailing together in order to bring forth that last consummate specimen of God's handiwork, the Human Soul." [6]

The same process could be seen in history, where evolution slowly eliminated dependence on force and brought peaceful, moral, industrial society to a dominant position in the world. From the past Fiske turned to the future to picture a time when the spiritual in man would more and more prevail over his brute inheritance. Then, after many ages, yet surely and inevitably, warfare would be eliminated and there would be peace on earth for all men. "Now what," he asked his audience, "is this message of the modern prophet but pure Christianity?—not the mass of theological doctrine . . . but the real and essential Christianity which came, fraught with good tidings to men, from the very lips of Jesus and Paul!" [7]

[5] JF, "The Destiny of Man Viewed in the Light of His Origin," in *Studies in Religion* (Boston, 1902), pp. 1–84.

[6] JF, "Destiny of Man," pp. 19–20.

[7] JF, "Destiny of Man," p. 73.

Fiske closed with a brief allusion to the topic under discussion, immortality, in which he recapitulated the arguments of his earlier essay on the "Unseen World," arguing that while science did not prove the existence of an after life, it could never disprove it. "I believe in the immortality of the soul," he assured his hearers, "not in the sense in which I accept the demonstrable truths of science, but as a supreme act of faith in the reasonableness of God's work." [8]

There was little new in the speech, few ideas that Fiske had not previously presented in his *Cosmic Philosophy* or his essays, and he was quite surprised when some reviewers suggested that he had carried out a major shift of position. The actual differences were more a matter of tone and emphasis, and they had come to Fiske so naturally across the years that he was unaware of any divergence from his earlier position. The idea that man was the goal of evolution was implicit in his earlier work, but he had never so definitely pointed the moral of this conclusion. He had in his *Cosmic Philosophy* spoken of the congruence of his evolutionary faith and the essence of Christianity, but he did not there define this essential Christianity. In his 1882 speech at the Spencer dinner he had defined the essence of religion as belief in two propositions, that God ruled the world and that God was the source of ethical ideas. This was probably also what Fiske meant by "essential Christianity." But he did not, in his Concord adresses, specify what he meant, and he avoided all overt references to Herbert Spencer's "Unknowable," with which he had previously identified his essential religion.[9]

Fiske's ambiguity made it difficult for his hearers to determine whether the essence of Christianity he praised actually contained what they valued most in their religion. The ringing tones in which he now clothed his remarks and the confident manner in which he asserted that Christianity was the final religious position beyond which no evolution was possible, impressed many as quite different from the praise of Christianity in his *Cosmic Philosophy*. In fact, however, his ideas had not so much been revised as transmuted to a new emotional level, stated in tones which reflected Fiske's own

<hr />

[8] JF, "Destiny of Man," p. 82.

[9] JF, "Preface" to "Idea of God," in *Studies in Religion;* especially pp. 99–109. JF, "Evolution and Religion," in *Excursions*, pp. 271–272.

desire for assurance, and clothed in language that often echoed the rhythm and wording of the King James Bible. The peroration of the address carried the tone to its ultimate point. "If the foregoing exposition be sound, it is Darwinism which has placed Humanity upon a higher pinnacle than ever. The future is lighted for us with the radiant colours of hope. Strife and sorrow shall disappear. Peace and love shall reign supreme," Fiske assured his auditors. "The dream of poets, the lesson of priest and prophet, the inspiration of the great musician, is confirmed in the light of modern knowledge; and as we gird ourselves up for the work of life, we may look forward to the time when in the truest sense the kingdoms of this world shall become the kingdom of Christ, and he shall reign for ever and ever, king of kings and lord of lords." [10]

Brought out by Houghton, Mifflin and Company as a small one-dollar book in the fall of 1884, Fiske's address drew wide attention, mostly from the lay press. Not until his next volume on religion appeared did religious journals take Fiske seriously. Not all lay reviewers were pleased. To the rigidly naturalistic critic of the Chicago *Dial*, this essay seemed to "damage whatever claim the writer may have had to the title of philosopher," since Fiske tried "to entertain the fundamentally opposed conceptions of the principle of organic evolution on the one hand, and of the unique position of the human species on the other." The *Literary World* reviewer, too, found Fiske unconvincing. But other notices in general circulation magazines were more laudatory. The *Critic* called it "fresh, vigorous and thought-provoking," and proclaimed that "it will confirm many, who now believe, in holding fast to the faith." Asa Gray in the *Nation* summarized and quoted extensively from Fiske, though limiting himself to mild praise. William Dean Howells welcomed the book in *Harpers' Monthly*, though a trifle amused to find "Mr. Fiske unable to language his thoughts of infinity at supreme moments except in the words of the old Book of those Semitic tribes so remote from Darwin." [11]

[10] JF, "Destiny of Man," pp. 83–84.
[11] Chicago *Dial*, 5:177 (November 1884). Boston *Literary World*, 15:284 (Nov. 15, 1884). *Critic*, 5:182 (Oct. 18, 1884). *Nation*, 39:426 (Nov. 13, 1884). *Harpers' Monthly*, 72:808–809 (April 1886). Reviews in religious periodicals are noted in the following chapter.

III

Encouraged by the interest in his first contribution, the managers of the Concord School invited Fiske to join their 1885 seminar on the topic "Is pantheism the legitimate outcome of modern science?" Fiske gladly accepted, but again deviated from the suggested topic. Rather than answer the question, he chose to elaborate his own theological ideas and describe the view of God he thought was the legitimate outcome of modern science.

Writing rapidly at his summer home at Petersham, Fiske produced in fifteen days the sixty manuscript pages he read at Concord on the evening of July 29. To show the idea of God he thought the world view of contemporary science did support, he organized his essay about two contrasting concepts, opposing an immanent concept of God to that which saw Him as transcendent. By a transcendent God he meant one essentially discontinuous with the universe, residing outside it, and related to it only as the will or even the whim of the deity dictated sporadic interventions to alter the normal course of events. By an immanent God he meant one whose relation to the universe flowed directly from the essence of His own nature, who therefore followed regular and dependable courses of action, of which the laws of science were partial though necessarily incomplete descriptions. It was of this deity that it made sense to say, as Fiske had in his earlier essay, that evolution was "the way in which God makes things come to pass." Since the cosmic process expressed the will of God, the generalizations which described that process must of necessity elucidate the will of God. Spencer's version of evolution, still to Fiske the greatest generalization of all, was preeminently the way in which God chose to act.[12]

Fiske identified the concept of a transcendent God with the ideas of orthodoxy against which he had revolted in his youth—with an irrational and vindictive Being who put man into a world in which he was incompetent to save himself or do good by his own efforts, and who then damned most men for this failure while intervening to save a few from eternal torment. In this concept only exceptions

---

[12] JF, "The Idea of God as Affected by Modern Knowledge," in *Studies in Religion,* pp. 89–210. Manuscript Draft Notes for the Idea of God, HHL.

to the normal course of events could testify to the power of God, while any extension of the realm of nature shown to be ruled by law and order limited the area in which He could act. Fiske argued that this was also the concept held by eighteenth-century Deism which, while making God less irrational, had limited Him to the function of creator and prime mover who started things off but thereafter refrained from intervention. Now that nineteenth-century science had replaced the concept of creation at a single stroke (common to both orthodoxy and Deism) by the concept of creation as a process going on continually through all time, it was no longer sensible to think of the action of God as limited to the moment of creation and to special and unusual interventions thereafter. Rather the immanent concept, picturing God at work continuously, was the idea best in accord with modern science and the moral demands of the age.

The concept of immanence permitted Fiske to rehabilitate still further the teleological ideas towards which he now leaned. Although the idea of final cause might, as he had vigorously argued in his *Cosmic Philosophy,* be of no value as an instrument of scientific research, it now seemed to him a legitimate deduction from the dramatic tendency he saw at work in the cosmic process. If it was the process itself which expressed the will of God, then any goals discernible in the process were clear expressions of the intention of God. As he had the year before, Fiske argued that man was the intended goal of the entire long history of the universe revealed by geology and astronomy. Thus he revived, while restating, the Paleyan concept of design. "Paley's simile of the watch is no longer applicable to such a world as this. It must be replaced by the simile of the flower. The universe is not a machine, but an organism, with an indwelling principle of life. It was not made, but it has grown." [13]

Fiske was not the only one to explore these ideas. With a varying emphasis and more concern for effect on doctrine, Theodore Thornton Munger in his "New Theology" used the concept of immanence to rehabilitate the meaning of older religious ideas, especially the

[13] JF, "Idea of God," p. 184.

concept of the fatherhood of God and the divine love for man, to him the central part of the Christian message. Fiske properly credited A. V. G. Allen's *The Continuity of Christian Thought* as the source of his historical sketch of the role of the ideas of transcendence and immanence in the development of the early Christian church. Three of Fiske's fourteen chapters summarized Allen's work. These identified the concept of transcendence with what Allen termed the "Roman Theology," which stressed original sin, the weakness of man, and the juridical functions of God. Allen traced this approach from St. Augustine through the Catholic Church to Calvinism. Immanence Allen identified with the "Greek Theology" stemming from Athanasius, which stressed man's union with God through Christ. A. C. McGiffert said of these two opposed concepts that "the theological use of the words is modern, dating only from the nineteenth century, but the ideas for which they stand are very old." This idea had appeared in ancient Greek philosophy and had affected religious thinkers and philosophers of all ages. What Fiske added to Allen was a stress on the congruence of this idea of God with the view of the universe he had derived from his readings in science. He assured his audience that what was usually termed the conflict of religion and science was really a conflict between higher and lower concepts of God. Thus evolution merely came to the aid of the better part of the Christian tradition, rather than attacking it.[14]

Most of the sources of Fiske's mature religious ideas were American. Although an analogous development of "modernism" occurred in England, and Fiske was at all times conscious of English opinion, it was not a major influence upon him. Fiske continued to read and admire Herbert Spencer, the main English influence on his thought; nothing pleased him more than letters or remarks indicating that Spencer approved of his later works. Yet he quietly jettisoned aspects of Spencerism that did not fit his new orientation. The term "Unknowable," and the implication that Christianity was

---

[14] Quotation from A. C. McGiffert, "Immanence," in *Encyclopaedia of Religion and Ethics,* 7:167 (1915). JF, "Idea of God," pp. 145–168. A. V. G. Allen, *The Continuity of Christian Thought* (Boston, 1884). T. T. Munger, "The New Theology," in *Freedom of Faith* (Boston, 1883), pp. 3–44.

something the race would outgrow, disappeared from Fiske's writings. It was from Americans like Munger and Allen that he drew the concepts which best expressed his new attitude.[15]

On more than one occasion Fiske showed his determination to keep a middle path between the radicals and the rigidly orthodox. When Moncure Conway resigned as pastor of the radical South Place Chapel in London, Fiske was invited to replace him. Although he had gladly spoken from the South Place pulpit on his various visits to London, the invitation had little attraction and Fiske politely rejected the offer.[16]

When requested by the Nineteenth Century Club of New York to speak on a panel with T. B. Wakeman, a religious positivist, and Chauncey Depew, an orthodox believer, Fiske read part of his *Idea of God*. During the debate that followed he defined his position "by saying that with whatever Depew had said *that was essential* to Christianity I fully agreed; that I had expected to find such agreement; that, however, I had *not* looked for an ally in Wakeman." This did not satisfy Depew, who felt that Fiske's ideas were an assault on the Bible, and Depew responded with a highly emotional defense of his faith later widely reprinted by American and British Bible societies. Yet Fiske felt he "had the full sympathy of the audience." Although rigid believers in the absolute and inerrant inspiration of the Bible could not accept Fiske, those seeking a more moderate path found him attractive.[17]

To answer critics who accused him of renouncing his earlier ideas or who found themselves unable to distinguish Fiske's position from pantheism, he wrote a lengthy preface to the published edition of his second Concord address in which he denied both charges. In refuting the latter criticism Fiske carefully defined pantheism as a total identification of God with the universe. In contrast, Fiske's idea of God did not limit Him to the universe but saw Him as at the same time within and greater than the universe. Thus the laws

---

[15] Fiske's continuous worship of Spencer, while he gradually diverged from him, can be clearly seen in the prefaces to Fiske's various religious essays.

[16] Conrad Thies to JF, Oct. 20, 1884; JF to Thies, May 21, 1885, HHL.

[17] Quotations from JF to Abby, Mar. 15, 1886, HHL (italics in source). C. M. Depew, *Orations and After-Dinner Speeches* (New York, 1896), pp. 522–523; *My Memories of Eighty Years* (New York, 1924), p. 401.

of science were not a complete description of God, but were accurate and valid insofar as God was involved in the universe. The crux of the dispute lies in the definition. If Fiske's interpretation is accepted, his disclaimer of pantheism is unimpeachable. However, those who attacked Fiske felt that identification of God with any aspect of the universe limited Him by implying that some part of divinity was subject to the constraints of space, matter, and time.[18]

In arguing that he had not altered his basic position, Fiske called attention to the few sentences in his *Cosmic Philosophy* which could be interpreted as admitting teleology into the universe or which approached the idea of a personal God. Finding evidence for a personal God was difficult, for one of the clearest religious attitudes in the book had been his denial that thinking of God as a person was in any way legitimate. But he had now reached the conclusion that "the utter demolition of anthropomorphism would be the demolition of theism." In order to assert that his ideas had not altered Fiske devoted several paragraphs of his introduction to an unconvincing assertion that his critics had misunderstood him when he called for the "deanthropomorphization" of God.[19]

While Fiske tried to mask the changes in his thinking and to deny that any significant change had occurred, he was justified in claiming that he had not altered as much as his readers believed. His religion was still basically naturalistic, his intellectual conception of God a deduction from a scientific view of the universe. The logical transition between his *Cosmic Philosophy* and the essays of the 1880's was not too great. It was for emotional rather than logical reasons that Fiske now preferred to think of God as in some ways a person rather than a "deanthropomorphized" being. Fiske used the loopholes he had left in his earlier acceptance of the Spencerian world view to escape the mechanistic picture of the universe toward which that view tended. In his *Cosmic Philosophy* he had asserted that the world of matter was not commensurable with the world of spirit and mind, and had tended to describe the essence of the universe as spiritual rather than material. All he had to do in order

---

[18] JF, "Preface" to "Idea of God," pp. 92–94.
[19] JF, "Preface" to "Idea of God," pp. 94–98. Quotation from "Idea of God," pp. 173–174.

to arrive at his new position was to stress these aspects even more, so that he could speak of the spiritual aspects of the universe as controlling all. Religion had always been important to Fiske's thought. Now he gave it full pre-eminence and devoted his future philosophical and scientific writing to aspects of religious thought.

Yet Fiske tended to deny even these minor changes in his thinking. He could not admit them without weakening the belief in his own superior correctness which was his main defense against a world that did not treat him as well as he thought he deserved. The actual transition in his attitude to religion was a steady one, with no marked breaks, but with two periods of accelerated change. The first of these periods came while he was working out the intellectual implications of his position while writing his *Cosmic Philosophy*. In this period he definitely abandoned the admiration for Comte that had continued since his Middletown days, ceased calling himself an "infidel," and adopted the term "cosmic theism" to describe his religion. The second period of more rapid change occurred in the years immediately preceding the writing of his two Concord essays, as he sought emotional comfort in facing his personal problems and found it in a new way of looking at evolution which "came with such vividness as to seem like a revelation." [20] The most significant result of this change was less in the logical aspects of his thought than in the emotional realm. The idea that the process of evolution had a fixed, moral end made it easier for Fiske to find a religious comfort and encouraged him to think of God as a person. It strongly affected the tone in which he referred to religion. Once polemic had been marked in Fiske's treatment of his opponents, and the inner rewards of faith had seemed less important than the use of religion to explain the universe. Now he tended to praise the values he found inherent in all religion and to present his own approach in pious terminology that made its naturalism palatable to audiences desiring to find some acceptable way of holding on to what they valued in traditional religious ideas while adapting to the modern world.

IV

Fiske's shift helped make his religious writing popular, but it was

[20] "Preface" to "Idea of God," p. 101.

not the only factor in his success in attracting listeners and readers. A comparison of Fiske's speeches with the addresses given by other participants in the seminars at Concord is instructive. All who spoke agreed with Fiske in defending the credibility of immortality and rejecting pantheism in their replies to the questions posed by the leaders of the Concord School. Their essays were widely reported and many appeared later in print. Each of the men who shared the platform with Fiske in 1884, A. P. Peabody of Harvard, William Torrey Harris, Thomas Davidson, and R. A. Holland, agreed with him that modern science had not disproved immortality. Yet Dr. Peabody contented himself with drawing a few analogies between scientific and religious beliefs. The other three presented rigorously logical expositions of their points of view, one of which the Boston *Transcript* correspondent described in terms only too applicable to all: "The contribution of Dr. R. A. Holland to the subject was from the standpoint of the dialectic, and to all who fully understood it, it was an unanswerable argument." Hegelian logic was in keeping at Concord, where the audience expected it and might be able to understand it, but it would not attract less intellectual groups.[21]

Four of the six papers read at Concord in 1885 were published in Harris's *Journal of Speculative Philosophy*. Each of these four, A. P. Peabody, Edward Montgomery, G. H. Howison, and W. T. Harris, brought forth a definition of materialistic pantheism which they rejected and which they claimed science could not establish. None tried to develop any extended positive conclusions. Only Fiske and Francis Ellingwood Abbot, the sixth speaker, went further than the immediate question and expounded a positive religious position in harmony with science. In an expanded version of his speech, published under the title of *Scientific Theism,* Abbot used abstract philosophical terminology to argue that, since science revealed a self-existing and self-determining system of objectively real relations and things, the universe thus described must be considered an intelligent, infinite, living, self-consciousness, and thus a definite spiritual person. This God was "essentially knowable *per se,* and actually known to the precise extent to which science had discovered the immanent relational constitution, or organic idea, of Nature itself."

[21] Boston *Evening Transcript,* August 1, 2, 4, 1884. Quotation from Aug. 2, 1884.

Like the others, Abbot specifically rejected materialistic pantheism as a valid adjustment to science. Both in 1884 and 1885 the Concord lecturers advanced ideas and attitudes similar to Fiske's. But what they stated in dry, abstract terms, Fiske presented in lucid wording which made effective use of traditional symbols of Christian faith.[22]

Fiske used his talents as a stylist to achieve a maximum response from his audience. In his early history lectures he had learned to glory in the feeling of control over his audience and to treasure emotional responses to his ideas. He developed an almost automatic technique of saying what he believed in a manner that would please his listeners. Always writing under intense pressure to finish and earn money, he had little chance to revise or modify. He had to, and did, get the effect he was after the first time he tried. Writing automatically, Fiske was not conscious of shifting in religious belief and he felt greatly surprised that so many people thought that he had in effect repudiated his earlier views.

In the eighties his reputation was growing. Although he had only begun to attain success as a lecturer, the publicity surrounding his tours had begun to turn him into a celebrity. And, most important in gaining attention for his religious views, he was presented to his audiences not as a simple historian, but as a philosopher and scientist. His essays and *Cosmic Philosophy* formed the basis of his claim to scientific stature. Few among his auditors had the competence to judge his qualifications. It was enough for him to quote remarks by Darwin and other famous men praising him, for laymen to accept his claims. Even preachers and theologians were "laymen" in this sense, as they had discovered to their intense discomfort when they tried to disprove evolution scientifically. They were, no more than their parishioners, in a position to evaluate Fiske's pretensions to scientific standing. Although a majority of those attending Fiske's lecture audiences were educated, they had for the most part been trained in schools and colleges where the classics formed the heart of the curriculum. Few had any scientific training, either in school or outside; few saw any difference between an investigator and a popularizer. The spectacular failure of the religious attack on

---

[22] *Journal of Speculative Philosophy,* 19:337–384, 407–428 (October 1885). F. E. Abbot, *Scientific Theism* (Boston, 1885), quotation from p. 203.

Darwinism had damaged the intellectual prestige of clergymen; the prestige of the scientist was high. When Fiske spoke as a scientist showing his listeners how science supported religion he was listened to with respect.

Fiske's two little books on religion were eagerly purchased and read. How widely they sold is not now determinable; we have only the general statement of Fiske's publisher, made of these and two later volumes on religious themes, that "none of his books have reached a wider audience, or have been read with more profound interest." As lectures they were also well received all over the country. In August 1884, shortly after the first Concord address was given, Fiske repeated it in the Unitarian Church at Petersham and "was *astonished* at finding that the farmers were enthusiastic about it." [23]

As word of Fiske's new attitude to religion spread, he received many invitations to speak on Sunday in churches along his lecture route. Almost always the response was favorable. While many of these churches were Unitarian or radical Congregationalist, others were more conservative in their approach to Christianity. The appeal of Fiske's naturalism to orthodox believers did not depend solely on his merits as a speaker or on the minor shifts he had carried out. To understand his success it is necessary to put his lectures into historical context and consider the changes that affected major religious denominations in the last decades of the nineteenth century.

[23] "Publisher's Note," in *Studies in Religion*, page v. JF to his mother, Aug. 20, 1884, HHL (italics in source).

CHAPTER NINE

ORTHODOXY
IN TRANSITION

The wide approval of Fiske's religious essays by audiences drawn from many denominations can be explained only if the changes which took place in these denominations are taken into consideration. After the bitter debate of the 1870's over evolution ebbed, Fiske's ideas began to seem useful to members of orthodox denominations. Reviews of his two books by religious periodicals provide a convenient index of the reactions of various American religious groups to the concept of an immanent God ruling the universe in orderly patterns of developmental change; their comments on his work indicate how this idea met the needs and desires of thinkers and believers.

The hysterical tone of the earlier discussion of evolution and the problems which science raised for religion had almost passed away by the 1880's. Articles or books, like those of Benjamin Tefft, arguing that Darwinism was nothing more or less than atheism now received a cool reception. *The Origin of Species* had been out twenty years and *The Descent of Man* almost ten; their hypotheses had clearly won scientific and general acceptance, yet the predicted death of Christianity had not occurred. Religious periodicals now favored articles proving that evolution and religion were compatible. Although a scattering of intransigeant voices went on arguing that evolution was false or, at least, unproven, more and more writers began to explore the possibilities and consequences of an accommodation of religion and evolution.[1]

Unsettling ideas arising out of the study of comparative religion and Biblical criticism—the other two scholarly stimulators of controversy in the nineteenth century—were not especially prominent in this decade. Comparative religion, with its clear implication that Christianity was not unique and might not even have a more valuable revelation than that of any other major religion, had so far affected mostly the radicals. Extensive serious discussion of criticism as a problem of faith was still rare outside the Free Religious and Unitarian press. A warning for the future appeared in 1887 when the International Sunday School Lessons for the year were chosen from the sections of Genesis dealing with the history of the patriarchs. Religious periodicals invited distinguished scholars of their denominations to prepare expositions of the lessons for young readers and found to their horror that they were flooded with critical articles. But, except for a brief period of embarrassment while the magazines secured more suitable reading matter for youth, no disturbance arose and the scholars went quietly back to work, for the most part still unhindered.[2]

Liberal wings within orthodox denominations showed the most interest in the new ideas. In the first stages of the conflict over evolution both new and old schools had joined in denouncing this concept of science, but as the general acceptance became clear, the more liberal thinkers began to search for ways to use evolutionary ideas to support their positions. Properly handled, these concepts could make their opponents' stands old-fashioned and obsolete, while portraying their own ideas as the way to the future. But before doing so it was necessary not only to assert that science did not conflict with religion, but also to show how religious ideas could

---

[1] B. F. Tefft, *Evolution and Christianity* (Boston, 1885); see review in *Methodist Review*, 67:480–481 (May 1885). The shift in attitude can be sampled in *American Church Review*, 36:25–40 (October 1881); *Mercersburg Review*, 35:145–168 (April 1888); *Methodist Review*, 67:283–285 (March 1885); *Princeton Review*, 12:29–47 (July 1883); *New Englander*, 42:51–64 (January 1883); *Baptist Quarterly Review*, 14:185–200 (April 1881).

[2] *Methodist Quarterly Review*, 69:447–451 (May 1887).

survive in the universe which modern science postulated. For this purpose the concept of immanence proved very valuable and attracted many thinkers in the various denominations.

II

All major American religious groups reacted to the concept of an immanent God ruling the universe in orderly patterns of developmental change, which Fiske stressed in his essays, but the manner of reaction and the extent of influence varied widely. The spread of this approach to religion can be seen, in part, in the reactions to Fiske's essays.

To Unitarians, and especially to the radical wing of that church involved in the activities of the Free Religious Association, Fiske seemed much too orthodox. B. F. Underwood, editor of the *Index,* which served as the voice of the F.R.A., vigorously attacked Fiske's first Concord address. At that time Underwood thought Fiske had undertaken a major revision of the Spencerian approach to religion that so many "Cosmists" among the F.R.A. found congenial. Only after Fiske's elaborate denial of any major alteration in his earlier views did this group grudgingly welcome his work. Propagation of the concepts of the immanence of God and an optimistic view of man and the world had been one of the effects of the activity of the F.R.A., which took them up in forms more extreme than Fiske liked. They did not need his teleological version of evolution to convince their adherents. Although Fiske's second essay, *The Idea of God,* received no adverse criticism from the F.R.A., neither did it win great praise.[3]

Even the more conservative *Unitarian Review* found Fiske too orthodox at first glance. N. P. Gilman attacked *The Destiny of Man* in the April 1885 issue, but T. R. Slicer came to Fiske's defence the following month, calling the book "a genuine contribution to the hopes of the human heart concerning the unseen world." When *The Idea of God* appeared even Gilman applauded. "The book contains much more sound thought than *The Destiny of Man,* and

[3] *Index,* 16:76–77 (Aug. 14, 1884); and 16:111, 114–115 (Sept. 4, 1884); 16:160–161 (Oct. 2, 1884); 16:225–226 (Nov. 6, 1884); 17:297 (Dec. 17, 1885); 17:75–76 (Aug. 13, 1885).

is not disfigured by any final bow to Orthodoxy," he told his readers, ignoring the fact that there was no significant difference in language or ideas between the two works.

Fiske received greater praise from Unitarians than from the F.R.A. because his work had more meaning for these less radical thinkers. Within the ranks of those who had never left the Unitarian church for the F.R.A., Transcendentalists and Parkerites found nothing startlingly new in Fiske's essays. The concept of immanence had obvious affinities with the Emersonian Over-soul, and none of Fiske's other ideas went much beyond the positions already reached before the Civil War. Conservative Unitarians, whose attempts to maintain a special position for Christ in the religious thought of the denomination had caused the F.R.A. schism of the sixties, were the group most attracted by Fiske. They were then engaged in trying to reunify the denomination, a process not fully successful until the nineties, and hopefully explored intellectual as well as organizational means of reconciliation. The pages of the *Unitarian Review* mirrored the shift in attitudes that this process entailed. When started in 1874, the periodical printed the views of the conservative wing but, as efforts to iron out denominational differences went on, it invited contributions from the radicals, and articles explaining the findings of comparative religion and Biblical criticism proliferated in its pages. Fiske had seemed a prophet to the radicals in the seventies. In the eighties he attracted conservative Unitarians because he seemed a symbol of the way the radical wing, both outside and inside the denomination, would modify its position and make compromise possible. They eagerly welcomed all such evidence.[4]

[4] Reviews of Fiske by N. P. Gilman are in *Unitarian Review*, 23:382–383 (April 1885), and 25:93–94 (January 1886); by T. R. Slicer in 23:474–475 (May 1885). G. W. Cooke, *Unitarianism in America* (Boston, 1902), chaps. VII–VIII. The views taken of denominational developments in this chapter are based primarily upon a survey of denominational journals. For the above paragraph many issues of the *Unitarian Review*, vols. 1–36 (1874–1891) contain valuable illustrations, and items of interest appear in *The New World*, vols. 1–9 (1892–1900), and the *Monthly Religious Magazine*, vols. 21–51 (1859–1874). Citation of all relevant articles would unnecessarily inflate the footnotes, and only the names of periodicals used and occasional illustrative articles will be cited in the footnotes that follow.

III

New ideas caused more dissension among Calvinist denominations than among Unitarians, and their response to Fiske's essays reflects this difference. The strains of adaptation to new concepts showed up clearly among Congregationalists and Presbyterians. These denominations had been modifying their doctrinal positions all through their stay on American soil. Divisions had opened within the sects before the Civil War, and controversies flourished after peace returned. Attempts by liberals to use evolutionary concepts to advance their position brought on many disputes in the closing decades of the nineteenth century, and at the same time speeded the penetration of orthodox denominations by ideas similar to those Fiske popularized.

The most searching examination of Fiske's essays came from men who had already begun to explore the ideas he advocated. By the time his essays appeared a number of Congregational and Presbyterian intellectuals had examined the concepts Fiske advanced, but with a greater interest in doctrine and dogma. To such thinkers Fiske's work lacked logical rigor and failed to consider essential problems. George Harris, a modernist professor at Andover Theological Seminary, expressed the attitude of such men clearly in his reviews of Fiske's essays.

For Harris, Fiske failed to solve the central problem which evolution posed for Christianity, that of defining the function of Christ in an evolutionary scheme. "It is not quite clear what place, if any, Mr. Fiske accords to Christianity," Harris noted in his discussion of *The Destiny of Man.* "Were Jesus and Christianity phases of development, mere results of the past, or were they new agencies brought into the world from God for the accomplishment of his eternal plan for humanity? Is Christianity a mere concomitant or is it a potent and indispensable cause of progress?" Harris's reaction to Fiske's second essay was no more favorable. Although he welcomed support for theism from an evolutionist, he still found Fiske's logic defective. Harris willingly accepted the views of science on the nature of the universe and adapted his religious concepts to accord with them, but he insisted that the only valid idea of God had to be "a truth of reason" and not just a deduction from natural science.

He concluded that the book was "receiving a warm welcome on account of the opinions it advances rather than for the reasoning it advances in favor of that opinion." [5]

The most vigorous group among liberals using concepts related to Fiske's were the intellectual descendants of Horace Bushnell. These men, of whom Theodore Thornton Munger and Washington Gladden may be taken as exemplars, carried further the stress on the current world, the testing of religious theories by the use of reason and Christian experience, that Bushnell had begun. They succeeded in making the views of their master, regarded with deep suspicion before the Civil War, dominant within Congregationalism. Although Bushnell rejected evolution as incompatible with religion, his followers saw no logically compelling reasons to do so. As Munger tried to arrange the insights of Bushnell into a comprehensive theological pattern which he termed "The New Theology," he found evolutionary ideas useful. Applying the idea of evolution to the history of the Church, he could deal with both Scripture and the older theology as parts in a continuous revelation of God in which his own ideas were the latest and therefore best. The concept of development permitted him to speak reverently of doctrines and dogmas which did not appeal to him, and to praise their historical role, rather than simply reject them. Munger stressed the power and responsibility of man in this world and placed ethics at the center of his religous position. His God was immanent, involved in the world, and preeminently a father to man, dealing with him in terms of paternal love, rather than the all-powerful Creator and omniscient Judge of early Calvinism.[6]

Washington Gladden showed far more interest in the social consequences of the "new theology" than did Fiske. Where Munger explored the intellectual consequences of Bushnell's ideas, Gladden moved toward views that would later be termed the "Social Gospel." If man was not inherently evil, but capable of good, and if the

---

[5] *Andover Review,* 3:84 (January 1885); 5:98–100 (January 1886).

[6] Horace Bushnell, "Science and Religion," *Putnam's Monthly Magazine,* 1:271 (March 1868). T. T. Munger, *The Freedom of Faith* (Boston, 1883), *The Appeal to Life* (Boston, 1877), *Horace Bushnell* (Boston, 1899), *Essays for the Day* (Boston, 1904).

history of the universe recorded his progress and testified to his strength, then it was man's responsibility to use his power for good ends. The Kingdom of God, which more orthodox thinkers placed in the after-life or identified with the body of the Church on earth, became the consummation toward which the world was working. Evangelical thinkers before the Civil War had looked forward to turning America into an earthly Kingdom by converting all its citizens to active Christianity, and had spread revivals across the land to attain this end. Now Gladden spoke as if America were already essentially Christian. The course of history and the labors of previous generations had prepared the way; one had only to apply principles that everyone now accepted to bring the Kingdom to realization in America. Gladden's Social Gospel proposed to ameliorate and eliminate the ills which a rampant industrialism and a little-understood urbanization had brought to America.[7]

Before the end of the century most younger Congregationalist and Presbyterian theologians joined Munger and Gladden. Almost the entire faculty of Andover Seminary and such luminaries as James T. Whiton of Meadville Theological Seminary, George A. Gordon, Newman Smyth, H. C. King of Oberlin, Levi L. Paine of the Bangor Seminary, Lyman Abbott, and Jeremiah L. Dinan all contributed to what they variously called the "new theology" or "modern movement" or "progressive orthodoxy." Earlier proponents of the adaptation of religion to science had frequently left the orthodox denominations and gravitated to the Unitarians, the Free Religious Association, or one of the "Cosmist" churches. But these men all agreed that their place was inside traditional denominations. And evolution seemed to support their theological position within their sects, rather than to threaten it.[8]

Probably more immediately influential than any theologian were active ministers like Henry Ward Beecher, who commanded a large

---

[7] Washington Gladden, "The Social and Industrial Situation," *Bibliotheca Sacra,* 49:383–411 (July 1892); *Applied Christianity* (Boston, 1886), *Ruling Ideas of the Present Age* (Boston, 1895), *How Much is Left of the Old Doctrines?* (Boston, 1899), *Recollections* (Boston, 1909).

[8] Lyman Abbott, *Reminiscences* (Boston, 1915). G. A. Gordon, *My Education and Religion* (Boston, 1925). Newman Smyth, *Recollections and Reflections* (New York, 1926).

audience as the most renowned preacher of his day. Reared in a strict Presbyterian household, Beecher moved far beyond the ideas of his father in the course of a lengthy preaching career in which he more and more emphasized the emotional values of religion. His idea of Christianity centered around the concept of love, which he used in ways that, even though they might at times be sentimentally vapid, resulted in highly effective preaching. Even before Fiske's later essays, Beecher had read Spencer and proclaimed himself a convert to evolution. In his own book on science and religion he contended that evolution, as a record of continuous progress, demonstrated God's love for man. Difficulties, such as the effect of Darwinism on the cherished argument from design, he brushed aside with epigrammatic assertions: "Design by wholesale is grander than design by retail." His chief follower, Lyman Abbott, frequently quoted and praised Fiske. Abbott's interest in the doctrinal consequences of ideas led him to support views of dogma in his *Theology of an Evolutionist* that approximated those advanced by the disciples of Bushnell.[9]

Discussion of such ideas led to bewilderment among laymen, a sense of strain, and some denominational strife. One of the clearest examples of the strain was the so-called "eschatological controversy" among Congregationalists. This conflict began over a simple point and illustrated the way any modification of doctrine, no matter how slight, aroused the fear that it threatened all religion. Those who felt that the most significant aspects of Christianity were its ethics and gospel of love became uncomfortable with the "eschatological" doctrine that a heathen who died without an opportunity to learn of Christ was thereby doomed to eternal torment, no matter how upright a life he had led and regardless of whether he would gladly have accepted Christ if given the chance. To evade this dilemma, several theologians advanced the idea that God might, out of divine love, offer a second probation after death to upright heathen who

---

[9] H. W. Beecher, *Evolution and Religion* (New York, 1885), quotation from p. 115. Beecher, "Progress of Thought in the Church," *North American Review*, 135:99–117 (August 1882). Lyman Abbott, *The Evolution of Christianity* (Boston, 1892), *Christianity and Social Problems* (Boston, 1896), *The Theology of an Evolutionist* (Boston, 1897), *H. W. Beecher* (New York, 1903), *Reminiscences* (Boston, 1915).

had not had the chance to hear of Christ earlier. They did not say that God would or must, merely that He might do so if He so chose. Yet this deviation from strict Calvinism embroiled the Andover Seminary—where the majority of the faculty supported it—in an intense controversy. The American Board of Commissioners for Foreign Missions protested furiously that this new doctrine "cut the nerve" of mission activity and refused to accept graduates of Andover for its mission stations. The Board of Visitors of the Seminary in 1886 unsuccessfully tried to remove six senior faculty members on charges that this belief violated the oath to uphold Calvinism which all professors were required to take.[10]

Actually, this modification of the concept of probation by the Andover professors was only a minor aspect of their systematic attempt to adapt older doctrine to nineteenth-century views, in which they explored the ideas of Fiske, as well as more radical religious innovations. Articles in the *Andover Review,* which these men edited during its brief nine-year career, especially the two series of editorials entitled "Progressive Orthodoxy" and "The Divinity of Christ," showed that at the center of their thinking lay a stress on God's love and goodness. Working out from this they discerned a function for Christ's life and sufferings. "It reveals God . . . as the God of love, eternally existing in the warmth of affection, and known to us in tenderness, in sympathy, in sacrifice, through which we learn to love God because He first loved us." This revelation validated the ethical system of Christianity and taught men to love the good. To fit the world view of the century, the love of God had to be universal and the sacrifice of Christ available to all; here entered the idea of a possible second probation for upright heathen, which became the occasion for controversy. In the course of their work these theologians brought under consideration almost every major religious idea current in the nineteenth century. They discussed the immanence of God, the role of evolution, and Biblical criticism. Social Christianity, with its emphasis on the coming of the Kingdom in this world, and its interest in the settlement house and

[10] W. J. Tucker, *My Generation* (Boston, 1919), pp. 90–221. F. H. Foster, *The Modern Movement in American Theology* (New York, 1939), pp. 16–37. D. D. Williams, *Andover Liberals* (New York, 1941).

other forms of aid to the victims of an industrial society, especially attracted them.[11]

The *Andover Review* praised Fiske's conclusions, but disagreed with his naturalistic method of proof and his blithe dismissal of traditional doctrine in favor of "essentials." The editors' interest in defending new religious ideas led them to give Fiske's works a searching examination.

Fiske received more casual treatment in Congregational magazines less interested in propagating new views. Such journals showed more interest in results than methods. The *New Englander,* organ of Connecticut Congregationalism, which had found Fiske's *Cosmic Philosophy* worthy only of parody, ignored Fiske's first essay, but then reviewed the second twice. Samuel Harris welcomed *The Idea of God* as a "serious, dignified, and respectful" contribution to religious thought. Frank Sewall, examining the same book at greater length later in the year, found much to praise, while regretting Fiske's reliance on naturalistic methods to support his conclusions. Sewall insisted that revelation had to be called to the aid of nature to attain a proper religious basis. *Bibliotheca Sacra,* which had been moved from Andover to Oberlin in 1884 to escape the influence of "progressive orthodox" teachers, never reviewed either of Fiske's books.[12]

The lesser interest of these two reviews in Fiske's works did not mean that they were unconcerned with problems of adjusting theological doctrine to the new ideas. The issue was a live one for all Congregationalists. The *New Englander,* which had shown Bushnellian leaning before the Civil War, objected to the speed with which Andover carried out its modifications. Although agreeing with Munger and Andover that adaptations of theology were needed, contributors to the journal felt that a restatement of old ideas, rather than a new theology, would answer the needs of the

[11] *Andover Review,* vols. 1–19 (1884–1893), especially serial editorials entitled "Progressive Orthodoxy," May 1885 to December 1885 (published under same title, Boston, 1885), and "The Divinity of Christ," May 1892 to January 1893. Quotation from *Andover Review,* 18:408 (October 1892).

[12] Samuel Harris, in *New Englander,* 45:88–91 (January 1886), quotation from p. 91. Frank Sewall, in *New Englander,* 45:434–440 (May 1886).

age. Yet before the journal discontinued publication in 1892, most of the "new" ideas received favorable presentation in its pages.[13]

Bibliotheca Sacra, which reacted violently to Andover's views, had itself played a mediatorial role during the dispute over Darwinism earlier. George Frederick Wright, editor from 1884 to 1921, contributed many articles in the seventies explaining evolution. A close friend of Asa Gray and a geologist of stature himself, Wright followed his mentor's lead in insisting that while Darwinism was true it in no way affected religion. In his revealing essay, "Some Analogies between Calvinism and Darwinism," Wright went further and argued that the world views of the two were in agreement. "The Calvinist has long stood in the breach, and defended the doctrine that order is an essential attribute of the divine mind," he told his readers. Wright thought no great change necessary to fit Calvinism for the nineteenth century—certainly not more than the new-school Congregationalists and such evangelical theologians as Charles Grandison Finney had carried out before the Civil War. In effect, Wright wished to stop the revision of Calvinism at the point it had reached in his youth. But this he could not do, not even in the pages of his own magazine. All through the eighties he denounced the Andover movement as heretical. Yet as the decade drew to a close, and even more in the nineties, *Bibliotheca Sacra* began to carry articles arguing for many of the same concepts and approaches toward which Andover had led the way. These major theological journals of the Congregationalists indicate the way the ideas that attracted Fiske penetrated all reaches of the denomination before the end of the century. Even the conservative *Bibliotheca Sacra* moved reluctantly with the tide.[14]

In contrast to the Congregationalists, Presbyterian periodicals were less in touch with wider currents of thought. When they did

[13] *New Englander,* vols. 17–56 (1859–1892).

[14] *Bibliotheca Sacra,* vols. 16–59 (1850–1902). G. F. Wright, *The Logic of Christian Evidences* (Andover, 1880), *Studies in Science and Religion* (Andover, 1882), *C. G. Finney* (Boston, 1893). *Scientific Aspects of Christian Evidences* (New York, 1898), *Story of My Life and Work* (Oberlin, 1916), "Some Analogies between Calvinism and Darwinism," *Bibliotheca Sacra,* 37:48–76 (January 1880), quotation from p. 54.

become aware of them they showed some acceptance, but also much stern refusal to compromise. Both the *Biblical Repertory and Princeton Review* and the *American Presbyterian Review* treated Darwin with disdain. In the seventies the *Princeton Review* (which had dropped the first half of its name by then) told its readers that those who accepted the doctrines of the scientists and philosophers of science "must reject those of Moses, Isaiah, Paul and John, and our Lord Jesus Christ." Yet in the eighties this review began to print articles assuring its readers that evolution was not necessarily materialistic and calling for a greater use of the insights of science by religion. This review was wholly laudatory to Fiske and welcomed his *Destiny of Man* and *Idea of God* as "signs of the positive religious tendency of the age." However, the *Presbyterian and Reformed Review* in the nineties still sternly rejected any basic compromise with old-school Presbyterianism, insisting that God was better understood as an active sovereign rather than as a universal father, viewing man as essentially corrupt and evil, and limiting the redemptive work of Christ to the small body of the elect.[15]

Sects deriving from European Calvinism, like the German Reformed Church, were not unaffected by the new ideas. William Rupp and S. N. Callender contributed articles to the *Mercersburg Review* defending a universal view of Christ's atonement and the concept of divine immanency. But these issues appear to have aroused little bitterness, and did not exert much divisive force among this group of Calvinists.[16]

The pace of change was most rapid in the Congregationalist churches. The loose organization of the denomination permitted individual ministers and theologians to experiment freely. Although splits in congregations, or dismissals of ministers who moved too fast for their parishioners, were not unheard of, a minister had full

---

[15] *American Presbyterian Review* [and other titles], 13 vols. (1859–1871). *Biblical Repertory and Princeton Review* [and other titles], 39 vols. (1859–1888). *Presbyterian and Reformed Review*, vols. 1–13 (1890–1902). Quotations from *Princeton Review*, 5:547 (July 1876), and *New Princeton Review*, 1:296 (March 1886).

[16] *Mercersburg and Reformed Review*, vols. 11–35 (1859–1888). Only an incomplete file was available to the author.

freedom to modify his theological position as long as he kept his congregation convinced of the value of his innovations.[17]

Change came slower among Presbyterians, where a superior organization kept watch over the actions of individual ministers and churches; indeed, among old-school Presbyterians, change hardly began at all during the nineteenth century. Although this organizational rigidity slowed the pace of theological innovation, it could not prevent it, and in fact intensified the struggle that resulted when controversies did come into the open. Presbyterians produced the greatest crop of heresy trials. The controversy over evolution in the seventies had aroused less heat among Presbyterians than among Congregationalists, for the ministers who led this movement tended to shift their affiliation into the less strict denomination. But when the crisis raised by the advance of Higher Criticism of the Bible came to the fore, in the nineties, it irritated conservative Presbyterians into launching heresy charges against the ministers and scholars who led the movement.[18]

Congregationalist and Presbyterian reviews and journals devoted more space to vigorous discussion of ideas similar to Fiske's than those of any others among the "orthodox" denominations. Only Unitarians and religious radicals exceeded them in this regard. Behind this concern lay a proud tradition of intellectual endeavor, an expectation that every believer would be able to justify his faith rationally, and a sense of occupying a position of leadership in American life and thought. Those who were conscious of this tradition desired rational and clear statements of doctrine which would be modern and up-to-date without losing the values associated with their old beliefs. But doctrinal clarification, especially in an atmosphere in which any deviation from historic doctrine implied outright and total subversion, inevitably produced bitter controversy.

Among Calvinists, as among Unitarians, Fiske won the greatest praise from those interested in healing denominational differences. His work lacked sufficient rigor to appeal to those actively engaged

[17] G. A. Gordon, *My Education*, pp. 212–261. Abbott, *Reminiscences*, pp. 447–486. Abbott, *Beecher*.

[18] R. E. Thompson, *A History of the Presbyterian Church in America* (New York, 1895), pp. 243–283.

in modifying doctrine and he was far too naturalistic to satisfy the most rigidly orthodox, who ignored him. But those seeeking a middle path were much encouraged by Fiske's optimistic view of the nature of the universe and by his solemn assurances that science supported the best part of religious beliefs. From this middle group Fiske drew his most ardent supporters.

IV

Episcopalians welcomed Fiske's essays, for they too reacted in the 1880's to the new theological ideas Fiske popularized, though they did so in a manner which illustrated the differences between this denomination and Calvinist sects.

The *American Church Review* praised Fiske's *Idea of God,* saying he "deserves the thanks of scientists and Christians for the able and clear and in general satisfactory manner in which he has handled his subject." The only complaint was that Fiske still remained too Calvinistic in his approach to religion; the reviewer termed his interpretation of church creeds and doctrines too rational. In interesting contrast, the English *Church Quarterly Review* reacted unfavorably to Fiske's essays. Their reviewer saw in Fiske's failure to rely on revelation a rejection of the true essence of the Christian tradition.[19]

Members of the Episcopal Church shared with the Congregationalists and Presbyterians the social leadership of America. As leaders they, too, felt some need to be modern and abreast of the time. But as they were less committed to an intellectual approach, the discussion of new views stirred little controversy within their ranks. Their religious attitude tended to stress ritual and tradition rather than logic or theology. It is indicative of the interests of this group that the most original contribution by an Episcopalian to the "new theology," and one which greatly attracted Fiske, was A. V. G. Allen's *The Continuity of Christian Thought.* Allen, a professor at the Episcopal seminary in Cambridge, Massachusetts, carried out a lengthy survey of church history to prove that the new ideas were

[19] Reviews of *Idea of God* in *American Church Review,* 48:200–202 (August 1886), quotation from p. 202; and in *Church Quarterly Review,* 22:251–253 (April 1886).

merely the latest stage of a Christian tradition reaching back to hoary antiquity. Thus the book developed a method of satisfying the Episcopal desire to maintain stability and tradition, while at the same time keeping up with the latest trends in modern thought.

The *American Church Review,* chief theological organ of the Episcopal Church, showed similar tendencies. Like all orthodox journals, it had reacted with hostility to new currents of thought in the sixties and seventies, attacking scientists as infidels, and terming their work "totally at variance with the teachings of religion." But, when writers in the eighties began to present related ideas within a Christian framework, the review found much to praise in the work of Fiske, T. T. Munger and A. V. G. Allen. In an examination of the doctrinal effects of immanence W. W. Newton concluded that the concept supported ritualism even more than rationalism and provided adequately for the emotional needs of the worshiper. More than one author drew on Bushnell's insights.[20]

Although new theological ideas were not without opposition within the denomination (the *American Church Review* carried a lengthy criticism of Allen in 1885[21]), modernism aroused no great controversy. The "new theology," and its claim of being the latest in progressive thought, might bolster the Episcopalian's sense of social and intellectual leadership, but it was not central to the religious life of the denomination. The strong desire for tradition and stability that marked this group made problems arising from ritual and liturgy more exciting than the intellectual approach of theologians—or even Fiske's popularizations.

V

Baptist and Methodist periodicals paid little attention to Fiske's work in the eighties. The *Baptist Quarterly Review* never referred to him, while the *Methodist Review* ignored Fiske's writings until the late nineties, when it began to feel embattled by even more

[20] A. V. G. Allen, *The Continuity of Christian Thought* (Boston, 1884). W. W. Newton, "The Theology of Today as It Centers in the Doctrine of the Incarnation," *American Church Review,* 42:58–80 (July 1883). *American Church Review,* vols. 12–53 (1859–1889), quotation from 24:288 (April 1872).

[21] John J. Elmendorf, "The Continuity of Christian Thought," *American Church Review,* 46:340–371 (October 1885).

radical figures. Then it carried a condescending notice of a new edition of the *Idea of God,* praising it as "a small but solid book." [22] The attitude of these journals toward Fiske paralleled the reaction of their denominations to the ideas for which he spoke.

Baptists and Methodists remained more aloof from the religious changes of the eighties than the Calvinist denominations. Methodists had always stressed the ability of man and his freedom to strive effectually for salvation; Baptists, too, had been affected by such ideas. Nineteenth-century advances seemed less of a challenge to this view of man than to that of Calvinist groups. But more significant than theology in explaining the slowness of these sects to react to new ideas was their position in American life. The centers of strength of both denominations lay in rural areas and among the native American lower-middle and working-class population of the cities. These social groups were least exposed to the new ideas of the century, and those who ministered to them had little need to grapple with modern trends. Not until the nineties, when they vigorously reacted to Biblical criticism, did these sects show much response to the characteristic doctrinal changes of the century. Then many violently rejected the whole pattern of liberal religious ideas.

The *Baptist Quarterly Review,* which had attacked Darwin with vigor, began to argue in the eighties that evolution and religion were compatible, but it did not look with favor at the attempts of modernists to alter Christian doctrine. "We have no need of the New Theology, for the old is better," wrote President A. H. Strong of the Rochester Theological Seminary—who would himself later contribute to the penetration of his denomination by related ideas. The Reverend H. O. Rowlands rejected it as certain to die out. "The masses *profess* to believe it, but they cannot be induced to trust it, nor risk much on its gilded sentiments; hence the churches advocating it are not attended by the masses," he asserted. This remark, while it probably reversed the order of causation in its explanation of the affinity of modernism for upper-class churches, did testify to some interest in theological change within the denomination. Walter

[22] *Methodist Quarterly Review,* 80:344 (March 1898).

Rauschenbusch, who in 1897 would be added to the faculty at Rochester by President Strong, was minister of a Baptist church in New York City in the eighties and concerned over the evils created by rapid urban growth. As he reached out for ideas which would help explain the misery he saw about him in the slums and also provide a basis for action to try to cure them, he found the concepts of Gladden and Munger useful. Especially putting stress on the responsibility of man to use his power to help bring about the Kingdom of God on earth, he elaborated the doctrinal ideas which made his 1917 *A Theology for the Social Gospel* the best articulated and closely reasoned exposition of the ideas of the Social Christian wing of the modernist movement.[23]

Such figures were in a minority among Baptists and Methodists in the eighties, although examples can be found in both denominations. The *Methodist Quarterly Review,* which had earlier attacked Darwin, Lyell, and Spencer as threats to religion, began to call for a truce in the late seventies, when the failure of the religious assault on Darwinism became evident. Its writers viewed the development of the "new theology" with suspicion, while at the same time editorials hopefully discerned Arminian elements in the Andover movement. By the nineties articles appeared arguing that Wesley had used the idea of the immanence of God long before Congregationalists thought of it. Paralleling and going beyond the tendencies of the denomination were such men as Bordon P. Bowne, head of Boston University's Philosophy Department from 1876 to 1910. Bowne's early work attacked Spencer's view of evolution, but in the late eighties he worked out his own theistic version of science, stressing immanence. The continued development of his thinking brought on a trial for heresy (but not a conviction) early in the twentieth century. The application of Higher Criticism of the Bible to the New Testament aroused the ire of the *Methodist Review* in

[23] *Baptist Quarterly Review,* vols. 1–23 (1867–1890). Walter Rauschenbusch, *A Theology for the Social Gospel* (New York, 1917). A. H. Strong, "The New Theology," *Baptist Quarterly Review,* 20:29 [n.s. 9] (January 1888). H. O. Rowlands, "The Present Drift in Eschatology," *ibid.,* 22:407 [n.s. 11] (October 1889), italics in source.

the nineties, and furious repudiations of this aspect of "liberal" religious thought echoed through its pages. Not until then did the journal find anything to praise in Fiske.[24]

VI

Religious groups like the Lutherans, Jews, and Catholics, whose primary appeal was to immigrants, either ignored Fiske or attacked his work. These groups showed relatively little concern over new patterns of thought, for most of their communicants remained unaffected. Where an interest can be found, it is among what can loosely be termed "Americanizing" wings—among Reform Jews or among Catholics concerned to have their church appear truly American to the dominant Protestant majority in whose midst they lived.

The major concerns of Lutheranism in the years after the Civil War were necessarily the problems of holding the flood of immigrants from Germany and Scandinavia within the church, of adapting religious habits formed in state-supported churches to a land where only voluntary effort could ensure survival, and of dealing with splits along national lines as Scandinavian and German Lutherans set up a variety of independent synods. Not until after 1900, by which time second and third generations had become influential in church affairs, did doctrinal matters become important divisive issues among various Lutheran synods.[25]

Among Jews, only leaders of reform showed an interest in ideas related to those Fiske popularized. Orthodox Jewry, concerned primarily with holding the immigrant to his ancestral faith, remained unaffected. Rabbi Isaac Meyer Wise, while rejecting Darwinism in his 1876 *Cosmic God,* had used aspects of the idea of evolution in his 1871 essay, "Reformed Judaism," to justify adapting Jewish religious practices to the modern world. In 1885, Kaufmann

[24] *Methodist Quarterly Review,* vols. 41–84 (1859–1902). B. P. Bowne, *The Philosophy of Herbert Spencer* (New York, 1874), *The Philosophy of Theism* (New York, 1888).

[25] A. R. Wentz, *A Basic History of Lutheranism in America* (Philadelphia, 1956), pp. 114–136, 175–247. P. W. Spaude, *The Lutheran Church under American Influence* (Burlington, Iowa, 1943), pp. 216–273, 362–377, 397–402.

Kohler urged Jews to accept "the results of modern investigations on both the fields of natural science and of Biblical and comparative religious research." The same year, the famous Pittsburgh Platform, which became the basic statement of Reform belief, used similar language. But theological ideas were of less consequence to Reform than its attack on ritual and the traditional Jewish way of life. The rejection by the Pittsburgh Platform of Mosaic and Rabbinic law as an unalterable guide to life was the center of the controversies that document evoked, rather than the rationalizations used to support the rejection. Insofar as religious ideas similar to those of Fiske affected Judaism, they were not major influences.[26]

The most urgent tasks facing American Catholics were taking care of the masses of Catholic immigrants who poured into America during the last decades of the century, preventing differences in national origin from affecting church unity, and defending Catholicism against the pressures of a predominantly Protestant environment. Theological problems were much less significant. Those who discussed ideas similar to Fiske's were either theologians desiring to refute concepts that appeared incompatible with Catholic doctrine, or else preachers desiring to convert American Protestants to Catholicism and interested in using modern religious ideas to present Catholicism as a religion fully abreast of current thought.

The first category of interest motivated the *American Catholic Quarterly Review* to endlessly attack Darwin and Spencer, and to reject the idea of development in religious doctrine. Contributors vigorously asserted the traditional Catholic tenet that the Church had preserved a "deposit of faith" unchanged since the days of the Apostles. Immanence appeared only as a form of pantheism to be denounced. The journal never reviewed Fiske, but a thirty-six-page examination of his *Idea of God* from a similar point of view

[26] I. M. Wise, *The Cosmic God* (Cincinnati, 1876), "Reformed Judaism," in *Selected Writings of I. M. Wise* (Cincinnati, 1900), pp. 260–351. Kaufmann Kohler, *Backwards or Forwards* (New York, 1885), p. 21. *Proceedings of the Pittsburgh Rabbinical Conference, Nov. 16, 17, and 18, 1885* (n.p., 1923). Fiske's only recorded lecture in a Jewish synagogue (an 1895 address on evolution) was given in the Temple Berith Kodesh of Rochester, New York—a citadel of extreme Reform; Blake McKelvey, *Rochester, the Quest for Quality* (Cambridge, Mass., 1956), pp. 117, 129.

appeared in the Catholic University *Bulletin* for January 1897 and attempted a point-by-point refutation of Fiske's assertion that religion had evolved.[27]

The *Catholic World,* a popular monthly founded by Father Isaac T. Hecker, a New Englander converted to Catholicism who devoted much of his life to trying to bring the rest of America to his new faith, exemplified the second approach. This review at first paid little attention to science but, as the victory of Darwin became clear, carried articles praising the work of St. George Mivart, an English Catholic who tried to modify Darwin by arguing that at most the body of man could be explained by evolution, while only the direct intervention of God could produce the mind and soul of man. In the nineties, under Father Hecker's successor, the Reverend A. F. Hewit (also a convert from Calvinism), the magazine printed articles explaining some of the results of Higher Criticism.

But these ideas were only a small proportion of the magazine's contents and were dropped as soon as the Pope began to condemn them. After the Encyclical "Providentissimus Deus" in 1895, Father Hewit repudiated the attempt to work out a Catholic version of Biblical criticism. After the excommunication of Mivart, the magazine dropped the subject of biological evolution. When the Pope, in the Apostolic Letter "Testem Benevolentiae" in 1897 condemned "Americanism" (the name applied to the idea attributed to Father Hecker, that Catholicism should be modified to make it more palatable to Americans), the magazine's editors publicly hailed the papal dictum that Catholicism was uniform and unalterable. In Europe, condemnation of "modern" ideas resulted in a series of apostasies or excommunications of leading Catholic modernists. In America, where the usefulness of such ideas as instruments of Catholic apologetics attracted priests, rather than any inherent attractiveness in the ideas themselves, supporters easily sacrificed "modernism" to preserve church unity.

The treatment of Fiske by the *Catholic World* illustrates its opportunistic attitude to modernism. The reviewer of Fiske's *Idea of God* attacked him for "the indecent way in which he mixes up

[27] *American Catholic Quarterly Review,* vols. 1–33 (1876–1908). Reverend E. T. Shanahan, *John Fiske on the Idea of God* (Washington, 1897), reprinted from the Catholic University *Bulletin* for January 1897.

the names of profound scholars and saints in the same category with infidels and scoffers," and rejected his conclusions as "bald pantheism —Spinoza in an *Atlantic Monthly* dress." Yet, when it served an immediate purpose, the magazine did not hesitate in 1901 to use a quotation from Fiske to contradict atheistic scientists, even though it had earlier rejected the reasons by which Fiske arrived at his views.[28]

VII

No denomination remained wholly unaffected by the theological trends of the nineteenth century. Within each sect individuals struggled to find intellectual formulations that would permit them to adapt to the world view encouraged by the advance of science without abandoning ancestral religious beliefs. Interest was strongest in churches serving an educated body of believers, who thought of themselves as occupying the top of the American social ladder, and who felt an obligation to provide intellectual and social leadership for the nation.

Almost all of those involved accepted the idea that lay at the center of Fiske's thought—that of a universe essentially controlled by fixed laws discernible to science. In the earlier part of the century this concept had affected in its full vigor only the most rationalistic wings of American religion. As the triumph of the scientific explanation of the world continued, it became something every intelligent man was expected to believe. The vigor and fury of the clerical attack on Darwin merely served to make more people aware of the scientific position. While the great mass of immigrant and native American church members might still go on unconscious of the ways of thinking which lay at the base of science and looking at the practical applications of science around them as in some way akin to magic, those stimulated by religious controversy to examine the matter themselves could not maintain such an attitude. They faced the problem of finding a meaningful place for God in a world which seemed self-determining.

The concept of immanence that attracted Fiske was the most

[28] *Catholic World*, vols. 1–75 (1865–1902). Quotations from Reverend H. A. Brann, "Dude Metaphysics," *ibid*, 42:635 (February 1886). See also, *ibid.*, 74:431 (January 1901).

widely accepted solution of this problem. A universe ruled by un-alterable law seemed to put God too far away from the believer to serve as an object of worship. This had been the flaw in Deism, which reduced God to a first cause. In the popular versions of the Newtonian universe that penetrated American religious thought in the eighteenth and early nineteenth centuries, the concept of special creation had helped moderate this, for if the characteristic traits of each species were the result of a direct thought of God, they demon-strated divine forethought and love. Evolution, by explaining species in terms of a general process which included even man, threatened the feeling of direct relationship with God. It was this aspect of evolution, even more than the way it brought Genesis into question, that made the religious debate over Darwin so bitter. Immanence—seeing God as present in all parts of the process—made the universe more habitable to man. The way in which Fiske revived teleological views and pictured man as the intended goal of the entire process further aided accommodation to the new ideas.

Such an approach helped retain emotional values in religious ideas, but it also entailed certain losses. The function of prayer changed, and the use of ceremonial increased in the later nineteenth century. If universal laws were the outstanding expression of the divine personality, prayers for direct intervention had little use; prayer thus tended to become a contemplative rather than an active process, an attempt to find union with God and to draw from His presence strength and direction for the life of the believer. Church services, even among evangelical sects which had long been sus-picious of ritual, used more ceremonial and began to stress liturgical aspects. Massed banks of flowers about the pulpit, to introduce a note of beauty into bare New England meetinghouses, and carefully chosen music during the services became more common.[29]

As conceptions of God and universe altered, so too did ideas of man's relations to the world and God. It became more difficult to think of man as inherently evil. This was especially a problem for

[29] The Prebsyterian experience is revealing; see Thompson, *History of the Presby-terian Church*, pp. 226–242. The problem was discussed from a Congregationalist viewpoint in E. S. Parsons, "Prayer in a Universe of Law," *New Englander*, 55:362–366 (October 1891).

the Calvinistic sects so heavily affected by the new ideas. Those who adopted an optimistic view of man's nature did not agree on its relation to current problems. Fiske, who held all his life to the Spencerian laissez faire position, did not think man's acts could alter the world. Even though Fiske expected a millennium in the distant future, as inevitable law steadily improved man, he thought it beyond human power to hasten the coming of that day of glory. No more than the state could affect the working of economic law could man alter the decrees of an immanent divinity. That Fiske's religious liberalism did not involve any political or economic reform made it all the more palatable for those in his audience who stood highest in the American social and economic hierarchy. But to others a view of man which gave him power to do good also entailed the responsibility of doing everything possible to hasten the coming of the Kingdom of God on earth. Out of this approach stemmed the Social Gospel and its attack on the evils of industrialization and urbanization.

The inner message of Fiske's religious essays remained basically secularistic. In this he had not changed from his youthful conclusions on first exploring the religious significance of science. His view of God was a deduction from the scientific ideas he accepted; his religion "purified" of nonscientific dogma. Although he specifically proclaimed that his belief agreed with what he called essential Christianity, he never explained the position of Christ in his "pure" religion. If God was immanent in the world and in direct contact with man, it was difficult to explain the role of a Savior, the need for divinity to take on flesh in order to speak to man. More orthodox thinkers who explored the concept of immanence struggled with this problem, but Fiske ignored it.

Yet despite this basic secularism and the difference between his "essential Christianity" and the religion which most Americans professed, Fiske became one of the most popular lecturers on religious themes in the nation. Religious periodicals praised his books and cited him as an authority. Where before he had been a hero only to extreme religious radicals, he now became an attractive adornment of more orthodox pulpits.

Fiske's first great advantage in convincing listeners was his claim to be a scientist. That he had little justification for his assertion did not affect his audience. Despite their education, most were unable to evaluate his pretensions. The failure of the massive attempt by preachers and theologians to prove that evolution was scientifically incorrect had damaged their position of intellectual leadership, and scientists tended to inherit the mantle of authority the churchmen had lost. Although theologians might explore the same ideas as Fiske in a more rigorous, as well as more Christian, manner, Fiske's claim to speak as a scientist aroused greater interest in his words and made his assertions more convincing.

Fiske's reputation as a philosophical interpreter of history aided general acceptance of him as a religious philosopher. His letters reveal that in many cases the sponsors of his religious lectures were the same people who supported his historical tours. Not only Unitarians and "Cosmists," but Congregationalists, Presbyterians, and Episcopalians joined to help him find halls for his talks and invited him to speak in their churches. These were the denominations most easily penetrated by the religious ideas that Fiske presented. Thus his historical work brought him to the attention of those most likely to be interested in his religious position.

Fiske's reputation as a scientist and philosopher among groups interested in accommodating religion to modern science merely prepared the way for his success. It is not in itself sufficient to explain it. Fiske could not have called forth such widespread praise for a basically secularistic view had his audiences not been able to hear in his lectures more than he said. Fiske by the late eighties had achieved almost total empathy with his audience; he had become a master at phrasing his ideas in words which would please his listeners. Nowhere in his work did this talent show itself to greater advantage than in the way he used traditional Christian language and symbolism to express a secularistic view of religion.

Where other men used rational and logical approaches, and tried to face the difficulties which their ideas involved, Fiske avoided all such aspects of his topic and concentrated on the positive side of his message. He said that science directly supported religion. His auditors were not likely to realize that his religion actually depended on science and would have to be altered as scientific ideas changed.

He said that the essence of Christianity was unassailable; few went on to explore the way his "pure" religion differed from the historic Christianity they wished to preserve. His audience, listening to him in churches where the minister often explored similar ideas from a Christian standpoint, was not likely to doubt the obviously sincere man in the pulpit who spoke in words that echoed the accustomed language in which God and Christ had always been preached in those halls. They could easily assume that, since Fiske spoke as a scientist and a philosopher with a greater claim to authority than their own minister, and since he phrased his conclusions in even more positive terms, he had actually succeeded in demonstrating what their minister could only suggest. They could depart in the comforting belief that they had heard a convincing proof that the Christianity of their childhood was the religion best suited to the modern world.

Fiske did not alter in any significant way once he had assimilated Spencer. He had little more to offer in the way of religious ideas in 1885 than he had had a decade earlier. The most significant change was in the tone in which he presented his ideas. But in a time of uncertainty, of search for a basis for religious security, this proved to be enough. For the churches had altered more in the preceding quarter-century than Fiske had. What seemed radical and infidel when Fiske first expressed it, won wide acceptance as a major defense of Christian faith when presented in a more sympathetic manner. That his audience could react in this way to Fiske's lectures testifies to the speed with which American orthodoxy had altered in these years. The debates over the "new theology" sufficiently weakened older doctrines and confused believers so that Fiske's passionately expressed secularism seemed a support for faith. Without these changes in American religion Fiske would probably have been largely ignored. In a time of uncertainty and perplexity his confident assurances had immediate value.

This was Fiske's major contribution to American thought and his most valued service to American life in the nineteenth century. What his audiences thought they heard Fiske say permitted those who wished to hold on to their beliefs to feel that they now had an intellectual basis for doing so. It justified the considered judgment of a student of American religion who lived through these years that "at a time when . . . Christian theism in America was threatened with abandonment by a host of thoughtful minds, it was he more than any other writer, who turned back the tide." [30]

[30] J. W. Buckham, "American Theists," *Harvard Theological Review,* 14:274 (July 1921).

CHAPTER TEN

THE MEANING
OF AMERICA

Not until Fiske began to put into print his vision of the meaning of America did he finally achieve the income he desired. By the end of the 1880's new publishing contracts and lecture tour profits combined to solve his most pressing financial problems.

The collapse of his 1885-1886 tour under the management of Major James B. Pond marked the low point in Fiske's affairs. Thereafter his slow, steady cultivation of the type of listener he had already attracted resulted in consistently profitable trips. Although he never achieved the mass audience he dreamed of, his pleasing material and growing reputation brought out more of his usual audience than ever before; skillful management made his efforts rewarding.

Shortly after his contract to write a multivolume history of the United States for Harper & Brothers broke down in 1885, two new commissions from other publishers came in. D. Appleton & Company, in which his friend E. L. Youmans was influential, hired him to serve as associate editor and assist James Grant Wilson in preparing a multivolume cyclopaedia of American biography. Later in the year Fiske contracted with Ginn & Company of Boston to condense Washington Irving's *Life of George Washington,* and write a preliminary sketch of the history of the United States to the birth of Washington, as well as a supplement on events after his death. The whole would be a brief synopsis of United States history to 1865 suitable for the use of school children.[1]

The main burden of editing the Appleton biographical cyclopaedia fell on Wilson and his staff in New York. Fiske, in Cambridge, had only to arrange for work by local experts, write a few sketches of outstanding historical figures, and read proof and check for accuracy some of the articles. For this part-time work (Fiske was expected to put in only two weeks a quarter at his various tasks) Appleton paid Fiske $2,000 a year during the three years he assisted the project. When he was in Cambridge and could use the facilities and staff of the Harvard library, Fiske had little difficulty in keeping up his side of the bargain. But when off on lecture tours he tended to fall behind. After Fiske's 1887 trip to the West Coast, Wilson asked in a marginal note to Fiske's letter requesting an advance on his quarterly $500, "Do D A & Co think they should pay Fiske for a *quarter* in which he has only corrected some proofs and written Hutchinson article, about one and a half printed pages, perhaps two or three days work?" Appleton did; and shortly thereafter Fiske gratefully acknowledged receipt of the check. Fiske used the articles he prepared for the cyclopaedia as the basis for new lectures. He developed from them a series entitled "Scenes and Characters in American History," which included talks on Jefferson, Hamilton, the Tyler family, and other distinguished Americans connected with the post-1789 period he had not yet reached in his own historical work.[2]

Ginn & Company promised Fiske $750, with a $50 bonus if he completed the condensation of Irving on schedule. Fiske expected to finish by the end of September 1886. In the middle of that month he began to draw advances from Ginn, and before he finally turned in all his manuscript the following March he had drawn almost all the payment in advance.[3]

[1] JF to his mother, Sept. 1, 1885; JF to J. G. Wilson, July 23, 1886; JF to Ginn & Co., Sept. 16, 1886, HHL.

[2] JF to J. G. Wilson, July 23, 1886, Sept. 6, 1886, Oct. 18, 1886, Dec. 21, 1886, Apr. 27, 1887, July 30, 1887 (Wilson's quoted remark is on margin of this letter), HHL. JF to M. S. Snow, Dec. 26, 1887, WUA.

[3] JF to Ginn & Co., Sept. 16, 1886, Feb. 28, 1887, Aug. 17, 1887, HHL.

Fiske's difficulties with the work were not limited to the excess time he put in on it. Even before he completed his task, he and the publisher quarreled over the title. Fiske's efforts pleased Ginn, who liked the prologue and epilogue so well that he proposed to market the entire book as a "History of the United States" over Fiske's signature. The sharp protests of Fiske, and his threat to withdraw his name from the title page if the work was so mislabeled, finally led Ginn to settle on a more accurate description of the contents, "Washington and His Country." [4] Shortly after settling this point, Ginn began to press for changes in the section dealing with the Civil War. He had sent out galley proofs of the book to prominent educators, and Southern protests that Fiske was too favorable to the North disturbed the publisher. Ginn wrote urgently to Fiske asking him to adopt a less controversial attitude that would increase acceptance of the book by schools in the South. Fiske resisted for several months, refusing "to emasculate it in deference to the Slave Power," but telling Ginn he could make any changes he desired if he left Fiske's name off the title page. This Ginn did not want to do and he kept up the pressure until September 1887, when Fiske compromised sufficiently to replace his reference to John Brown's "religious fervour" by the phrase "fanatical fervour," and to substitute the term "Confederacy" for "rebellion." Ginn did not think these modifications solved the problem. He requested further changes and suggested ending the book earlier to avoid the Civil War entirely. Fiske refused. In his final letter he tartly remarked, "You may have observed that Rev. E. E. Hale makes his History of the U.S. stop with the peace of 1815, in order to *avoid giving offence.* That is only a half measure, however. To write a history of this country, without offence to anybody, one should stop at 1492." [5]

Even more significant than these two commissions were Fiske's contract with Houghton, Mifflin and Company. This was the successor to Ticknor and Fields, who had published Fiske's early essays in the *Atlantic Monthly,* as well as to Osgood & Company, the publishers of his *Cosmic Philosophy.* Although Osgood lost some of his

[4] JF to Ginn & Co., Feb. 22, 1887, Feb. 28, 1887, HHL.

[5] Quotations from JF to Ginn & Co., Apr. 26, 1887, Sept. 12, 1887, and May 21, 1888, HHL (italics in source).

enthusiasm for Fiske and permitted the English house of Macmillan alone to put out Fiske's 1879 volume entitled *Darwinism,* Fiske's religious writings aroused the interest of Houghton. The house published the first of his Concord lectures in 1884. The same year they brought out another volume of essays, *Excursions of an Evolutionist,* as well as taking over *Darwinism* from Macmillan. The senior partner, Henry Oscar Houghton, had a strong interest in religion, and his house published many significant works by outstanding religious writers. The firm distributed the *Andover Review,* and issued books by religious radicals like Lyman Abbott and Washington Gladden, as well as sponsoring more orthodox works. In 1885 Fiske's *Idea of God* appeared in the *Atlantic Monthly,* which Houghton owned, before being marketed in book form. When, in the following years, Houghton also began to publish Fiske's historical works, he used the same method of presentation. In 1886 and 1887 the *Atlantic* printed the nine chapters to which Fiske's treatment of the years 1783 to 1789 had grown; the book was published as *The Critical Period* in December 1888. In December 1887, the month after the last of these nine articles appeared, the *Atlantic* began to print Fiske's fourteen chapters on the American Revolution, running the work until December 1890.[6]

In 1888 Henry O. Houghton became aware of the difficulties Fiske faced in completing his history because he needed to lecture continuously and take on odd jobs that had little direct relation to his major work. Houghton offered to place Fiske on a salary basis that would enable him to concentrate on writing. In return, all copyrights on work done would be the property of the publisher. At first this salary amounted to $5,000 a year, with Fiske promising to limit himself to three months' lecturing each year. Later it was raised to $6,000 and Fiske agreed to cut back his annual tour to two months.[7]

Fiske's history was only one of the multivolume projects Hough-

[6] *A Sketch of the Firm of Houghton Mifflin & Company Publishers* (Cambridge, Mass., 1890). *A Catalogue of Authors whose Books are Published by Houghton, Mifflin and Company* (Boston, 1901). Horace E. Scudder, *Henry Oscar Houghton* (Cambridge, Mass., 1897), pp. 58–63.

[7] George H. Mifflin to JF, June 23, 1896, HMCo papers, 10:548–551. F. J. Garrison to G. H. Mifflin, Nov. 12, 1898, HMCo papers, 21:374–375.

ton Mifflin financed. The firm had a subscription book department which effectively disposed of books by direct solicitation of customers, either by mail or by door-to-door selling. This method permitted efficient and profitable sales of multivolume works, and the publishers showed considerable initiative in developing series for this department. Among the works whose creation they aided were the four-volume *Memorial History of Boston* and the eight-volume *Narrative and Critical History of America,* both edited by Justin Winsor. They were engaged in the eighties in putting out a series of biographies under the title "American Statesmen," which became standard reference works. A series of state histories and one of biographies of American religious leaders also appeared under their imprint. Although all these series were cooperatively written and not the work of one man, as Fiske's multivolume history would be, this arrangement did not involve any major problems in merchandising. As in the American Statesman series, individual volumes could be sold by the trade book department as written, and the full set then handled by the subscription department when complete. In addition, illustrated editions issued in limited numbers were especially profitable when sold by mail or door-to-door solicitation. When finished, Fiske's history would be a useful companion to the collected works of the great New England writers that Houghton had taken over from his predecessors, and which he successfully marketed across the nation.[8]

Fiske's work appealed to the head of the firm, who had publicly expressed a preference for "writers whose books have a steady sale from year to year, rather than a phenomenal or sensational sale for a short period." Houghton had begun life as a printer and had only gone into publishing later; he much preferred works which provided his printing press with a steady, predictable demand to those which posed difficult problems in meeting rush orders. Since Houghton felt confident that Fiske would provide works that he could sell steadily and profitably, he offered generous terms.[9]

The contract went into effect on January 1, 1889. Fiske was then

---

[8] *The Firm of Houghton Mifflin*, pp. 39–40. *Catalogue of Authors*, pp. 153–176.

[9] Quotation from "Mr. H. O. Houghton on American Literature," *Publishers' Weekly,* 39:46 (Jan. 17, 1891).

at work on a brief history of the American Revolution intended for use in schools. This he delivered to his publishers as the first piece of work on which they had copyright control under the pact, and they published it as *The War of Independence* in 1889. Fiske's *American Revolution* (already appearing in the *Atlantic*) was paid for on a royalty basis when published in 1891, as his *Critical Period* had been when it appeared in 1888. Fiske agreed to include the only other completed section of his history, the part on the colonization of New England, under the terms of his salary agreement. Since his *American Revolution* took all available space in the *Atlantic*, Houghton brought out *The Beginnings of New England* in 1889 as the second published portion of the history. Aside from some time spent producing a school textbook, *Civil Government in the United States,* published in 1891, Fiske now turned to the earliest portion of American history and concentrated on the volume that would stand first in the collected works. *The Critical Period* benefited greatly from being published just before the centennial celebrations of the Constitution got under way. If the volume on the discovery of America could come out just before the celebrations scheduled in 1892 to mark the four hundredth anniversary of Columbus's voyage, it would also gain from the interest aroused by these ceremonies.[10]

From this point on the Houghton Mifflin Company tended to take over the place in Fiske's financial concerns formerly occupied by his mother; once more he had someone to whom he could turn when his problems became more than he could handle. All through his life Fiske had shown the habit patterns of a child who avoided responsibility for failure by calling upon a sympathetic elder. His mother had aided him generously during the life, and immediately after the death, of her second husband, when her means permitted. The providential interventions of Mrs. M. A. Edwards and Mrs. Augustus Hemenway carried Fiske through periods when he could find no way to solve his own problems. He seems to have come to believe such interventions and aid were his due; his reaction to each crisis was not to reform the habits that led to difficulty, but to search

[10] F. J. Garrison to G. H. Mifflin, Nov. 12, 1898, HMCo papers, 21:374–375.

for someone to bail him out. The worst period of his life had been the years after the death of his stepfather, when his mother could no longer come to his support. In the years ahead he would find the Houghton firm as generous as his earlier benefactors, though its motives were not the same.

The firm desired to see Fiske complete his series in the briefest time possible and willingly provided financial support in addition to his salary to make this feasible. Fiske repeatedly demanded and received large advances on the copyrights of his early works which were still on a royalty basis. In practice his publishers permitted him to engage in much outside work to supplement his salary. They allowed Fiske to write a biography of his friend E. L. Youmans for another publisher and also allowed him to contribute articles to periodicals they did not own. Fiske's lecture tours frequently approached closer to five or six months a year than the two to three months to which his agreement limited such activity.[11]

II

The most important factor in Fiske's success in drawing readers and listeners was the attraction exerted by his vision of the meaning of American history. An examination of what he had to say indicates the reasons why a significant element in American society enthusiastically hailed him as the greatest historian of his day.

Fiske's attitude to New England is central to his vision of America. This was the section of the country he understood best, the one with which he felt most in sympathy, and from whose viewpoint he looked at the rest of the nation. This attitude alone would make *The Beginnings of New England* a key work, even if Fiske had not fittingly chosen to include in this volume an explicit presentation of the complex of ideas that informs every one of his histories. An analysis of the work reveals Fiske's basic conception of history, and shows why Fiske thought of himself as a philosophic and scientific historian. It also helps explain why a work that concentrated largely on narration of colorful incidents could impress

[11] G. H. Mifflin to JF, June 23, 1896, HMCo papers, 10:548–551; June 2, 1897, HMCo papers, 10: 906–907.

general readers as "novel, and fresh in treatment, philosophical and wise," and be praised by a scholarly reviewer for its "interesting and philosophical brevity." [12]

"I have purposely omitted many details which in a formal history of that period would need to be included," Fiske stated in his preface. "It has been my aim to give the outlines of such a narrative as to indicate the principles at work in the history of New England down to the Revolution of 1689." [13] To Fiske, his concrete illustration of these principles made his work a philosophic history. He presented them explicitly in the opening chapter of the book, "The Roman and the English Idea," which drew upon some of the concepts Fiske had already explored in his religious essays and in his *American Political Ideas.* It contrasted the Roman idea of building empires by conquest and forcible incorporation of alien peoples with the English method of nation-making that incorporated new peoples through representation. The Roman method inevitably led to tyranny and corruption. The English, by adopting and developing the Teutonic idea of representation, achieved what neither the cultured Greeks nor the powerful Romans had been able to create. They built a large and efficient state that left its individual members free, and thus was inherently progressive. Fiske briefly surveyed political history from ancient times through the development of England, organizing his presentation around the conflict of these two ideas, with the climax coming in the Puritan revolt that prevented Stuart despotism from destroying this glorious English idea of self-government. The Puritan movement, including the migration to America, had a vital role in preserving freedom for the entire world.

Fiske thus restated in a secular manner, modifying to bring it into accord with nineteenth-century attitudes, the sense of mission that had motivated the Puritans themselves. He quoted with approval various Puritan expressions of this idea. "It was the simple truth," Fiske told his readers, "that was spoken by William Stoughton when he said in his election sermon of 1688: 'God sifted a whole

---

[12] Quotations from reviews of *Beginnings* in the Boston *Post,* July 26, 1889, and Frederic Bancroft in *Political Science Quarterly,* 4:522 (September 1889).

[13] JF, *The Beginnings of New England* (Boston, 1902), pp. vii–viii.

nation, that He might send choice grain into the wilderness.' " [14]
The Puritan concept was essentially religious; by following God's
ordinances their state would serve as a saving remnant for the rest
of the world. But to Fiske the significance of Puritanism was that
it prevented the destruction of liberty in the last free state of
Europe, even while despotism succeeded in stamping out the remaining vestiges of representative government on the Continent.
Yet more, Puritanism carried the Teutonic idea of government to
a new land where there would arise a new nation "equipped as no
other nation had ever been, for the task of combining sovereignty
with liberty, indestructible union of the whole with indestructible
life in the parts." [15]

The first chapter set out the leading ideas and provided a philosophical frame. The rest of the book graphically traced the incidents
which marked the transmittal of English political concepts to
America through the founding of the New England common-
wealths in the seventeenth century. In a swiftly moving narrative
replete with colorful incidents, Fiske described the decision to
emigrate, the first settlements in Massachusetts, the forging of the
New England Confederacy, difficulties with the Indians leading to
King Philip's War, and the resistance to Stuart attempts to end
Massachusetts self-government that led to the Revolution of 1689.
He sketched the political developments and briefly related them to
his introductory chapter. New England worthies were flatteringly
portrayed in terms which could not fail to gratify the filial pride of
their descendants among Fiske's audience.

Through the whole narrative ran a sense of providence, of divine
forethought. The book was thus an exposition of the destiny of
America as planned by an immanent divinity, and served as an
expansion of his first Concord lecture which had explained the
destiny of man in terms of the plans of such a deity. [16] Fiske placed
as his motto on the title page a quotation from Edward Johnson's

[14] JF, *Beginnings*, p. 174. Fiske misdated Stoughton's sermon; it should be 1668,
not 1688 (the error appears in all editions and was not corrected when Fiske revised
the book in 1898).

[15] JF, *Beginnings*, p. 56.

[16] See JF, *Studies in Religion* (Boston, 1902), pp. 59–66, and *Beginnings*, pp.
viii–ix.

Wonder-Working Providence of Zion's Savior in New England
(1654): "The Lord Christ intends to achieve greater matters by this
little handful than the world is aware of," and the entire volume
was a secularized version of this sentiment. Fiske, indeed, warned
against taking this idea too literally; against trying, as did the
original settlers, to see God's hand in every minor event. This made
for too strict a criterion of judgment to please Fiske, for his admired
New Englanders often lapsed from the highest standards. Rather
each event should be judged in the context of the times. On this
basis Fiske could urbanely defend the barbarities which New Englanders visited on the Indians and their persecution of those who
disagreed with them in religion; these were a product of the times
and a measure of how far the Puritans were a part of them. The
hand of God appeared in the advancement of the political principle
of free government. Here the Puritans were far in advance of their
contemporaries and prepared the way for the future as they set up
self-governing townships, federated them by provincial assemblies
freely elected by the towns, and then went on to form a confederacy
of the major provinces which in a crude and imperfect way foreshadowed the later American union. In this process of centralization
of power through federalism, New England improved on the
British model and led the way to a state greater than any yet
existing. As the United States would develop along lines laid down
by the Puritans of New England, so too England itself would be
influenced by its Puritans into granting greater freedom to its
subjects, and thus prepared for the peaceful expansion of the British
Empire. In time the whole world would follow this lead and what
was only crudely and imperfectly revealed in New England would
become the road to a millennium of peace and prosperity for all
mankind.[17]

It was in this sense that Fiske thought of his work as a contribution to philosophic history. He felt that he had found the underlying
principle, the immanent design, of New England history in this
gradual evolution of the idea of self-government with representation, an idea which permitted the necessary increase in central power

[17] JF, *Beginnings*, especially pp. 304–310, 341–347.

to meet the needs of a large state while preserving the freedom of the individual. In the light of this the reader could easily interpret the wealth of anecdote in which Fiske narrated the settlement and early development of New England. Those who did so had no difficulty in understanding the closing words of the book: "In the events we have here passed in review, it may be seen, so plainly that he who runs may read, how the spirit of 1776 was foreshadowed in 1689." [18]

Since it was philosophical in this sense, Fiske felt his book was also a contribution to scientific history. To Fiske science meant primarily an attempt to arrive at general laws that would explain the over-all trends of the universe. He had little interest in the demand for careful investigation and painstaking accuracy through which his contemporaries who desired to write scientific history transformed the methods of this discipline. Although a few men, like Henry and Brooks Adams, also felt attracted by the search for laws ruling the past, the majority of historians seem to have thought of science primarily as a methodology, as a way of investigating the world. They engaged in exhaustive searches for new source material, carefully assessed and validated these sources, and published their results in monographs examining in detail some narrow aspect of their field of study. When they did turn to over-all generalizations and explanations, many of the scientific historians adopted the same Anglo-Teutonic hypothesis which Fiske used. But it was not the center of their concern and they did little with it; methodology was closer to their hearts. Fiske, who had almost no interest in science as a method, preferred to leave to others the careful investigations designed to determine the facts as accurately as possible. While the pressure of financial need spurred him to write very rapidly, he would in no case have cared to search out original sources before sitting down to compose. Fiske desired large generalizations and explanations. He was quite content to draw his factual illustrations from the work of other historians.[19]

[18] JF, *Beginnings*, p. 347.
[19] W. S. Holt, "The Idea of Scientific History," *Journal of The History of Ideas,* 1:352–362 (June 1940). H. H. Bellot, *American History and American Historians* (London, 1952), pp. 1–40. *Historical Scholarship in the United States, 1876–1901, as Revealed in the Correspondence of Herbert Baxter Adams,* W. S. Holt, ed. (Baltimore, 1938).

Fiske made no secret of this attitude. His footnotes candidly confessed it. Although the bibliographical essay he appended at the end of his book devoted six pages to listing primary sources, he made little use of such material; it is unlikely that he had many of the books available to him in the rooms in St. Louis where he wrote most of the book. The first edition had forty footnotes in its two hundred and seventy-eight pages. Of these, thirteen were either explanatory in nature or contained cross-references, and twenty-three cited secondary authorities for quotations and statements, while only four referred the reader to primary sources for the period; and these were mostly quaintly worded titles, cited to amuse the reader rather than call his attention to major sources of information. Of the twenty-three secondary citations, seven were to John A. Doyle's *The Puritan Colonies.* Fiske had urgently requested a copy from Henry Holt early in 1887, before the American publication of Doyle's history, and carried the unbound sheets which Holt sent him along on his speaking tour for use while writing his lectures.[20] In his discussion of the English background, Fiske cited most frequently Samuel Rawson Gardiner. Interestingly, Fiske did not use the ten volumes covering the years from 1603 to 1642 that Gardiner had published by the time Fiske wrote. Rather, he referred to the small elementary survey entitled *The First Two Stuarts and the Puritan Revolution, 1603–1660,* which Gardiner had written for the Longmans, Green & Co. student series "Epochs of Modern History." Doyle and Gardiner were Fiske's main reliance for factual material. These were supplemented by Fiske's phenomenal memory in a manner indicated in a marginal note (omitted from the printed version) on Fiske's manuscript of his history of New England. Citing his source for a detailed description of English mistreatment of Separatists, he says, "I think I took the above from Leslie Stephen's Dict. Nat. Biog., s.v., Barebones, Praisegod." [21]

Since Fiske did not attempt to be scientific in his use of sources or mastery of detail, any criticism of his work on the grounds of

[20] JF to Henry Holt, Feb. 21, 1887, Mar. 9, 1887, HHL.
[21] Manuscript version of *The Beginnings of New England,* p. 54, HHL.

factual inaccuracy is really irrelevant to his purposes. He could be no more accurate than the writers to whom he turned for his facts. If he found reliable surveys, or if easily available monographs permitted him to correct the large-scale works upon which he mainly depended, Fiske usually came out well. Where his trusted guides erred, he did too. He could draw on Justin Winsor of the Harvard library to guide him and, since Winsor was an expert bibliographer, Fiske usually based his books on the best previous studies. Given his attitude and the speed with which he needed to work, the relative infrequency and minor nature of the errors Fiske fell into are more remarkable than the fact that he did tumble consistently, as his professional reviewers never hesitated to point out.

To Fiske his history was scientific both because it pointed out large generalizations and because he drew these over-all patterns from the work of men hailed in his day as scientists. The two most important influences on *The Beginnings of New England* were Edward Augustus Freeman and Herbert Spencer. Freeman was a historian to whom the leaders of "scientific history" turned for guidance. Johns Hopkins University inaugurated its series of monographs in history and political science by printing as the first number an address which Freeman had given during his trip to the United States, entitled "An Introduction to American Institutional History." Fiske took from Freeman his concept of the Anglo-Teutonic roots of the idea of freedom and self-government, as did many of his more academic contemporaries. But where they also followed Freeman and other German and English founders of scientific history in adopting the methods of careful source study, along with the over-all view, to Fiske methodology seemed unimportant.[22] Fiske worked out a detailed application of his mentor's view to the American experience, and to him this appeared sufficient. Fiske drew from Spencer his vision of the way in which New England's development would serve as a pattern for the future, adding to Spencer's idea of evolution towards universal peace a concrete illustration of how this would come about.

Fiske had found generalizations which he believed his work

[22] Holt, "Scientific History."

showed fitted the facts of the past. They also served to explain the present and helped predict the future—not in detail, but in the large general patterns that he admired. Here, then, was evidence that his work was scientific in the truest sense; he treated history as a science of man which followed laws and permitted prediction, as natural science did. These laws could not provide precise detailed predictions or mathematical statement, but, then, neither did Spencer's version of evolution, which Fiske felt certain was a scientific law in the highest possible sense of the word.

This was the only work of history in which Fiske stated his ideas so explicitly. There was no need to do so again; once they were in print they were a matter of record and did not have to be repeated in each succeeding volume. To reiterate his vision of the destiny of America each time he came to a concrete illustration of it (and to Fiske everything he wrote on American history was such an illustration) would have risked boring his audience. The same scheme of ideas informed each of his works. Each shared, "so plainly that he who runs may read," the same vision of the way America fulfilled the purposes of an immanent deity by its progress towards a continental state ruling with effective power while preserving the freedom of the individual.

Reviewers enthusiastically hailed Fiske's book. Except for Catholic critics, who disliked Fiske's view of their church, all found his version of the meaning of the American past attractive. The Reverend P. O'Callaghan objected that "how Protestant attempts at acquiring power to persecute others is a struggle for the cause of liberty, while Catholic attempts at keeping that power is religious tyranny, has not been made clear by Mr. Fiske or by anyone else." But Protestant lay and religious reviewers found the book convincing. Although many noted, as did *Harpers' Monthly,* that "it is not a contribution of fresh facts," they were also prone to accept that periodical's praise of the "charm of Mr. Fiske's clear style, vast knowledge, and right perspective." Frederic Bancroft in the *Political Science Quarterly* added scholarly approval to the chorus. "Palfrey, Bancroft, Doyle and Ellis have written more satisfactorily of all or a part of New England Puritanism," he noted, "but none of them has put together the leading facts in such interesting and philosophical brevity as is done in this book." English reviewers praised the edition which Macmillan brought out there.[23]

Although popular, *The Beginnings of New England* was not Fiske's best-selling book. Nevertheless, it did sell some 27,000 copies in Fiske's lifetime, a substantial figure for a work professedly scientific and philosophical. Since Fiske's audience consisted primarily of New Englanders, and their descendants or imitators, it is not difficult to understand their interest in the book and willingness to accept the view of the meaning of American history that it presented.[24]

III

Preceding *The Beginnings of New England* in date of publication was the work which now stands last in Fiske's connected series of historical volumes, *The Critical Period of American History, 1783–1789*. In method this book fell midway between the stress Fiske placed upon his conceptual scheme in his *Beginnings* and the almost bare narrative of *The American Revolution*. He organized it about a thesis—that the period in question was the most critical of all in American history, for these years decided whether or not the great political ideas brought to America by the New England migration would be carried on to even greater heights. These events "determined a century ago that the continent of North America should be dominated by a single powerful and pacific federal nation instead of being parcelled out among forty or fifty small communities, wasting their strength and lowering their moral tone by perpetual warfare, like the states of ancient Greece, or by perpetual preparation for warfare, like the nations of modern Europe." [25]

[23] Boston *Post*, July 26, 1889. *Atlantic Monthly*, 64:566–569 (October 1889). *Book Buyer*, n.s. 6:211 (July 1889). *Nation*, 49:178–179 (Aug. 29, 1889). *Harpers' Monthly*, 79:802 (October 1889). *Andover Review*, 12:223–225 (August 1889). *Unitarian Review*, 32:183–184 (August 1889). *Catholic World*, 50:842–843 (March 1890). P. O'Callaghan, "New England and the Formation of America," *Catholic World*, 64:344–354 (December 1896), quotation from p. 346. *Political Science Quarterly*, 4:522 (September 1889). London *Athenaeum*, Oct. 4, 1890, p. 447. *English Historical Review*, 5:608 (July 1890).

[24] JF, *Beginnings* (Boston, 1900), p. ii.

[25] JF, "Preface" to *The Critical Period of American History, 1783–1789* (Boston, 1902), p. ix.

This thesis has intrigued professional historians and attracted
more scholarly attention to this volume than to any other that Fiske
wrote. But it is worth noting that the thesis which most historians
choose to discuss, and many to attack, is not usually stated in the
form given in the preceding paragraph. Fiske's thesis is more often
cited as if what he said was that this was a period of crisis and
despair and depression, which spurred the nation to seek remedies,
and for which the authors of the Constitution in their great wisdom
found a cure. Scholars showed a tendency to prefer this simplified
version from the start. In 1890 a German scholar wrote that "Mr.
Fiske clearly and eloquently describes how the energy of a handful
of intelligent, patriotic men saved their country from the threat of
destruction." [26] But the full intent of Fiske's thesis went beyond this.
It was not only a crisis of trade and credit and politics caused by the
lack of effective federal government, it was also the most crucial
period in the evolution of the world-organizing idea which was
America's greatest gift to the future of the world. Some failed to
grasp this idea and fought against it for local and particularistic
advantage. Others, wiser and better able to grasp and understand
the great trends of history, worked to further the federal principle
and brought into being the most powerful and perfect expression
of it the world had ever seen.

In its simpler form the thesis has been easily refuted, for Fiske
never examined the facts for himself to see if they really fitted his
interpretation. Like most of his work, Fiske wrote *The Critical
Period* rapidly, making no attempt to check sources or to find out
if the causal relations he postulated between events could be demonstrated. In 1912 Edward Channing, in the relevant chapters of the
third volume of his *History of the United States,* easily demonstrated
that Fiske had over-estimated the post-Revolutionary-War depression and failed to see that it was over and recovery under way before
the Constitutional Convention met. Without violating the facts it
might have been possible to interpret the call for the Constitutional

[26] F. C. Philippson, "Die Politische Krisis der Vereinigten Staaten nach Beendigung
des Unabhängigkeitskrieges," *Vierteljahrschrift für Volkswirtschaft, Politik, und
Kulturgeschichte,* XXVII (1890), Band iii, seite 2: "Wie das Land durch die Energie
einer Handvoll einsichtiger, patriotischer Männer, vor dem drohenden Untergang
gerettet wurde, wird von Herrn Fiske klar und warm geschildert."

Convention as an expression of reviving trade and a desire for expansion, rather than as a despairing attempt to end a crisis period. Though Channing clearly showed Fiske's factual inaccuracies, historians have continued to attack Fiske's volume. As late as 1950 Merrill Jensen indicated in the preface to his *The New Nation* that he specifically intended it as a correction of Fiske's errors and interpretations.[27]

Since it can be checked against specific facts, the narrower form of Fiske's thesis is easily refuted and needs heavy modification to bring it into accord with what is now known. Fiske, as always, had turned to other historians for his information. In this work his major reliances were George Bancroft's two-volume *History of the Formation of the Constitution of the United States* and the first volume of John Bach McMaster's *History of the People of the United States*. These he supplemented with information obtainable from biographies, from monographs, and even from local legends. Fiske's handling of his material lacked critical acumen. His treatment of the Shays Rebellion in Massachusetts illustrates his method of work.[28] Fiske added nothing to the accounts in Bancroft and McMaster, except for one detail, and that detail was incorrect. He said that Shays was captured in the battle of Petersham on February 4, 1787; actually Shays escaped and fled to Vermont. Neither Bancroft nor McMaster fell into this error, nor can it be found in the one contemporary source on the rebellion that Fiske cited in his bibliography, G. R. Minot, *The History of the Insurrections in Massachusetts*. Fiske further compounded his error, and at the same time indicated its source, when he included a picture of the "House in Petersham where Shays was Captured" on page 197 of his 1898 illustrated edition. Apparently Fiske had heard this "fact" as a local legend while at his summer home in Petersham and, without checking to see whether Shays actually was captured, uncritically accepted it. Similarly he accepted with inadequate evaluation the material on the post-war depression he found in general histories. None of the

[27] Edward Channing, *A History of the United States*, III, *The American Revolution, 1761–1789* (New York, 1940), pp. 431–527. Merrill Jensen, *The New Nation* (New York, 1950), pp. xi–xiii. R. B. Morris, "The Confederation Period and the American Historian," *William and Mary Quarterly*, 3rd ser., 13:139–156 (April 1956).

[28] JF, *Critical Period*, pp. 214–217.

men he consulted had made any special study of the economic situation; political development and foreign affairs drew most attention, while McMaster added some new social detail. In these works he found continuous references to the post-war depression and drew from them concrete illustrations to point and make more graphic the sense of constitutional crisis he desired to convey to his audience. He also assumed causal relations between his facts that a closer examination would have revealed as untenable. But no one had made such an examination, and Fiske's misconceptions went unchallenged for some years.

Fiske's full thesis on the nature of the "Critical Period" is a corollary of the philosophical principles which he had set forth in *The Beginnings of New England*. Again the specific facts illustrated the nation's and the world's progress towards universal peace and prosperity through the evolution of federal states. He tried to show how in the years from 1783 to 1789 the United States repeated on a higher level and in a more advanced form the experience of the abortive New England Confederacy that he had sketched in his *Beginnings*. Attempts to refute this thesis by asserting that Fiske garbled the real course of events miss his main point. His critics would be more effective if they realized that his interpretation is too simple an explanation of the complexities of history. Its major fault is not that it fails to correspond to the true situation; had his sources given him a more accurate picture of the life of the decade, Fiske could easily have adapted his thesis to the facts. It is just here that the main flaw lies. The full thesis is so broad and indefinite that it can be held whatever the facts might be. Like Spencer's law of evolution, it is so generalized as to be a blank form on which anything can be written and which explains nothing about the actual course of history. It was effective because it gave listeners and readers a picture of themselves that pleased them.

Without exception, contemporary reviewers praised the book and accepted its thesis at face value. This enthusiastic reception of his first published book of history established Fiske as a major figure in American historical writing.[29] His thesis has continued to in-

[29] *Atlantic Monthly*, 58:122–123 (January 1889). *Book Buyer*, n.s. 6:21–22 (February 1889). *Critic*, 14:3–4 (Jan. 5, 1889). Chicago *Dial*, 10:31–32 (June 1889).

trigue historians because it does have some valid insights. The political developments of the 1780's and the way these stem from the past growth of the nation is one of the major aspects of the period, one which must be explained by a satisfactory interpretation of the specific events of these years. Though few today would accept Fiske's interpretation as he wrote it, it has been a lasting contribution to history in the stimulation it provided students to investigate sources and think about the period. It has also left a permanent impression upon the popular mind. No book of Fiske's is more frequently referred to today, both in the popular press and in scholarly works, than *The Critical Period*.[30]

The third work in Fiske's historical series to appear in book form was his two-volume treatment of the American Revolution, published by Houghton in 1891 after being serialized in the *Atlantic Monthly* in fourteen installments. Although now sold as an independent history, these chapters on the years 1776 to 1783 had not originally been intended to stand by themselves. They were the section Fiske wrote in London while at work on his projected "Short History," describing the military and diplomatic aspects of the war. Earlier chapters were to have set the stage and shown the origins of the revolt, as *The Critical Period* showed the immediate consequences. Fiske had used these chapters as lectures at the Old South in 1884 because he badly needed money and had not time to write special talks for the occasion. "I was greatly surprised at the interest thus shown in a plain narrative of events already well known, and have never to this day understood the secret of it," he wrote in his preface.[31]

Without exception, every general reviewer praised its philosophical frame. Many of them undertook to explain the popularity and

---

Harpers' Monthly, 78:661 (March 1889). *Nation*, 48:55–56 (Jan. 17, 1889). *Andover Review*, 11:212–215 (February 1889). *Catholic World*, 49:279–281 (May 1889). London *Athenaeum*, Jan. 8, 1889, p. 727. *Nineteenth Century*, 26:324–327 (August 1889). *English Historical Review*, 5:388–390 (April 1890).

[30] Jensen, *New Nation*, pp. xi–xiv. Morris, "Confederation Period," pp. 145–146. Vernon Nash, *It Must Be Done Again; the Case for a World Federal Union* . . . *Illustrated by Excerpts from John Fiske's "Critical Period of American History"* (New York, 1940).

[31] JF, *The American Revolution*, 2 vols. (Boston, 1902), I, p. xi.

interest of the lectures, at which Fiske had expressed surprise. Charles C. Starbuck told the readers of the *Andover Review* that "the narrative, while perfectly plain, and not seeking after startling effects or mysterious explanations, is so penetrated with a genuine sense of the genetic connections of things, that it takes on a teleological luminousness which cannot fail to be fascinating." The most thorough discussion was H. L. Osgood's review in the *Political Science Quarterly*. Writing as a man fully imbued with the new spirit of history, Osgood found the work unsatisfactory. He objected to concentrating upon battles at the cost of ignoring significant developments in Congress, within state administrations, in finance, in foreign affairs, and in the minds of men. "As treated here the colonial revolt seems to be an isolated American event, having no clear connections with the general course of the world's history." Held up to thorough, professional standards of historical workmanship, Fiske did not rank high. But the bulk of Fiske's readers were uninterested in such standards; and those who had read his earlier work and accepted the vision of the meaning of American history they found there, had no difficulty in discerning that the same connection with world history was implicit in this work, too.[32]

The readership which these three historical works drew probably did not greatly differ in composition from the audiences who turned out to hear them in lecture form. Circulation of his books spread Fiske's fame to areas of the country which he never personally penetrated, but the core of those attracted was still likely to be composed of descendants of New Englanders who found his interpretation of the American past pleasing to their pride of ancestry. In addition would come those desiring to imitate them and any others who accepted the New England group as the natural intellectual leaders of the nation. When given in lecture form, Fiske's histories attracted the upper levels of society and their imitators, where those who looked to New or Old England for social and

---

[32] *Book Buyer*, n.s. 8:259 (July 1891). *Critic*, 18:308 (June 13, 1891). Chicago *Dial*, 12:135–138 (September 1891). *Nation*, 53:72–73 (July 23, 1891). *Andover Review*, 16:205–208 (August 1891), quotation from p. 205. *Presbyterian and Reformed Review*, 3:390–392 (April 1892). *Political Science Quarterly*, 6:725–727 (December 1891), quotation from pp. 725–726. *English Historical Review*, 8:163–168 (January 1893). London *Spectator*, 67:469–470 (Oct. 10, 1891).

cultural leadership were the major group. In religion such people tended to be either Episcopalians, Unitarians, or members of the Calvinist denominations affected by the new religious thought of the time. There was thus a significant overlap betewen the two audiences, those who were drawn to Fiske's histories and those who valued his religious works, as there was also in the ideas which Fiske presented under the headings of history and religion.

Fiske's religious essays used the concept of an immanent God to support an abstract view of the destiny of man which his historical writing concretely related to the American scene. The destiny of America and the destiny of man were identical, for America led man toward the goal indicated in the religious lectures. And, in this process of leadership, New England ideas took first place. The core of his audience found this world view very flattering, for it put them and their ancestors in the key position in the nation and the world, and justified in universal terms their claim to the intellectual and social leadership of American life. Fiske's admirers were quite happy to believe that the result of a philosophic and scientific investigation of history proved that they were the peak and goal toward which all past evolution had been working, and also the best promise of a millennium to come. They showed their enthusiasm for this view of history in their attendance at Fiske's lectures and their purchases of his books, which combined to make him the most popular and the best-paid historian of his generation.

CHAPTER ELEVEN

THE EXPLOITATION
OF SUCCESS

John Fiske's ideas did not develop after the 1880's. The underlying concepts of his histories did not alter and his religious essays merely expanded upon the Concord lectures. Except for his *Discovery of America,* in which he tried to demonstrate his ability to use scholarly technique, Fiske's writings simply repeated and amplified in a less convincing manner what he had done earlier. Although his lecture methods remained the same, the patient exploitation of procedures he had worked out earlier continued to bring ever-increasing returns.

The praise which his first published books on American history drew from reviewers increased Fiske's attractiveness as a lecturer. His operations became nearly institutionalized and his regular tours of the country took on some aspects of a one-man travelling university extension. His lecture trips always lasted longer than the two or three months to which he had agreed to limit himself in his contract with Houghton, Mifflin and Company. In both 1891 and 1892 he was on the road for four months, in addition to engagements about New England that required no formal touring. Stopping at important cities year after year, he gave widely advertised courses of public lectures and interspersed these with single addresses or series of talks at schools and colleges in the vicinity, as well as "parlor courses" given in the homes of society matrons for their friends or for women's clubs. His week was normally full, for even though no profit-making engagements were possible on the Lord's day, Fiske frequently read parts of his religious essays at various churches, and even occasionally accepted invitations to give sermons.

As the demand for his services grew, he found it harder to work out convenient itineraries; the schedule of his tours grew very complex. In one week he gave several lectures in both Buffalo and Rochester, shuttling back and forth between the two cities and making a side trip to a girls' school at Aurora. On another occasion he scheduled simultaneous series in Baltimore and Philadelphia, commuting several times a week between the two cities.

Fiske's chief sponsors remained the socially prominent, with New England names conspicuous among them. St. Louis, Milwaukee, Buffalo, Cleveland, and other cities where he had intimate connections among the New Englanders who were part of the social and economic leadership, became even more profitable than before. Similar sponsorship in New York now produced lucrative crowds in the lecture hall. Chicago, which he had previously found difficult territory, also became profitable. Fiske now fully realized potentialities for success that had been present even during his time of desperation in the early eighties. The difference was that a decade of word-of-mouth advertising by community leaders, extensive newspaper publicity, and complimentary reviews of his books in religious and literary journals had made him a celebrity in his own right. Where earlier he had drawn only a small portion of those desiring to emulate the social and intellectual leaders, now he attracted enough of such people to provide himself with a large income.[1]

Fiske had a steadily growing list of talks available that would entertain, edify, and stir the national pride of his audiences. He made use of his books in progress, along with the results of his work

[1] JF to Abby, Mar. 16, 1890, Mar. 23, 1890, Feb. 18, 1892, Mar. 3, 1893, HHL; and Mar. 1, 1892, LC. JF to Henry Holt, Dec. 2, 1890, May 3, 1895; JF to H. A. Richmond, Oct. 29, 1890, Dec. 3, 1890, HHL. JF to Mrs. Anne C. Botta, Jan. 21, 1891, Jan. 29, 1891, HUL. Manuscript Itinerary of Lecture Course in Spring of 1892; JF to William Wilcox, July 7, 1892, HHL.

for the *Appleton Cyclopaedia of American Biography,* to provide lecture materials. From his forthcoming volume on the discovery of America came talks on the voyages of the Norsemen to America, on the ideas of ancient geographers, on the work of Columbus, and a defence of the veracity of Americus Vespucius. His histories of the Southern and Middle Colonies, as well as his work on eighteenth-century New England, were first given as lectures.[2] Fiske did not discard all lectures based on earlier books. As late as 1899 he still advertised six extemporaneous lectures on the American Revolution. The existence of a manuscript lecture on the early days of New England suggests that this, too, was a subject he kept in his repertoire.[3]

When Fiske had to prepare lectures for special occasions when he could not use material already on hand, he added the new lectures to his battery of available talks. In 1892, on his second trip to the West Coast, Fiske prepared for the centennial celebration of Captain Robert Gray's discovery of the Columbia River an address on the exploration and early settlement of Oregon that he was still giving in 1899. On December 16, 1893, he and his wife, mother, and daughter were guests of honor at a dinner to commemorate the Boston Tea Party given in Delmonico's restaurant by the New York State branch of the Sons of the American Revolution. The Ministers from the Netherlands and Greece, the President of Princeton, the Secretary of the Navy, and Carl Schurz were lesser luminaries who also addressed the gathering. Following the speeches, his hosts gave the Fiske family a reception at the Hotel New Netherlands, which featured a reproduction of the tea ship *Dartmouth* and the serving of "untaxed tea." Fiske gave the main address of the evening, a talk

[2] The best listing of Fiske's lecture material is in a printed circular which Fiske sent to Henry A. Richmond on Mar. 23, 1899, HHL. While the circular is undated, it was prepared before March 1898. The lectures based on the *Appleton Cyclopaedia* material were published after Fiske's death in volume I, *Scenes and Characters in American History,* of his *Essays, Historical and Literary,* 2 vols. (New York, 1902). See also, JF to Richmond, Dec. 22, 1891; JF to Abby, Feb. 9, 1894, HHL, and Manuscript List of *Cyclopaedia* articles, U.C.L.A. Library.

[3] Manuscript article on New England, HHL. Articles included in vol. II of Fiske's *Essays* were apparently also drawn from manuscripts Fiske kept on hand for possible lecture use.

on the significance of the Boston Tea Party that he later frequently repeated.[4]

For use in schools that desired only single lectures, Fiske prepared a talk on John Milton and an address entitled "Old and New Ways of Treating History." The latter was remarkable in its praise of ways of writing history which Fiske himself rarely practised. The "old" history he described was history as literature. Although Fiske lauded its highest examplars, Thucydides and Gibbon, the contrast between James A. Froude's inaccurate literature with Edward A. Freeman's careful source studies and acute generalizations with which the essay opened, showed clearly where Fiske's preference lay. His description of the methods worked out by his contemporaries to expand the amount of available information and to increase the accuracy of historical writing, displayed Fiske's awareness of an ideal he seldom followed in his own work.[5]

Fiske's lecture tours produced highly satisfactory financial results. His precise income is not recorded in the surviving records, but he seems to have been earning between $4,000 to $6,000 a year by his lecturing to supplement the $6,000 that his agreement with Houghton, Mifflin and Company brought him. In 1891, F. M. McKay, the chairman of a committee of University of Illinois trustees seeking a new Regent for that institution, asked Fiske to take the position. McKay told him the trustees would go as high as $10,000 a year, but Fiske turned it down saying that this sum was "much less than I now earn by literary work which I should have to give up." The year he turned down McKay's offer Fiske agreed to give his mother $500 annually so that she would not have to dip into her capital to provide for living expenses, warning her that the money was solely for her use and that if he found her helping any of her

[4] See circular accompanying JF to Richmond, Mar. 23, 1899; JF to Abby, May 4, 1892, May 16, 1892, HHL. *Critic*, 22:418–419 (Dec. 23, 1893), describes the Delmonico affair. The tea party address appears in *Essays*, II, 161–193. The Oregon oration in a revised version is in *Unpublished Orations* (Boston, 1909), pp. 17–62.

[5] JF, "John Milton," *Essays*, II, 35–67; "Old and New Ways of Treating History," *Essays*, II, 1–33. JF to Abby, Apr. 15, 1894, LC. See also essays on E. A. Freeman and Francis Parkman in JF, *A Century of Science* (Boston, 1902), pp. 187–254, 255–274.

late husband's relations, "it would affect my *feelings* with regard to the whole situation very seriously." [6]

Yet despite his large income, which increased even further in his last years, making him one of the best-paid writers of his day and undoubtedly the highest-paid historian of his generation, Fiske still found himself in financial difficulties. An illness while on tour in 1891 reduced Fiske's earnings; he had figured his budget so closely that before the trip was over he began to regret his generosity to his mother. "That $500 to mother is going to be a deadly pull," he wrote his wife. Money was again short in the Fiske household and when he sent Abby fifty dollars from St. Louis later in the spring he urged her to "squeeze it till it squeals." An income running upwards of $10,000 a year, in pre-inflationary days of the gold dollar, untouched by any income tax, might seem sufficient even for Fiske's large family, but it remained characteristic of Fiske that no matter how high his income went, he always spent more than he made.[7]

Part of the drain on his finances came from the tragic illnesses which had begun to strike his children in the previous decade. His eldest son continued to require treatment all through the nineties, and the cost of male nurses to take care of him while at home, and sanitarium fees when he was away, ran high. In one year it exceeded $2,000. Although Abby's wealthy bachelor brother aided Fiske in meeting these payments, they did strain Fiske's resources. Anxiety and concern for his son became a recurrent note in his letters.[8]

But necessary medical expenditures and the costs of feeding, clothing, and housing a large family did not exhaust the expenses of Fiske's household. He now felt able to provide his family not only with what they absolutely needed, but with what he thought their social position deserved. This included trips to Europe, private tutors for the older boys, an expensive preparatory school for the youngest child, and formal coming-out parties for his daughters to

[6] F. M. McKay to JF, Apr. 5, 1891; JF to McKay, July 10, 1891; JF to his mother, Mar. 6, 1891, HHL (italics in source). JF to Abby, Apr. 9, 1890, Feb. 19, 1893, HHL, and Apr. 17, 1894, LC.

[7] Quotations from JF to Abby, Apr. 2, 1891, Apr. 15, 1891, HHL. JF to Abby, Mar. 14, 1891, Mar. 27, 1891, HHL.

[8] JF to T. H. Huxley, Aug. 5, 1893; JF to James Brooks, Aug. 8, 1893, Nov. 21, 1894; JF to Martha Brooks, Sept. 27, 1895, Nov. 2, 1893, Dec. 13, 1893, HHL.

introduce them properly into society. But one desire that was close to his heart he was never able to gratify; none of his sons received a Harvard degree. Three of the four boys entered Harvard. The eldest, Harold, had to drop out because of illness. Clarence, the second son, apparently never entered. The third, Ralph, failed to complete his first year. The youngest son, Herbert, after an education at St. Marks School, withdrew during his senior year at Harvard for reasons that do not appear on the record.[9]

Fiske's desire to maintain his wife and children in the style to which he felt they should accustom themselves in part explains his recurrent financial crises. But probably equally important was the scale of his own self-indulgence. Purchase of more books than he could afford had been a weakness since college days. Now that he could fully express his love of books, he began to do so in a luxurious manner. He bought first editions, replaced older copies with better or more lavish printings, and had many of his books rebound by a private hand binder, designing the leather cases himself. By the time of his death he had crowded over ten thousand volumes into his library and had to shelve many of his treasures two deep in order to find room for them all. Entertained by and associating with wealthy people on his lecture tours, Fiske admired and imitated their way of life. He wrote in glowing terms of the rare delicacies he ate in the fine restaurants of New York, St. Louis, Milwaukee, and other cities along his lecture route. Under this regime of self-indulgence, which increased as money became easier to get, Fiske's physical appearance altered, and his weight swelled up to nearly three hundred pounds, a tendency encouraged by his habit of spending much of his time sitting at a desk where he normally consumed two or three quarts of beer a day. And now that he was successful, he was not satisfied with just any beer. "As soon as you get this, order from S. S. Pierce *one dozen* quarts of Foster's Bass; and stand it upright in the store-room or wine-closet," he requested Abby

[9] JF to Mrs. Mary B. Walker, Feb. 17, 1890, PUL. JF to his mother, Nov. 12, 1891; JF to Shepherd Gilbert, Nov. 21, 1892; Herbert Spencer to JF, Dec. 13, 1894, HHL. Harvard Class of 1891, *Report,* 6:140 (1941). Harvard Class of 1896, *25th Anniversary Report* (Cambridge, 1916), p. xxi. Harvard Class of 1900, *Report,* 3:126 (1910).

while on his way home from a tour of the middle-west. "I shall
probally [sic] be thirsty on Saturday." [10]

II

Under these disturbed working conditions, distracted by family
illnesses and problems, traveling extensively to earn money, and
writing a school textbook on civics for the same reason, Fiske
completed his most extensive attempt to meet the canons of the new
methodology in history—his two-volume work, *The Discovery of
America.*

Fiske could approach closer to the scholarly ideal in this work
because of the extensive research that had already been done on
the subject. Interest in the age of discovery and exploration was
widespread; scholars had thoroughly discussed the problems involved and edited the significant sources bearing on the problems,
making them easily available in any of the great libraries of the
country. With his increased income, Fiske could purchase many
such collections for himself. His early interest in languages proved
useful, permitting him to consult works in many different languages.

Yet, despite the time and care Fiske put into it, and the warm
reception the book received, the work itself provided convincing
evidence that Fiske's true talent lay in popularization rather than
in original historical research and composition. The book was
strongest and most impressive where he summarized and illustrated
conclusions reached by previous scholars, least satisfactory when he
tried to introduce original material of his own.

The long first chapter (170 pages in the collected edition of 1902)
showed him at his best. Here Fiske set out to describe the American
Indians whom the discoverers and explorers met. He was acquainted with the work of leading anthropologists of the day due to his
long-standing interest in ancient languages and myths, which had
led him twenty years earlier to read up on Indian affairs. As early
as 1879, Lewis H. Morgan had thanked Fiske for a favorable review

[10] Quotation from JF to Abby, Apr. 21, 1891, HHL (italics in source). JF to
Abby, Apr. 1, 1885, Mar. 4, 1893, Mar. 29, 1894, Mar. 7, 1895, HHL, and Feb. 14,
1896, LC. JF to G. H. Humphrey, Feb. 16, 1901, HHL. "John Fiske's Library,"
Cambridge *Tribune,* Aug. 3, 1901.

of his volume on *Ancient Society,* calling it "the first direct and unhesitating recognition it has received from an American competent to judge its contents." Fiske built his first chapter about the work Morgan and Adolf Bandelier had done in investigating the social, political, and martial activity of the Indians of North America. These pages presented material unfamiliar to most professional historians, who tended to concentrate on political history and written records. Reviewers of the book almost universally praised this section, for Fiske summarized the Morgan-Bandelier reconstruction of Indian society in clearer language than the originators had used, making a significant contribution toward man's understanding of his past available to a wide audience that might otherwise have remained in ignorance of it.[11]

But when Fiske tried to do more than present the results of other people's work, he was far less satisfactory. In his second chapter he gave a lucid summary of what was known of the Norse voyages to America. He accepted, as did most historians, the truth of the voyages described in the Norse sagas, and also agreed with majority opinion in rejecting theories of continuous settlement by Norsemen in North America. But Fiske tried to do more; he tried to come up with a new proof of lack of long-term settlement. "If the Northmen had ever founded a colony in Vinland, how did it happen that the English and French in the seventeenth century, and from that day to this, have never set eyes upon a wild horse, or wild cattle, pigs, or hounds, or any such indication whatever of the former presence of civilized Europeans? I do not recollect ever having seen this argument used before, but it seems to me conclusive." This reasoning, with its assumption that domesticated animals left behind by an abandoned European colony must necessarily survive, and its attempt to call a lack of evidence conclusive proof, was not very convincing. Yet it was one of the few places where Fiske tried to make his work more than a lucid compilation of other men's views.[12]

If *The Discovery of America* had little value as a contribution to

[11] L. H. Morgan to JF, July 24, 1879, HHL. JF, "Morgan's Ancient Society," *North American Review,* 125:589–591 (November 1877). JF, *The Discovery of America* (Boston, 1902), I, xi–xiii, xvi–xvii, 1–170.

[12] JF, *Discovery,* I, 171–267, quotation from I, 254–255.

original scholarship, it was convincing evidence of Fiske's great talent for popularization. The book abounded with long discussions of points that had aroused scholarly controversy and contained extended considerations of the difficult problem of locating the geographic points mentioned by the early explorers. In his urge to make the work scholarly, Fiske included a multitude of footnotes in the approved academic manner, citing sources in many languages, and often giving the original of sentences he translated in the body of the work. That a scholar writing for the *Yale Review* should find such technical apparatus admirable is understandable. But that the book should also impress a nonacademic reviewer in the *Critic* as having at the same time "the fullness of an encyclopaedia, with much of the interest of a novel," is even more impressive. Barrett Wendell remarked that "it is a history of that fascinating kind which tells us, to be sure, little that was not known beforehand; but that shows us, so simply that we hardly realize we are being taught, where each scattered bit of knowledge belongs." Fiske's narrative skill easily carried the freight of scholarship with which he loaded the book. This became the best-seller among Fiske's works. Within six weeks of publication 7,000 copies were in print; before the end of the first year the total reached 11,000, and the book continued in good demand thereafter.[13]

The over-all conceptual scheme of this volume did not differ from that of Fiske's earlier works. His extensive narration of the growth of geographic knowledge helped demonstrate his belief that the discovery of America was not a special revelation, accomplished at one sweep by Columbus, but rather a gradual evolution. He did not try to make the course and goal of this evolution as explicit as he had in his *Beginnings of New England,* but readers had no difficulty discerning them. They appeared so clearly that the *Catholic World* protested against what "seems to be intended as the moral of his book. Spain's adherence to the old faith and the Inquisition caused her downfall. England's Protestantism gave her freedom of

[13] Quotations from *Critic,* 20:249 (Apr. 30, 1892), and Barrett Wendell, *Stelligeri and other Essays* (New York, 1893), p. 23. T. S. Bacon, "The Character of Columbus," *Yale Review,* 1:244–257 (November 1892). *Publishers' Weekly,* 41:826 (May 28, 1892). Boston *Evening Transcript,* Dec. 23, 1892.

thought and made her the foremost nation of the world." To the reviewer such reasoning was "quite antiquated"; to Fiske it revealed the true inner meaning of the whole American experience.[14]

The range of scholarly competence Fiske displayed in citations bristling with quotations in strange languages and in his informed handling of anthropological material, much of which was new and exciting both to historians and general critics, impressed all reviewers. Although they did point out minor weaknesses, on the whole they spent more time praising the excellencies of Fiske's work. E. G. Bourne in the *Political Science Quarterly* lauded "its thorough and conscientious scholarship and its engaging style." E. J. Payne in the *English Historical Review* similarly found much more to praise than to criticise. Lay reviewers were even more impressed.[15]

Fiske, however, was not pleased with the reception of his book. Unlike the reviews of *The Critical Period,* which had mostly concentrated on the thesis of the volume and had been uniformly complimentary, critics of his *Discovery* did point out flaws in the workmanship. The anonymous *Critic* reviewer, while praising the book in the generous terms quoted earlier, also remarked that he could "see the clay as well as the iron in the feet on which this work of art stands so gracefully." This infuriated Fiske into writing to his wife, "Bless you, don't mind what the *Critic* says; it don't know enough to go in when it rains." The *Nation* reviewer similarly mixed some reservations with his praise, which Fiske explained by telling a correspondent that "it has in some way taken a dislike to me, and never loses an opportunity of saying something unpleasant about me. Therefore . . . I discount in advance what the "Nation" says and do not mind it." Although almost every competent reviewer expressed some reservations about the work, the main tenor of their articles was highly laudatory. They recognized that the work was primarily a popularization, but the level of accomplishment was so high that it increased their respect for Fiske's scholarly abilities. Where his earlier work had diverged from the

[14] *Catholic World*, 55:460 (June 1892).
[15] *Political Science Quarterly*, 8:166 (March 1893). *English Historical Review*, 7:764–766 (October 1892).

trends of academic history, this book impressed scholars by showing Fiske's ability to use their methods.[16]

Fiske's success won him many academic and professional honors. Both Harvard and the University of Pennsylvania awarded him honorary degrees in 1894. Oxford University in England invited him to lecture on seventeenth-century New England at a special summer session in 1894. Although Fiske accepted the offer in April and permitted news of it to appear in literary journals, he withdrew reluctantly in July. He did not have enough money to make the trip and had to continue preparing the lectures on the early history of Virginia he would give at the Lowell Institute in Boston during the spring of 1895.

Annoyed by the mild academic strictures on his book, Fiske never again tried to use sources so extensively or footnote as thoroughly as he had in *The Discovery of America*. He remained essentially a solitary figure in the historical world and took little part in the round of professional societies and activities that grew up as scholarship became recognized as a full-time profession in the latter part of the nineteenth century. This was not for lack of opportunity. Fiske was a member of many societies that frequently requested him to participate in their activities. When invited to join the editorial board of the *American Historical Review*, Fiske turned down the offer on the ground that he had no time. He refused requests to contribute articles to the journal. He never appears to have attended any meetings of the American Historical Association. Fiske gratefully accepted the honor of election to membership in the Massachusetts Historical Society, but he soon decided that attendance took too much effort. He attended only one meeting and never contributed to the work of the society. Nor did he take an active

[16] Quotations from *Critic*, 20:250 (Apr. 30, 1892); JF to Abby, May 9, 1892, HHL; and JF to Henry Vignaud, June 12, 1893, Vignaud Papers, William L. Clements Library, University of Michigan. Reviews of *Discovery* are in *Book Buyer*, n.s. 9:162 (May 1892); Chicago *Dial*, 12:9–11 (May 1892); *Harpers' Monthly*, 85:480 (August 1892); *Nation*, 54:449–451 (June 16, 1892); *Popular Science Monthly*, 41:416–418 (July 1892); *Sewanee Review*, 1:102–104 (November 1892); *Methodist Review*, 74:673–674 (July 1892); *Presbyterian and Reformed Review*, 4:509–511 (July 1893); London *Athenaeum*, July 30, 1892, pp. 152–153.

role in any other society he joined or which elected him to honorary membership in the nineties.[17]

III

As the nineties progressed, Fiske's reputation as a religious lecturer increased. Many churches on his route asked him to give lay sermons on Sundays. Where once he had been most attractive as a preacher to radical Unitarians, now his fame spread out to other Protestant groups affected by modernist trends. More or less orthodox congregations among the Calvinist sects welcomed him, and he noted with delight that his books were used in conservative Sunday Schools to convince the young that their religion fitted a world ruled by science. The names of Episcopalian ministers appear among his hosts on tours and (though this is not clearly indicated in the letters) they may even have joined the spreading ranks of clerical sponsors of his lectures. Wherever he went, Fiske found that his fame as a religious thinker had gone before him and audiences eagerly turned to him as a guide.[18]

To fill his need for lectures on religion, Fiske worked up three speeches which he gave over and over from coast to coast. Since his Sunday sermonizing brought in no money, he found it difficult to put aside much time for religious writing. Though all three lectures existed in at least partially complete form as early as 1892, Fiske went on giving them until a financial crisis in 1899 made it advisable to publish them.[19]

The first of the three to be given publicly was a brief attempt to defend his attitude towards the problem of evil. He used this lecture, parts of which may have been written in the late eighties, in

[17] JF to Abby, Apr. 3, 1894, Apr. 15, 1894; JF to his mother, July 25, 1894, HHL. *Book Buyer*, n.s. 11:289 (July 1894). JF to J. F. Jameson, Aug. 6, 1895, Jameson *Papers*, LC. HMCo to JF, Dec. 20, 1895, HMCo Papers, 10:441. C. F. Adams, "Remarks by the President," Massachusetts Historical Society, *Proceedings*, 2nd series, 15:180–182 (1901, 1902).

[18] JF to Abby, Feb. 18, 1892, Mar. 29, 1892, Apr. 13, 1892, May 16, 1892, Mar. 4, 1893, Mar. 19, 1894, Apr. 12, 1897, HHL; Apr. 15, 1894, LC. JF to his mother, Mar. 3, 1896, HHL.

[19] JF to Abby, Mar. 14, 1892, HHL. The three lectures were published in 1899 as *Through Nature to God*.

1892. In his 1874 *Cosmic Philosophy* Fiske had taken the tough-minded position that if the existence of evil made it impossible to think of the world as the creation of an omnipotent personal God, he preferred to hold on to the idea of a monistic universe and abandon the concept of a personal God. He modified this position in the eighties, as his religious development, under the impetus of personal and family difficulties, led him to a greater appreciation of the value of a personal God. Now he had to explain how pain and evil could exist in a universe ruled by law and order, in which the guiding spirit was an immanent deity working for righteousness. In this essay Fiske elaborated the solution he had suggested in his Concord lectures. He denied the essential meaningfulness of evil and argued that, looked at in the long view, over the great expanse of evolutionary time, what appeared to be evil in the short run was the necessary accompaniment and condition of the final good end. Thus Fiske concluded that what was usually thought of as evil was, to the man of true vision, really for the good.[20]

The existence of evil, Fiske assured his audience, "is purely relative, yet it is profoundly real, and in a process of perpetual spiritual evolution its presence in some hideous form throughout a long series of upward stages is indispensable. Its absence would mean stagnation, quiescence, unprogressiveness." But he comforted any listeners who might find this an unacceptable version of social Darwinism by reassuring them with a rosy view of the future, for "the nature of evolution also requires that it [evil] should be evanescent. In the higher stages that which is worse than the best need no longer be positively bad." He concluded that "the mystery of evil remains a mystery still, but it is no longer a harsh dissonance such as greeted the poet's ear when the doors of hell were thrown open; for we see that this mystery belongs among the profound harmonies in Gods' creation." [21]

Fiske turned to another aspect of this problem in "The Cosmic Roots of Love and Self-Sacrifice," and tried to refute those who did

[20] JF to Abby, Mar. 19, 1892, HHL. "Preface" to "Through Nature to God," in *Studies in Religion* (Boston, 1902), pp. 215–221. JF, "The Mystery of Evil," in *Studies,* pp. 225–267.

[21] JF, "Mystery of Evil," pp. 265–267.

not agree that the universe was organized to encourage morality. This lecture, which existed in at least rudimentary form in 1892, when Fiske included it in a list of his available speeches, was refashioned into a reply to Thomas Henry Huxley's Romanes lecture on the relation of evolution and ethics. In its new form it was given as the Phi Beta Kappa address at Harvard in 1895 and successfully repeated in many cities. Huxley had argued that the processes of nature were morally neutral, that no external standard for morals could be found in a contemplation of the cosmos, and that the only true guides to morality were produced by man and represented his greatest contribution to the cosmic process. Huxley effectively symbolized the way man found his rules of conduct in his image of the garden, where man's will determined what tendencies were to rule, as contrasted with the same piece of land in the wild state. Not by supinely permitting nature to take its course, but by fighting and altering those aspects he disliked, did man arrive at rules of behavior that civilized the world he lived in.[22]

Fiske found very disturbing the idea that the processes of nature had no necessary relation to moral ends. He could not accept Huxley's dualism and felt he had to contradict it in order to maintain his own belief that evolution not only validated moral codes but guaranteed their eventual triumph over transitory evil. He tried to refute Huxley by recalling his own favorite theory of the influence of lengthening infancy upon man and arguing that this theory proved that morals arose in the natural course of human evolution.

But arch-evolutionist Huxley had not denied that morals arose in the course of evolution and themselves evolved thereafter, so Fiske had to go further. From his idea on infancy Fiske then jumped to the conclusion that "the cosmic process exists purely for the sake of moral ends." This leap he accomplished by his teleological view that whatever came last in time was the goal towards which evolution had been deliberately working. "The moral sentiments, the moral law, devotion to unselfish ends, disinterested love, nobility of soul,—these are Nature's most highly wrought products,

[22] JF to Abby, Mar. 14, 1892, Mar. 20, 1895, HHL. T. H. Huxley, "Evolution and Ethics," in T. H. and Julian Huxley, *Evolution and Ethics, 1893–1943* (London, 1947), pp. 33–84.

latest in coming to maturity; they are the consummation toward which all earlier prophecy has pointed." In time the full goal would be achieved. "Below the surface din and clashing of the struggle for life we hear the undertone of the deep ethical purpose, as it rolls in solemn music through the ages, its volume swelled by every victory, great or small, of right over wrong, till in the fullness of time, in God's own time, it shall burst forth in the triumphant chorus of Humanity purified and redeemed." Although pleasing his audience and satisfying Fiske, his view that morality was the goal and purpose of the world could be no more than an assumption.[23]

The most characteristic of the three essays he entitled "The Everlasting Reality of Religion." In it Fiske recapitulated almost every significant religious position he had taken during his career. The date of composition is difficult to fix. Fiske said he thought of the main lines of argument while reading the controversy between Spencer and Frederic Harrison on the nature of religion, which would put it in 1884 or 1885, but it is unlikely that he actually wrote it until the nineties.[24]

Fiske opened the lecture with an invocation of his radical religious past. By defending Voltaire against charges of atheism he assured himself that he had not really changed, while impressing his audience by his originality in beginning a defense of religion by praising a man popularly thought an arch-atheist. But Voltaire's religion, even though not atheism, did not measure up to the demands of nineteenth-century science. Deism, like Calvinistic orthodoxy, left God outside the universe; while each had been a valid religious idea in its time, both were now outgrown. To accord with the modern world view of science, they had to be modified by the "Greek" concept of immanence, which brought God back into direct contact with the world as the internal ruling principle. Fiske rejected all materialistic interpretations and insisted that the basic reality of the cosmos was spiritual.[25]

---

[23] JF, "The Cosmic Roots of Love and Self-Sacrifice," in *Studies*, pp. 309, 324.

[24] JF, "Preface" to "Through Nature to God," in *Studies*, pp. 217–218. A briefer version of this essay appeared in the *Christian Register*, 74:815–817 (Dec. 12, 1895).

[25] JF, "The Everlasting Reality of Religion," in *Studies*, pp. 327–336.

Having thus cleared away past errors, Fiske moved on to more positive ground and categorically stated what he conceived to be the essence of all religion. He listed three principles which he thought could be found in all religion from its most primitive roots in the distant past to the highest developments of the nineteenth century. Each was indispensable; without all three there could be no religion. "Now in all ages and in every form of Religion, the theory has comprised three essential elements: first, belief in Deity, as quasi-human; secondly, belief in an Unseen World in which human beings continue to exist after death; thirdly, recognition of the ethical aspects of human life as related in a special and intimate sense to this Unseen World." [26]

After clarifying what he meant by religion, Fiske went on to ask whether these three ideas were in essence real. His answer was a ringing yes. He based his assertion upon the postulate that nature never made a false major step, and at all stages worked to bring about internal adjustments of living things that harmonized with the environment. To say that religion might be an internal adjustment with no real relation to the external world was "something utterly without precedent in the whole history of creation. All the analogies of Evolution, so far as we have yet been able to decipher it, are overwhelming against any such supposition." Thus the view of the universe derived from science proved that "of all the implications of the doctrine of evolution with regard to Man, . . . the very deepest and strongest . . . [is] that which asserts the Everlasting Reality of Religion." [27]

In this lecture Fiske showed the final way in which he combined the two impulses that had shaped his religious thought ever since his Middletown days. He had then been drawn to the Transcendentalists and theologians to whom the Reverend John Langdon Dudley had introduced him, as well as to the scientists and philosophers of science whose work he explored along with George Litch Roberts. He had long since repudiated Comte and Buckle, but he still asked of religion that it provide the coherent world view that had attracted him to these men. As his own religious ideas devel-

[26] JF, "Everlasting Reality," p. 358.
[27] JF, "Everlasting Reality," pp. 369, 371.

oped he drew closer to the Transcendentalists and he took his definition of religion in this oration almost directly from Theodore
Parker. This meant no great alteration in his basic approach. He
still drew his organizing ideas from science, though now reinter-
preting these concepts in a manner which better satisfied his emotional needs, and expressing his synthesis of the idealism of Theodore Parker with the agnosticism of Herbert Spencer in pious language that was far closer to that of theologians than that of scientists.

Though this mixture of Transcendentalism and Spencerian evolution theory satisfied Fiske and attracted audiences, it received
less favorable evaluations from many critics. Fiske's "scientific" proof
of religion aroused greatest interest when the volume containing
the three lectures appeared in print in 1899. All those with a religious inclination praised it, including the *Methodist Review* which
rejected the view taken of evil in the earlier lectures as unsatisfactory. The rare exception was John Bascom, who objected to the
narrowly naturalistic base upon which Fiske rested religion and
remarked that "it is amusing to see with what heartiness the orthodox are wont to pat Mr. Fiske on the shoulder as a doughty cham-
pion from the camp of the enemy whose dictum finishes discussion." [28]

Secularistically inclined reviewers were even less respectful than
Bascom. In *Popular Science Monthly,* now no longer edited by
Fiske's ally Youmans, the reviewer remarked that he did not have
"much faith in the method followed in" *Through Nature to God.*
An anonymous *Nation* reviewer of pragmatist inclinations sub-
jected the entire line of argument to scathing criticism. "The development of a wholly erroneous conception of the sun or moon,
or of another life, or of anything else which in some respects cannot
really influence the species, may be a 'true step,' providing it be
stimulating or tend to sustain life," this critic pointed out. He went

[28] John Bascom, Chicago *Dial*, 28:19–20 (Jan. 1, 1900). Favorable reviews appeared
in *Arena*, 22:294–295 (August 1899), and 25:365–372 (April 1901); *Century
Magazine*, 519:155–156 (November 1899); *Critic*, 35:734–735 (August 1899);
Methodist Review, 81:833–836 (September 1899); *New World*, 8:566–570 (September 1899); *Outlook*, 62:127–128 (May 13, 1899); *Poet Lore*, 11:309–312 (Spring
1899).

on to argue that since false ideas of religion would not necessarily lead to the death of believers or their failure to propagate, evolution would not eliminate such ideas. W. N. Guthrie in the *Sewanee Review* attacked Fiske's three postulates of religion as not justified by history. Much of the Old Testament did not share the second (belief in immortality) and had little of the third (stress on ethics), Confucius ignored the first (belief in God), and primitive Buddhism may even have denied all three. Guthrie noted that these three principles were, however, "the essentials of the Christian religion as understood by a large section of our cultured classes today." [29]

Guthrie's closing remark illustrates the changes in Christianity in the forty years following Fiske's revolt against orthodoxy. In the 1850's it was inconceivable that a view could be classified as Christian which had no place for a supernatural Christ; even Unitarians believed in this, while rejecting the Trinity. Now, to many churchgoers, a naturalistic view contained all that Christianity needed, as long as it supported ethics and held out some promise of immortality. Not everyone who listened to and applauded Fiske had reduced Christianity to this minimum level. Fiske's essentials were sufficiently vague and general, his phrasing adequately pious, to permit less acute auditors and readers to reach the comforting conclusion that they truly supported the creed which the believer desired to maintain.

Worth mentioning at this time, though not published until after his death, is Fiske's brief essay on immortality, *Life Everlasting,* originally given at Harvard in December 1900 as the annual Ingersoll Lecture. This was the final statement of Fiske's religious position, but it showed no noticeable advance in ideas over his 1876 *Unseen World,* despite an increased use of Christian terminology.

As he had a quarter century before, Fiske again made it clear that he did not believe that science could prove immortality. But it could not disprove it either. Fiske then used the series of analogies he had presented in his *Through Nature to God* to argue that the

[29] *Popular Science Monthly,* 56:268 (December 1899); see also letters from readers in 56:498–500 (February 1900). *Nation,* 69:118 (Aug. 10, 1899). *Sewanee Review,* 8:12–25 (January 1900), quotation from p. 18.

theory of evolution made it a distinct possibility. He then jumped easily from the assertion of possibility to the idea of certainty. "We are all agreed," he reminded his readers, "that life beyond the grave would be a delusion and a cruel mockery without the continuance of the tender household affections which alone make the present life worth living." This evidence, since it was inconceivable to Fiske that the universe might mock man, provided him with sufficient support for a confident faith in the survival of the soul after death.[30]

To the orthodox Congregationalist *Bibliotheca Sacra,* which had ignored Fiske's earlier essays, this now seemed "one of the most powerful and convincing defenses of the doctrine of immortality which have appeared since the speculations of modern science have raised new questions concerning it." Most religiously oriented reviewers praised the book, but the secular press tended to be more critical. To J. W. Chadwick, writing in the *Nation,* its affirmations were so pale and unconvincing that "it seems not impossible that some who go to this little book with a stout faith in immortality will come away from it with that faith perceptibly decreased." To this school, Fiske had merely succeeded in demonstrating how little scientists knew.[31]

Fiske was still engaged in the nineties in liquidating the religious controversies stirred up in the seventies by the theory of evolution. He was not alone in such an approach; outstanding writers like Henry Drummond and Joseph Le Conte similarly went on repeating in the nineties approaches to religious problems they had worked out earlier. What they had to say was by then fully acceptable to those concerned over such matters, and had been for almost a decade. Southern Presbyterians might hold the line and be willing to dismiss professors from their theological seminary if they accepted evolution, but in the North the center of religious controversy had moved on to a new area. A leader of "progressive orthodoxy" noted in 1891 that "we were bravely over our fright from evolution, and were beginning to breathe easier, but, before we are

---

[30] JF, "Life Everlasting," in *Studies,* pp. 377–420, quotation from p. 400.
[31] *Bibliotheca Sacra,* 59:206–207 (January 1902). *Critic,* 39:581 (December 1901). Chicago *Dial,* 32:126 (Feb. 16, 1902). *Harvard Monthly,* 3:166–169 (January 1902). *Methodist Review,* 84:166–167 (January 1902). *Nation,* 73:282 (Oct. 10, 1901).

fairly rested, we are taking new alarms from Biblical criticism." [32] Critical approaches to the Bible, which had been discussed for several decades, became the major disturber of religious peace in the nineties—every religious journal examined showed traces of the controversy it aroused. Although Fiske had written on such themes in the seventies, he contributed nothing to this debate. After some time, and some acrimonious discussion, theologians of liberal leanings began to accept the results of the application of principles of historical criticism to the New Testament. The concept of evolution in religion which these men had welcomed in the eighties made it easier for them to agree that even the Bible was the product of developmental change, and that the Gospels might contain ideas which the race had outgrown.

But fervent evangelicals, heavily represented in such denominations as Methodist, Baptist, and old-school Presbyterian, which had been least affected by evolutionary theology, found it difficult to accept such ideas. The greatest evangelist of the century, Dwight L. Moody, had been willing to associate with religious liberals, even though he never accepted their theological ideas. So long as they accepted Christianity as a saving religion, Moody could cooperate with them; to him, as to most revivalists, doctrine, as such, was not essential.

Biblical criticism of the New Testament widened the gap between evangelicals and liberals and made such toleration more difficult, if not impossible, in the future. Interpreting Christ as a human figure expressing primarily an ethical position, around whose striking life and death a set of mythical beliefs had been constructed by later and lesser men, as liberal theologians using Biblical criticism tended to do, would support a religion of ethics but not the religion of salvation preached by the evangelicals. In rural and lower-class urban America the reaction to the critics took the form of wholesale rejection of all ideas associated with modern-

---

[32] George Harris, "Ethical Christianity and Biblical Criticism," *Andover Review*, 15:461–471 (May 1891), quotation from p. 461. Henry Drummond, *Natural Law in the Spiritual World* (New York, 1884), *The Ascent of Man* (New York, 1894). Joseph Le Conte, *Religion and Science* (New York, 1873), *Evolution, Its Nature, Its Evidences, and Its Relation to Religious Thought* (rev. ed., New York, 1891 [1st ed., 1889]), *Autobiography* (New York, 1903).

ism. The evangelicals attacked not only Biblical criticism, but also the whole complex of theological concepts that religious liberalism had advanced. Although Fundamentalism as a movement did not really start until the twentieth century, the origins of the movement can be discerned in the nineties, though not in the years when evolution was the center of controversy.[33] To the evangelicals, who probably constituted the majority of religiously inclined Americans in the nineteenth century, Fiske had little appeal. Since his essays did not deal with the aspects of new ideas that most concerned them, they ignored his work.

IV

Fiske's plans for historical writing in the last part of the nineties carried him into areas of the American experience which until then he had left almost untreated. To round out his history of the colonies in the seventeenth century, begun in his *Beginnings of New England,* Fiske planned two books, one on the South and the other on the middle colonies. One or two more volumes on the eighteenth century would link these up with his already published work on the American Revolution and the period of confederation, forming a complete set of books covering American history through the formation of the Constitution. His work on the southern and Middle-Atlantic colonies involved Fiske in the consideration of ways of life he found much less admirable than those of his beloved New England.

Fiske had little sympathy with either area. While working on the southern book, he tried to extend his lecture tours into the South. Visits to New Orleans and the University of Virginia, speaking engagements in Kentucky and other southern states appeared on his lecture route for the first time. But Fiske did not find this experiment satisfactory. Financial results were not encouraging, the people were not to his liking, and the scenery too unfamiliar. "I was all day Sunday passing through the state of Mississippi, and a more dismal, wretched, woe-be-gone, out-at-elbows, down-at-heel country

---

[33] S. G. Cole, *The History of Fundamentalism* (New York, 1931). W. R. Moody, *D. L. Moody* (New York, 1900). Gamaliel Bradford, *D. L. Moody* (New York, 1927).

I have never set eyes on," he complained to his mother. "Compared with almost all other places, how beautiful New England is, and how clean and civilized! I believe I would rather die than live down here." [34]

These words clearly revealed the limits of Fiske's sympathies, a limit which caused difficulties when he tried to expand his view of American destiny to new areas. For he now had to show the relevance of the basic philosophical structure of his earlier work to the southern and middle colonies. To do so Fiske had to demonstrate how varying social and ethnic elements fitted the American evolutionary pattern he had laid out. But this he could not do, though he did make the attempt.

Once again he directed the reader's attention to God's plan for America, the development and expansion of English political ideas of liberty. Fiske interpreted Virginian local government as a reversion to the Teutonic past, though not in as pure a form as New England townships, since the extended settlement needed for plantations made counties more practical than smaller units. After briefly describing political development during the first decade of Virginia's settlement he assured his readers that "in the unfolding of these events there is poetic beauty and grandeur as the purpose of Infinite Wisdom reveals itself in its cosmic process, slowly but inexorably, hasting not but resting not, heedless of the clashing aims and discordant cries of short-sighted mortals, sweeping their tiny efforts into its majestic current, and making all contribute to the fulfillment of God's will." [35]

Fiske tried to use the ethnic similarity of the settlers in Virginia and New England as a means of understanding the South; he then employed the resemblances to justify treating Virginia as if it were only Massachusetts in a warmer climate. He insisted upon the homogeneity of population between New England and the South. "The distinction between Cavalier and Roundhead was no more a difference in respect of lineage or social rank than the analogous distinction between Tory and Whig." Thus, while accepting the

[34] Quotation from JF to his mother, Mar. 3, 1896, HHL. JF to Abby, Mar. 11, 1893, Oct. 26, 1895, Mar. 8, 1896, HHL.
[35] JF, *Old Virginia and Her Neighbors,* 2 vols. (Boston, 1902), I, 228.

myth of a great Cavalier migration to Virginia, Fiske could still argue that "the settlers of Virginia and New England were opposed to each other in politics, but they belonged to one and the same stratum of society, and in their personal characteristics they were of the same excellent quality." [36]

Fiske had already put on record his high estimate of the New England settlers and, when he said that Virginians shared "the same excellent quality," he undoubtedly meant to be flattering. But it is questionable that southerners would agree, or that they would find anything to attract them in Fiske's implied conclusion that the meaning of southern political development could best be seen in the more democratic evolution of a New England they disliked and distrusted.

The attempt to pass lightly over variations between the two areas of first settlement in America forced Fiske to ignore real divergences between the two regions. For Fiske the differences were far less significant than the ethnic similarity. Since both regions were English by descent, he preferred to emphasize resemblances and permit the distinctive qualities of the South to appear only in the colorful anecdotes with which he studded the course of his flowing narrative.

For the Middle-Atlantic region, treated in *The Dutch and Quaker Colonies in America,* Fiske's conceptual scheme proved even less useful. For now he had to deal with groups that not only experienced varying paths of evolution from that of New England, but were also of different ethnic origin. Yet they, too, had arrived at democratic results not unlike those of the "English" colonies. Fiske's explanation of this outcome was simple: the English imported democratic ideas when they conquered the Dutch colonies, which until then had been tyrannies ruled by agents of the Dutch West India Company. Fiske thought the ethnic variety of these colonies had hindered their democratic development. He had in an earlier book indicated his opinion that this heterogeneity explained the differing ways the colonies reacted to George III and his ministers when they attempted tyranny. In the ethnically homogeneous

---

[36] JF, *Old Virginia,* II, 14–15, 32, 34–51.

areas, "when the revolutionary war came, there were very few
Tories in the New England colonies and very few in Virginia; but
there were a great many in New York and Pennsylvania and the
two Carolinas." [37]

An adequate treatment of the religious diversity of this region
also eluded Fiske. He had little sympathy with those who emi-
grated to America in order to be able to carry on a sectarian life
in a manner of their own choosing. As a result his treatment of
pietistic sects presented the central aspects of their lives as mere
humorous peculiarities. He made effective use of the description of
New York City in the travel account of Dankers and Sluyter, two
advance agents of a minor pietistic sect who came to America to
find a location where their group could live its own religious life
undisturbed. But, when Fiske turned from the descriptive material
in the diary to sections where the opinions of the travelers entered,
he presented them as two comic Dutchmen loose in a strange
land.[38]

Similarly he found it difficult to deal with the Scotch-Irish immigrants. He discussed their contributions briefly in *Old Virginia*.
But, although he had promised to take up their work on the frontier
in his *Dutch and Quaker Colonies,* he devoted even less space in
this book to them. Never did he come to grips with the problem
of evaluating their differences from, or similarity to, his English
ideas, nor with the related problem that a consideration of this
group would have led to, that of determining the relation of his
concept of the evolution of American liberty to the Turner thesis
on the influence of the frontier which was currently attracting attention.[39]

The concepts of these two books were still attractive to Fiske's
old audience, even if southerners and other Americans who did
not think of themselves as primarily of New England origin might
not react enthusiastically to them. Those who desired to believe in

[37] JF, *The Dutch and Quaker Colonies in America,* 2 vols. (Boston, 1902),
especially, I, 230; II, 304–307. Quotation from *The War of Independence* (Boston,
1899), p. 12.
[38] JF, *Dutch and Quaker,* II, 86–101.
[39] JF, *Old Virginia,* II, 456–463; *Dutch and Quaker,* II, 410–414.

the identity of Americanism with the New England heritage, or the identity of religion with the abstractions of liberal Calvinism, did not see any decline in Fiske's work. But one did not have to be a southerner or desire to build a myth of aristocratic origins to find that Fiske had not dealt adequately with the unique aspects of the southern experience, nor did one have to be a descendant of Dutch settlers to see the accuracy of Mrs. Schuyler Van Rensselaer's devastating critique of Fiske's book on the middle colonies.[40]

In a lengthy analysis which appeared in the *North American Review* of August 1901 (with unfortunate timing, within a month after Fiske's death), Mrs. Van Rensselaer thoroughly demolished any pretensions to scholarship that Fiske might still have had. She noted that he had used only such sources as were most easily available, "and on scores of pages he shows that he was very careless even in the use of the narratives and documents that he did consult. His mistakes in matters of fact are frequent and sometimes very grave." She devoted some sixteen pages to detailing these errors, of which only two need be noted here, since they characterize Fiske's methods and indicate the way his sympathies and preconceived ideas affected his understanding of history.[41]

Fiske followed the portrayals of Dutch governors contained in Washington Irving's comic *Knickerbocker History*, ignoring the more reliable information in works cited in his footnotes. This made for entertaining lectures, but did not indicate a proper understanding of his subject or of scholarly method. She also proved that while Fiske said that the residents of New Netherlands petitioned

[40] Basically favorable reviews of *Old Virginia* appeared in: *Atlantic Monthly*, 81:274–278 (February 1898); Chicago *Dial*, 17:73–74 (Feb. 1, 1898); *Methodist Review*, 81:169–171 (January 1899); *Nation*, 66:36–37 (Jan. 13, 1898); *Outlook*, 60:818–820 (Dec. 3, 1898). Scholars qualified praise while pointing out errors: *American Historical Review*, 3:734–738 (July 1898); *Political Science Quarterly*, 13:334–338 (June 1898); *English Historical Review*, 13:367–368 (April 1898).

The reception of *Dutch and Quaker* was similar, although it is interesting to note that the *Critic*, after praising the original edition [36:366–367 (April 1900)], greeted the appearance of an illustrated edition with the complaint that Fiske lacked sympathy for his subject [44:478–479 (May 1904)]. In the interval Mrs. Van Rensselaer's critique had appeared.

[41] Mrs. Schuyler Van Rensselaer, "Mr. Fiske and the History of New York," *North American Review*, 173:171–189 (August 1901), quotation from p. 172.

for a New England style of local government, what they actually asked for was the form familiar to them from their homeland. Mrs. Van Rensselaer conclusively demonstrated that Fiske had failed to see or appreciate the burgeoning democratic spirit of the settlement that the despotic rule of the Dutch West India Company had failed to stamp out.

Fiske's basic philosophical position was probably more to blame for his misunderstanding of his material than his weakness as a scholar. Errors of fact were frequent in Fiske's earlier works. No attempt has been made to track down every mistake in his *Beginnings of New England,* but if a list were to be compiled it might well equal in length, if not exceed, Mrs. Van Rensselaer's indictment. Yet these errors had not distorted the significance of the events he narrated in that volume. Actually, Fiske's use of scholarly materials had improved, though none of his later books showed the same scholarship as his *Discovery of America.* Fiske had more monographic studies to draw on for his later works, due to the activity of academic historians in the closing decades of the century. He used many of the items in the Johns Hopkins University *Studies in Political and Historical Science* and seldom went wrong when summarizing their results. Thus his brief section on Maryland (whose early history had been thoroughly explored by Hopkins graduate students) won the praise of H. L. Osgood as the most accurate part of *Old Virginia.*[42] However, available monographs covered only minor parts of the extensive sweep of time and wide area over which Fiske carried his narrative. Fiske also cited more primary materials in his later volumes, but his exploitation of such sources was erratic, at times almost accidental. Fiske's use of certain documentary sets relating to the history of New York apparently depended on gifts from friends. Chance acquaintances met in the course of lecture tours suggested other vital sources to him. These materials provided much social detail, and his last books included chapters describing life in the colonies.[43]

Fiske's scholarly grasp, never too secure, had improved between

[42] *Political Science Quarterly,* 13:334 (June 1898).
[43] JF, "Preface" to *Dutch and Quaker,* I, vii–viii.

The Beginnings of New England and his *Dutch and Quaker Colonies*. He had better and more extensive monographs to draw upon, and was more aware of the possibility of using primary materials. If his lack of critical ability meant that he used these sources mostly for decoration and dramatic effect, this was no major change from his earlier practice. Not merely a failure of scholarship, but a failure in applying his philosophical scheme, explains the drop in quality between Fiske's earlier and later historical works.

Fiske interpreted the American experience as a divinely inspired growth in peace and freedom resulting from the predestined conquest of the continent by English political ideas. In this process New England was the leader and prime exemplar. Once he turned from New England (or from the revolutionary and constitutional periods, in which the contributions of all the sections were similar) Fiske had little sympathy for the people whose activity he described. He tried to fit them into his conceptual scheme by stressing the ways in which they resembled New Englanders rather than by examining the unique values which every group contributed to the American experience. Thus, to Fiske the English descent of Virginians was of far greater importance than what they actually did. He portrayed the Dutch as trying to imitate New England even when his evidence did not justify such a view.

Fiske need not necessarily have found this problem difficult. His conceptual scheme was sufficiently vague to be adaptable to almost any situation. It could easily have been adjusted to conform to the actual growth of liberty observable in the development of America's middle and southern colonies, had it been merely a logical conclusion about the meaning of American history. But Fiske's scheme expressed more than just logic. It was also his personal emotional reaction to his country and to history. Fiske treasured above all else the contribution of New England and its heritage from Old England. He tried to interpret everything in terms of the section of the country he found most congenial. Thus, in a vital sense, Fiske wrote as an ethnic historian celebrating the virtues of New England and its contributions to the United States in a way not too greatly different from that in which other ethnic historians might praise the Dutch, or Scotch, or German, or Irish influences upon American history. Fiske wrote with understanding about New England and about aspects of the nation's history in which his favored section was in step with the rest of the nation. When he wrote of other areas, Fiske felt little sympathy and the quality of his workmanship declined.

CHAPTER TWELVE

THE ASHES OF SUCCESS

By all objective measures the closing years of John Fiske's life were a time of great success. Honors poured in. His lecture tours became triumphal progresses across the land, and his income reached new and previously undreamed-of heights. He had become a celebrity, eagerly sought out both in Cambridge and while on tour.

Yet all his triumphs had a tinge of emptiness. Although he accumulated honors and popular approval, his scholarly reputation dropped. Even the enormous sums he now earned failed to match his ability to spend. And if his status as celebrity pleased, it too presented problems.

Awards of one sort or another arrived regularly in Fiske's last years. In 1896 the intellectual élite of Boston elected him to the famous Saturday Club. The Lowell Institute sponsored lecture presentations of his last three books of history. Harvard twice, in 1895 and 1896, asked him to lecture to students, after having presented him with an honorary Doctor of Laws degree in 1894. In 1899 Harvard alumni elected him to his third term as Overseer. The University of Pennsylvania gave Fiske a Doctor of Letters degree in 1894, and in 1901 Yale invited him to attend its 200th anniversary celebration in October and accept a Doctor of Laws degree. By 1900 the inner circle of the American Historical Association considered Fiske a possible candidate for the presidency of their organization. Both the Academy of Science of Brazil and the American Academy of Arts and Sciences, had elected him to membership. On the title page of the 1901 edition of his *History of the United States for Schools,* Fiske listed seventeen national and local historical associations to which he belonged. England, too, paid tribute to his fame. The committee organizing the millennial celebration of the reign of King Alfred asked him to speak on behalf of America at the dedication of a statue of the king in Winchester planned for the summer of 1901.[1]

Both at home and on tour, Fiske was now a celebrity. Young men traveled to Cambridge to consult him about their literary careers, interviewers sought his opinion on current events. Thinking of his honors and celebrity, Fiske might well have been pleased. But even fame proved to have its drawbacks. Outside demands on his time ate into hours he would have preferred to devote to his own affairs. The nation had not developed as he had anticipated, and interviews forced him to consider aspects of his age difficult for him to reconcile with his optimistic predictions about the future. Trends in urbanization, immigration, industrialization, and in national and international affairs disturbed him.

When asked by Houghton, Mifflin and Company to write a textbook on civics for use in high schools, Fiske organized the work about his favorite ideas on the way American local and federal government carried Anglo-Teutonic concepts and methods of rule to new peaks of development. But in this book he had also to consider problems faced by municipalities. "Our republican government," he noted sadly, "which, after making all due allowances, seems to work remarkably well in rural districts, and in the states, and in the nation, has certainly been far less successful as applied to cities." Instead of citizens ruling, corrupt political gangs controlled the large urban areas. He placed the blame on "the great mass of ignorant voters, chiefly foreigners without experience in

---

[1] JF to C. W. Eliot, Nov. 1, 1895, Oct. 24, 1896, HUL. JF to H. A. Richmond, Feb. 28, 1898; Alfred Bowker to JF, Sept. 9, 1900, HHL. C. W. Bowen to H. B. Adams, Nov. 24, 1900, in *Historical Scholarship in the United States,* W. S. Holt, ed. (Baltimore, 1938), p. 238. *The Later Years of the Saturday Club,* M. A. DeWolfe Howe, ed. (Boston, 1927), pp. vi–vii.

self-government, and with no comprehension of American principles and traditions." Fiske could see no simple way to cure this
breakdown in self-government. Although opposing a limitation on
the franchise, since he still believed that in time everyone would
assimilate his ideas, he did approve of plans to limit voter control
by making civic affairs partially nonelective. Thus, looking at the
way cities actually functioned forced Fiske to abandon part of his
dream of an automatic expansion of democracy.[2]

Urban development presented Fiske with phenomena that he
could only with difficulty fit into his vision of the future of America. The growth of large foreign-born, or second- and third-genera-
tion, electorates in cities, and the way such voters turned for leadership to men of their own group, rather than the New England
stock Fiske felt to be best qualified, was an aspect of American life
he found especially disillusioning. Out of this disquiet grew his
involvement in the immigration restriction movement.

In 1894 a group of young Harvard graduates who resented the
steady drift of power in the nation away from New England, for
which they blamed the immigration of "inferior breeds" from the
south and west of Europe, organized the Immigration Restriction
League to work for an ending of all immigration. After attempts
to achieve a complete halt proved politically impractical, the group
settled on the device of a literacy test as the best way to keep out
those whom they most disliked. Heavily infected with ideas of
racial supremacy and inferiority, they believed that some peoples,
such as Slavs, Latins, Greeks, and Hungarians, were inherently
illiterate. Thus a literacy test, while not halting all immigration,
would limit it to the lands they favored, Britain, Germany, and
the Scandinavian countries.[3]

While the version of racism which inspired the League was
much more virulent than the milder attitude Fiske had expressed
in his previous writing, he did not seem conscious that these ideas

[2] JF, *Civil Government in the United States* (Boston, 1902), especially pp. 105–151;
quotations from pp. 127, 147. First edition published in 1890.
[3] See Barbara M. Solomon, *Ancestors and Immigrants* (Cambridge, Mass., 1956),
and John Higham, *Strangers in the Land, Patterns of American Nativism, 1860–1925*
(Brunswick, N.J., 1955).

differed from his own. Intellectually, Fiske still held to the belief that the great Anglo-American community could assimilate any race, an idea that contradicted the basic belief of the League that certain races were inherently unassimilable and must be kept out of the United States. But the drift of power away from New England elements in the country disturbed Fiske as much as it did the young men. Having no clear idea himself of how to combat the aspects of American life he disliked, Fiske agreed to cooperate with those who thought they had.

The executive committee of the League, after trying for six months to get a prominent public figure to accept the presidency of their organization, and being refused by seven men, turned to Fiske in November 1894. Fiske accepted, but, so far as the records indicate, contributed only his name to the work of the League. In December 1894 the secretary was instructed to write to Fiske "saying that as he is an ex officio member of the executive committee, the committee will be glad to have him attend meetings, telling him when and where the committee meets, and that if that time is inconvenient the committee would be glad to know what time will suit him." But Fiske did not take the hint; he was never marked present at any session, not even the annual meetings which regularly reelected him president until his resignation in the spring of 1899. Fiske's national celebrity made his name useful in the publicity work of the League, but his own intense round of lecturing and writing left him no time to be more than a letterhead supporter and figurehead president.[4]

The rise in imperial sentiments that led to the Spanish-American War caused Fiske even more intellectual discomfort than did problems of immigration. Fiske's ideas on Manifest Destiny attracted many who leaned to expansion. His *American Political Ideas* and his later historical and religious works provided a theoretical justification for imperialism with their praise of America and England

[4] Manuscript Records of the Executive Committee of the Immigration Restriction League, Prescott Hall Papers, HUL; quotation from vol. I, meeting of Dec. 13, 1894. In his *Civil Government,* which he frequently revised in the nineties to keep it up to date as a textbook, Fiske retained in print a version of racism which varied from that of the League, since it stressed the ability of all races to become assimilated in time.

as the leaders of evolution and the predestined rulers of the globe. But Fiske expected that this predominance would be peacefully obtained through the voluntary adhesion of less-favored peoples; its great justification in his eyes was that such expansion would lead to universal peace and freedom.

To Fiske the outbreak of hostilities with Spain came as a shock, for this resort to force, even if he put most of the blame on Spain, seemed a regression from, and almost a flat contradiction of, his vision of the American future. When debate began to center about the annexation of the Philippines, Fiske at first joined those opposing American retention of the islands. But second thoughts soon assailed him as defenders of annexation appealed to Fiske's own ideas on the value of American political leadership for backward peoples. He cancelled a scheduled appearance at an anti-imperialist protest rally and began to support annexation. His vacillation revealed how uncertain Fiske was over how to apply his ideas to late nineteenth-century reality, how hard it was for him to face the way the nation had moved away from his vision of its ideal future.

In 1896, when Bryan captured the Democratic nomination for President, Fiske left the political party he had supported for nearly thirty years. Sound money was basic in Fiske's economic creed, and he backed McKinley. Fiske found many of the aggressive, rising industrialists uneasy company. Fiske had expected the triumph of industrialism to insure peace in the future. Not only had industrialism not done so, not only had it brought with it an increased immigration and urbanization he disliked, but he discovered that he also personally disliked many of the men who led the changes in industry. He had been flattered in 1885 when Andrew Carnegie gave a supper party in his honor, but thereafter he preferred to avoid his company.[5]

The steady stream of admiring visitors to his home satisfied Fiske no more than the contemplation of current events. Fiske still had to

[5] JF to Richmond, Nov. 4, 1896; JF to Gamaliel Bradford, June 14, 1898 [marked "never sent"]; JF to Abby, Jan. 21, 1885, Apr. 1, 1885; JF to Henry Holt, Apr. 8, 1896, HHL. W. D. Quint, "John Fiske in Cambridge," New York *Times Saturday Review,* Oct. 15, 1898. A. K. Weinberg, *Manifest Destiny* (Baltimore, 1935), especially chap. VIII.

work hard in order to keep up the flow of money. When callers came he often felt tired, and sometimes fell asleep while being interviewed. Above all he disliked people who tried to engage him in serious conversations. "He could not under ordinary circumstances be dragged into an oral discussion," his acquaintance, A. M. Davis, noted. Even among friends, Fiske "dearly loved not to chat, but to fold his legs and have his talk out," as George Perry remarked. Debate took too much effort; Fiske preferred to pontificate. Worries over his family continued. His third son, Ralph (the only one of his children to show signs of following Fiske in a literary career, who had had one poem and a translation from the French published), died suddenly in 1898 when only 27 years old. Harold continued to suffer relapses which frightened Fiske and strained family finances.[6]

Fiske's sedentary habits adversely affected his health, but did not diminish his enjoyment of life. As his weight approached three hundred pounds he found it hard to get around. Friends noticed a shortness of breath every time he had to climb stairs; his family worried and consulted doctors. For relaxation Fiske turned to his piano, to overseeing the work in his garden and conservatory, and to playing with his children (and now the grandchildren who had begun to arrive). Music remained his special love and he was never happier than when listening or joining his friends in musical evenings at which he could sing German lieder. J. K. Hosmer remembered listening with him to a Rubinstein sonata one summer afternoon, and watching "the great frame of my fellow-guest heave with emotion while his breath came almost in sobs as his spirit responded to the music." All of Fiske's friends testified to a quality of childlike freshness and spontaneity that he never lost during his

[6] Quotations from A. M. Davis, "John Fiske," in American Academy of Arts and Sciences, *Proceedings,* 37:675 (August 1901), and George Perry, "Great American Scientists, VIII: John Fiske," *Chautauquan,* 50:273 (April 1908). *Bookman,* 14:10–11 (September 1901). S. M. Crothers, "John Fiske," in *Later Years of the Saturday Club,* pp. 273–275. Ralph Browning Fiske, *The Count of Nideck,* adapted from the French of Erckmann-Chatrian (Boston, 1897), and "Petersham" [poem], *Atlantic Monthly,* 84:428–429 (September 1899). Boston *Evening Transcript,* June 16, 1898, June 18, 1898. JF to James Brooks, Nov. 21, 1894; JF to Martha Brooks, Sept. 27, 1895; JF to his mother, Aug. 30, 1897, HHL. C. B. Hoyt to JF, Sept. 27, 1892, Fiske Collection, U.C.L.A. Library.

life, which fascinated every acquaintance. Despite his age and bulk and burdens, Fiske could always relax and enjoy himself. As one friend remarked after his death, "His burly, bulky figure . . . sheltered a jovial soul, one that met life like a call to dinner, and whose appetite for living never failed." [7]

Even when Fiske traveled he took along work. Franklin Head, with whom Fiske regularly stayed for two or three weeks at a time while lecturing in Chicago, remembered him arriving "in a cab loaded inside and outside with big grip-sacks and dress-suit cases, eight or ten in number, and mostly full of music books and books of reference to use at his leisure hours in his historical work." As at home, Fiske consistently refused to discuss ideas at the dinner parties and receptions given in his honor after lectures. If pressed, he might extemporaneously present brief talks based on his most popular lectures. But whenever possible he would substitute a session at the piano where he could play or sing for his admirers the Schubert and Schumann songs he loved. At other times he would repeat from memory long extracts from his favorite English novels. [8]

Despite the social whirl of his tours, Fiske usually squeezed out two or three hours a day for writing. Often he managed to get more work done while on tour than amid the manifold distractions, both pleasant and unpleasant, of his home life. When he could, Fiske examined the special holdings of libraries on his lecture route. But these investigations were always haphazard; Fiske was unsystematic and he rarely seems to have bothered to take notes. When he sat down to write he depended mainly on the few reference books he had about him and upon a phenomenal memory for facts and

[7] Quotation from J. K. Hosmer, *The Last Leaf* (New York, 1910), pp. 176–177, and [anonymous], "John Fiske's Simplicity," *Atlantic Monthly,* 88:717–718 (November 1901). S. S. Green, "John Fiske," in American Antiquarian Society, *Proceedings,* n.s. 14:422 (October 1901). T. S. Perry, "Appreciation," *Atlantic Monthly,* 89:636–637 (May 1902). W. R. Spaulding, *Music at Harvard* (New York, 1935), pp. 194–195.

[8] F. H. Head, *John Fiske* (Chicago, [1902?]), p. 5. JF to Abby, Mar. 4, 1893, Feb. 27, 1895, Mar. 20, 1895, Mar. 30, 1895, Feb. 24, 1896, Jan. 24, 1897, Apr. 12, 1897, HHL.

dates that never failed to amaze his acquaintances. James Ford Rhodes recalled listening with wonder as Fiske held his own in an argument with several military historians that involved the tactical details of Napoleon's Italian campaigns. When Rhodes later expressed surprise at his knowledge, Fiske candidly replied: "It is all due to one book. . . . A few summers ago I had occasion to read Sir Edward Hamley's 'Operations of War' and for some reason or other everything in it seemed to sink into my mind and to be there retained, ready for use, as was the case tonight with his references to the Northern Italian campaigns." With such a memory Fiske needed to do little more than compile and try to put what he remembered into an organizational frame that would be meaningful to his listeners and convince them that he had demonstrated the true significance of the events he narrated.[9]

II

Fiske's expenditures continued to increase at their usual rate in the last years of his life. Despite his rising income he still had difficulty paying all his bills. He turned to his publishers for help and, with some reluctance as the total of his advances against royalties swelled, they came to his rescue. The company permitted Fiske to draw heavy advances against copyrights of books published before the salary agreement went into effect. By June of 1897 the debit against these royalties, which averaged little more than $1,000 per year, had risen to $6,830.[10]

Late in 1897, inspired by a suggestion from his Buffalo friend and former creditor, Henry Richmond, Fiske requested that Houghton, Mifflin and Company renegotiate his contract. He asked that the salary he had been receiving for the past nine years be treated as an advance on royalties of the histories and school books he had turned over to the publisher in these years. He also asked

[9] Quotation from J. F. Rhodes, *Historical Essays* (New York, 1909), p. 70. Henry Holt, *Garrulities of an Octogenarian Editor* (Boston, 1923), pp. 302, 343. Head, *Fiske,* pp. 11–12. S. S. Green, "Fiske," p. 423. W. D. Howells, "John Fiske," *Harpers' Weekly,* 45:732 (July 20, 1901). JF to Abby, Jan. 15, 1897, Mar. 15, 1897, HHL.

[10] G. H. Mifflin to JF, June 23, 1896, HMCo papers, 10:548–551; June 2, 1897, 10:906–907. JF to Abby, Apr. 18, 1897, HHL.

a further advance of $6,000 against future earnings of his existing copyrights, and an increase in the yearly salary schedule.[11]

The publishers, who were anxious to have Fiske's next two books in order to get a completed multivolume set on the Colonial period to merchandise by their efficient subscription department, agreed. They also raised his current salary to $1,000 a month while he wrote the next two books, and offered a bonus of a further $1,000 for each if completed on the date stipulated; this salary would be an advance against future royalties of the histories. Thus, if Fiske completed his work precisely on schedule, he would receive $15,000 as advance royalties on his *Dutch and Quaker Colonies* and $24,000 on his *New France and New England*.[12]

Fiske was jubilant at the terms of the contract. "Did the publishers do this willingly?" he asked Richmond rhetorically. "No. Why did they do it? Because I threatened to leave; and they preferred to surrender the advantage they had gained, rather than forego the advantages which they hope will come from my future work." He assured Richmond that his triumph over his publishers would permit him to live much more comfortably. "I can at once give up my annual lecturing journey! Hereafter I shall lecture only when I feel like it, just for a change of scene. No more three month stretches!" [13]

One year of reduced lecturing again disordered Fiske's financial arrangements. As always, Fiske's scale of living went on expanding, and family illnesses did not cease. Even the large salary Houghton, Mifflin and Company now paid him proved inadequate. In November of 1898 he notified his publisher that he wished to put into print three volumes of lectures which he had written and used in his tours of the previous two decades, but had until now withheld from publication. For these he desired to be paid by special arrangement.[14]

[11] F. G. G[arrison] to A. F. H[oughton], Dec. 6, 1897, HMCo papers, 21:49–56. JF to H. A. Richmond, Dec. 29, 1897, HHL.

[12] F. G. G[arrison] to A. F. H[oughton], Dec. 6, 1897, HMCo papers, 21:49–56; HMCo to Richard Stone [JF's lawyer], Dec. 9, 1897, 21:59–61, and Dec. 15, 1897, 21:64.

[13] JF to H. A. Richmond, Dec. 29, 1897, HHL.

[14] JF to his mother, Aug. 1, 1898, HHL. JF to Stuart F. Weld, Aug. 2, 1898, William L. Clements Library, University of Michigan. G. H. Mifflin to Mr. Dabney [HMCo's lawyer], Nov. 9, 1898, HMCo papers, 21:371.

Although annoyed by this new exaction, the company finally agreed to publish the books outside the salary agreement and pay for them separately, without deducting the royalties they earned from the outstanding advances which by then—January 1, 1899—totaled $19,469.81, and increased faster than earnings due to the $1,000 monthly payments. To insure the value of the completed set upon which they depended to pay off the debit position caused by these large advances, the company insisted that Fiske promise not to publish with any other house material which directly competed with the histories Fiske was writing for them.[15]

Apparently Houghton, Mifflin either did not know of, or did not think any conflict existed between, the work Fiske did for them and the three-volume history of the United States he wrote for Lea Brothers of Philadelphia. To make a multivolume world history which they had had translated from German more attractive to American purchasers, the Philadelphia publishers printed Fiske's three volumes as the concluding section of their twenty-four volume set. In these books Fiske drew heavily upon his earlier work for Harpers, as well as condensing material from his extensive Colonial history.[16]

III

Lack of data makes precise determination of the total circulation achieved by Fiske's books impossible. Only one statement of actual royalty figures is available, a memorandum prepared in the course of the 1899 negotiations giving earnings for the period July 1, 1898 to January 1, 1899. Analysis of this statement provides a basis for at least tentative conclusions on the sale of his works.

[15] HMCo to Mr. Dabney, Feb. 9, 1899, HMCo papers, 21:465–466; Feb. 11, 1899, 21:473–476; Feb. 21, 1899, 21:493a. Under this agreement the house brought out three books in 1899 and 1900, *A Century of Science* (1899), a collection of recent essays and lectures in which Fiske repeated his familiar views on Spencerian evolution and an assortment of other topics, *Through Nature to God* (1899), his three most recent religious lectures, and *The Civil War in the Mississippi Valley* (1900), the talks which Fiske had prepared in 1885 during his abortive attempt to win a place on the lyceum circuit and which he had gone on repeating in the nineties.

[16] JF, *The Colonization of the New World, The Independence of the New World, The Modern Development of the New World,* in *A History of All Nations,* vols. XXI, XXII, XXIII (Philadelphia, 1902).

Since the data cover the Christmas season, the best selling time of the year, they represent more than half of the yearly earnings of these books and cannot simply be multiplied by two to give an annual figure. The total royalties earned in the six months was $6,140.59. Of this sum, $1,070.20 came from illustrated editions, while $2,314.79 was from school texts; the sales of both these items depended on the steady pressure the publishers exerted through advertising and direct solicitation. Only $2,747.60 came from regular editions and reflected book store sales. The total earnings of all Fiske's books for the full year probably did not reach $10,000, an interesting contrast with the $12,000 salary the house paid Fiske. The publisher obviously depended upon effective merchandising of the full set of histories, when this was complete, to make the contract profitable.[17]

Unfortunately this statement does not give the figure which would be of greater interest than Fiske's money earnings; it does not tell how many copies of Fiske's works were sold. But it does give some slender basis for an estimate. Royalties of $2,747.60 on book store sales, at a rate of 15 per cent, and with most of Fiske's books selling at $2.00 a volume, indicates that fewer than 10,000 volumes were sold in six months. Making allowance for the fact that many of his books were in two volumes, and remembering that these six months contained more than half the year's business, leaves it as a reasonable conclusion that bookstore sales of Fiske's titles did not total 10,000 copies a year. To this should be added totals for illustrated editions and school books sold. In years in which a new title appeared (no new work by Fiske was published in 1898) bookstore sales would undoubtedly be higher. Estimating what Fiske's total sales were in a year could be no more than a guess.

The figure for bookstore sales is not really as low as it looks to eyes accustomed to the enormous sales which nonfiction titles attain today. In the nineteenth century the outstanding figures were mostly achieved by novels. Fiske was never a best-seller in this sense. Collection of information on sales of leading books did not begin until

[17] HMCo to Mr. Dabney, Jan. 27, 1899, HMCo papers, 21:457–458.

nearly the end of the century, so only a few of Fiske's books could have appeared on best-seller lists, but the fate of his *Dutch and Quaker Colonies* indicates the limited appeal of Fiske's work. The *Bookman,* the first magazine to regularly collect and print data on leading books, referred to it in November 1899, shortly after the book appeared, as "undoubtedly the leading book outside of fiction, and . . . already in good demand." Yet Fiske's book rated very low in the lists of five best-sellers which twenty-seven dealers across the country sent to the magazine. The listings for October sales (given in the December issue), mentioned Fiske once; the Albany book dealer put him in fourth place. In November the only mention was a fourth-place rating in Boston; in December the book was in fourth place in Pittsburgh. These three ratings were all. Compared with the fiction titles that dominated these lists (they did not segregate novels from nonfiction), Fiske did not have large sales. He had only a limited appeal to the middle-class public whose taste for sentimental novels determined best-seller status in these years.

Fiske drew readers from two groups—from the social élite who found his view of the meaning of the American experience attractive, and from those who desired to educate themselves and for whom the approval of social leaders and Fiske's lucid style combined to make his works a desirable vehicle by which to imitate upper-class cultural behavior. These two groups were not sufficiently numerous to put Fiske into a position to challenge the sales of novels; yet they undoubtedly made him the best-selling historian of his generation. No other historian even appeared in the *Bookman* lists during the period checked. And in reports on library reading compiled for the *Critic* from 1900 to 1903, Fiske showed steady popularity all over the country.[18]

None of Fiske's books sold more than 15,000 copies in their year of issue, and few among them went that high. But they were in steady demand thereafter, stimulated by Houghton, Mifflin and Company's merchandising of illustrated editions, by the publicity

[18] *Bookman,* vols. 1–17 (1895–1903), especially 10:284 (November 1899); 10:404–408 (December 1899); and 10:504–508 (January 1900); 10:600–604 (February 1900). *Critic,* February 1900 to February 1903, compiled lists of library reading favorites.

of Fiske's lecture tours, and by the purchase of further volumes by readers who found one title enjoyable. An average of 10,000 copies a year in bookstore sales during the last fifteen years of Fiske's life is probably not too far away from the truth. To this must be added the smaller sales previous to 1887, sales of textbooks and special editions, and the extensive merchandising of his collected works in the years after his death. What the total reached can only be guessed at: perhaps half-a-million copies, in all, during the years of greatest activity, though this may be a high estimate.

IV

Despite the salary from his publisher, augmented as it was by royalties from three new books and the contract with Lea Brothers, Fiske still went out on lecture tours which the failing health that plagued his last years rendered agonizing. His enormous bulk and shortness of breath after any physical exertion made the rigors of lecturing harder to bear than ever before.

Failing health, along with his usual problem of finding time for work in the round of social activity and travel which took up so much of his life, pushed Fiske further and further behind on his schedule for completion of the histories. He had guaranteed delivery of *New France and New England,* the last section in his series on Colonial history, for May of 1901, but by that date he had barely begun the process of revising his lectures into finished form. He had twelve lectures on hand, which he had given in Boston under the sponsorship of the Lowell Institute in the spring of 1901, but these still needed much work before appearing in book form. Fiske may have intended to expand them into two volumes, for his chapters of social history ("Salem Witchcraft," and "The Great Awakening") are disproportionately long in a single volume. Since Fiske revised only the first two chapters, we cannot be sure of his intentions in the matter. The unrevised part of the book was one of Fiske's weakest productions. He drew almost exclusively on Parkman. While his clear, easily understandable style was still with him, and he provided lucid descriptions of explorations and wars, he nowhere took up the most vital development in terms of his philosophical scheme—the slow and unexciting, but highly significant, growth of democracy during the first half of the eighteenth century. This Fiske might have in part corrected as he revised and expanded the book, but he never completed his work.[19]

Even the $12,000 a year that Fiske received from his publisher, and the substantial additional sums earned by lecturing and other writing, did not prevent him from running short of money. In December of 1900, while preparing his Lowell lectures on the eighteenth century and planning a revision of his earlier books for a collected edition of both his philosophical and historical writings, Fiske again needed an immediate loan. "The melancholy fact is," he told Houghton, Mifflin, "that unless I can count upon a special advance of at least $3,000 for the 15th, I must break off work this very morning and devote myself to meeting the emergency." His publishers sent the money, and Fiske wrote back gratefully, promising to repay it if he and the firm did not come to a satisfactory agreement on his projected eight-volume continuation covering the history of the United States from 1789 to 1865. One month later he wrote to Lea Brothers, asking them if they were interested in this new series and requesting information on how high they cared to bid against Houghton for it.[20]

Warned by his doctor to cut down on his activity and to rest, Fiske cancelled his usual travel plans in 1901 and turned down an offer to speak at Johns Hopkins. He limited his lecturing primarily to his talks before the Lowell Institute in Boston. With his health bad, progress on the revision of his lectures into book form was slow. He did some preliminary thinking on the address he would give in England for the Alfred Memorial dedication, sketching out a talk on the American development of the political ideas Alfred had illustrated in his work. In the spring of 1901, Fiske and his mother, who had become infirm in her old age, decided to combine their households. They had structural alterations made in her home at 90 Brattle Street, Cambridge, to provide a twenty-by-fifty-foot

---

[19] "Preface," to *New France and New England* (Boston, 1902), pp. v–viii.

[20] JF to HMCo, Dec. 13, 1900, Dec. 14, 1900; JF to Messrs. Lea Bros. & Co., Jan. 16, 1901, HHL. All three letters are copies in Fiske's own hand.

room in which Fiske would have sufficient space to shelve his many books.[21]

As his fifty-ninth birthday approached, Fiske was at work on his twenty-seventh book and planned still more. He was engaged in revising his *New France and New England*. In addition to his work on the Alfred Memorial lecture, he had begun to collect material for an autobiography, possibly for inclusion in the "Collected Works" Houghton planned to bring out. But these projects, like the extension of his *magnum opus* to include the history of the United States in the nineteenth century, and the revision of his *Cosmic Philosophy* that he planned, were still in the thinking, rather than writing, stage. Given time he hoped to complete the work he had on hand and go on to yet greater things. But he had no time.

In June of 1901, as Fiske and his favorite binder carefully supervised the movement of his books to the magnificent library at 90 Brattle Street, Cambridge experienced an extended spell of hot, muggy weather. The shortness of breath from which Fiske already suffered grew severe and his doctor urged him to leave the city to escape the heat. He and his son Herbert went by sea to the Hawthorne Inn at East Gloucester, Massachusetts, but the sea air failed to revive him. Early on the morning of July 4, 1901, with the celebrations of Independence Day echoing through his windows, John Fiske died. In accordance with his wishes he was buried in the village churchyard at Petersham, among New England worthies whose virtues he had celebrated, in a plot overlooking the quiet New England countryside he had loved.[22]

V

As a young man John Fiske confidently set out to win fame and wealth as a scholar and scientist. By the time of his death he had a substantial income and his obituary notices testified to his wide-

[21] JF to HMCo, Dec. 13, 1900, HHL. JF to D. C. Gilman, Dec. 14, 1900, Johns Hopkins University Archives. J. S. Clark, "Introduction" to JF, *American Political Ideas* (Boston, 1911), pp. xi–lxxv.

[22] JF to G. H. Humphrey, Feb. 16, 1901; JF to Ethel Fiske, May 1, 1901, HHL. *Atlantic Monthly*, 89:288–290 (February 1902). "John Fiske's Library," Cambridge *Tribune*, Aug. 3, 1901. *Harvard Graduates' Magazine*, 10:33 (September 1901). Boston *Evening Transcript*, July 5, 1901.

spread renown. Yet what he had achieved was not quite what he intended.

When Fiske entered Harvard College it had all seemed easy. Everything known was in books, and Fiske need merely read them to master all knowledge and be ready to add original contributions of his own. These contributions would clearly prove that he had been right and orthodox Middletown wrong. But without being fully conscious of what he was doing, Fiske modified his objectives as the need to support his family and increasing opportunities for free-lance writing led him to concentrate on financial rewards.

Fiske thought he was altering his methods rather than abandoning his scholarly goal. His *Cosmic Philosophy* deserved praise for the high quality of its popularization, but, except for some modest moments in the presence of his British idols, this was not the way Fiske thought of it. Most often he spoke of it as a synthesis in which he had not only brought together the ideas of other men, but had so combined and presented their concepts that he had shown himself their peer as a thinker. Similarly, Fiske thought of his historical books as scientific contributions to knowledge since they had an implicit philosophy that built upon the ideas of men who were leading scientific historians. Fiske's publicity referred to his lectures and writings in these terms, and this image won wide public acceptance.[23]

Many of the reasons for his deviation from his youthful plan were beyond Fiske's control. When he began his career, few scholars could pursue their studies without an independent income. Since Fiske had no private funds, and found nonliterary ways of earning a livelihood uncongenial, popular writing on serious subjects seemed a feasible way to work towards his goal. Marriage and the costs of raising a family of six children intensified the need to write rapidly in order to earn more money. This pressure reached a peak of

[23] Fiske's view of himself is best seen in two sketches based on data which he furnished: Edwin D. Mead, "John Fiske and his Philosophy," *Christian Register,* 65 (Apr. 6, 1886, Apr. 15, 1886, Apr. 26, 1886, May 6, 1886); and [M. A. DeWolfe Howe], "Biographical Sketch," preceding JF, *The War of Independence,* Riverside Literature Series, number 62 (Boston, 1897), pp. vii–xiv. [The latter sketch was written in 1894; see H. E. Scudder to JF, Mar. 29, 1894, HMCo papers, 8:337, and JF to Scudder, Apr. 1, 1894, M. A. DeWolfe Howe Papers, HUL].

tragic intensity in the 1880's when nervous breakdowns of his two eldest children caused heavy sanitarium and nursing expenses. That part of Fiske's money problems also stemmed from his own financial irresponsibility did not make the difficulties any less real, in fact it made them all the harder to solve.

But the pressure of events was not the only reason Fiske deviated from his goal. In some ways, these pressures actually aided him for, although Fiske would never have admitted it, he was actually better fitted by temperament and intellectual ability for a career as a popularizer than that of a scholar. The childlike sense of wonder and optimism, the phenomenal memory that permitted him to bring a wide though superficial knowledge to every topic he touched, combined with his relatively weak critical ability to make him much more effective as a transmitter of the ideas of others than as a discoverer or originator.

Fiske's character always showed remnants of the spoiled child of his boyhood. This was not entirely a weakness, for it made him an attractive companion. And, as Josiah Royce noted, "this childlike element in Fiske . . . was his strength. It was his wisdom. It gave him the collecting child's fondness for vast masses of details, side by side with the philosopher's love for interpreting the universe." Royce saw it as a major source of Fiske's popularity. "This childlike quality lighted up all his stores of information with its gentle enthusiasm. It won him the sympathy of numerous hearers to whom his opinions would have been repellent, or to whom his studies would have seemed hopelessly complicated, if his temperament had not assured them, through every tone of his voice, through every quality of his literary style, that his heart was cheerful, and that his faith was simple." [24]

But if his childlike temperament aided his success as a lecturer and made him a welcome friend, it had grave disadvantages as well. In his financial affairs Fiske showed a basic irresponsibility in continually borrowing more than he could have expected to pay by his own efforts, and then turning to his elders for rescue from the difficulties his own actions had created. It also adversely affected

[24] Josiah Royce, "John Fiske as a Thinker," *Harvard Graduates' Magazine,* 10:26 (September 1901).

his methods of work, which interspersed bouts of intense writing with long spells of social activity. When he wrote (and he did much of his writing, especially in the last two decades, while on tour or in the summer at Petersham), Fiske depended on his phenomenal memory to carry him through.

Of equal importance with his temperament in making Fiske's hope of a scholarly career unrealistic, was his faulty critical ability. This was more apparent in his later work than in his early philosophical writing, in which he could follow one main guide, Spencer, and evaluate everyone else in terms of his master. His late religious essays told more about his hope for comfort, of his desire for immortality, than they did about the logical basis by which he might have defended his views. They testified more to the strength of his faith than to the strength of his intellect. As a historian, Fiske wrote too rapidly and too easily; he accepted facts and interpretations without adequate evaluation. In all fields, once his emotions were involved, his critical ability disappeared.

In an age in which intellectual pursuits were in process of becoming academic professions, scholars found Fiske's work something of a puzzle, partly because of the wide range of subject matter he covered, but even more because the high quality of his popularization seemed to challenge the relevance of their own standards. Philosophers like Josiah Royce (who produced an objective, unflattering estimate of Fiske's value as a thinker) praised Fiske's historical work. Historians did not feel competent to judge his work in other fields, though many commented favorably on his philosophical and religious writing. It was easier to evaluate the activity of professional scholars who worked within clearly marked academic lines.

Reviews of Fiske's books in scholarly journals like the *American Historical Review* or the *Political Science Quarterly* showed the dilemma. Reviewers tried to apply scholarly standards of criticism on use of sources and accuracy of details. Measured by these criteria the books should have been rejected; yet such a verdict seemed unjust to the real value of the volumes, of which the reviewers were also conscious. This made it difficult to evaluate accurately the merits of Fiske's work while warning of his shortcomings.

In his last years the scholarly world became increasingly hostile to Fiske's work. By then the generation that felt grateful to him for what they had learned from his popularization of philosophy and biology, and who could see similar virtues in his historical work, had passed on. A new generation of men, trained in universities to follow the rigorous methods that transformed the craft of history into a profession, had come to the leadership of reviews and periodicals. Less interested in what Fiske actually accomplished than in the relation of his books to their areas of professional concern, they arrived at an unfavorable evaluation of his work that has since become the standard scholarly view.

This evaluation helped correct the naïve acceptance by so many of Fiske's contemporaries of his claim to be a great scholar and scientist. If Fiske's books had actually been the contributions to knowledge he dreamed of as a child, no more would need to be said. But, in fact, this is not their major achievement, and to make this the main criterion in evaluating them is to distort their real significance. Much more important than the failure of Fiske's books to measure up to scholarly standards was their success in expressing the reaction of significant groups in the United States to important changes of their time.

In his early years Fiske struggled with some of the problems generated by the spectacular advance in knowledge and the rise in popular estimation of natural science during the nineteenth century. In the field of biology Darwin's work on evolution provided a way of understanding the changing patterns of life. In physics the postulation of the laws of conservation and equivalency of energy seemed to provide concrete and detailed, yet simple, rules governing all the universe. As the century progressed, men tried to discover simple, over-all laws of a science of man which would bring psychology, sociology, and history to a state of clarity and predictability resembling that which physics had achieved. Much of Fiske's early writing informed his readers of discoveries in the social and natural sciences and discussed the implications of these new views. His great achievement was in providing a clear, concise account of these advances, especially the speculations of Herbert Spencer, in terms which could be understood by intelligent laymen, and in discussing the religious implications of these intellectual changes.

The altered concepts of the nature of the world and of man stemming from the scientific advance heavily affected religion. The meaning of God, the value of accepted doctrines, and the function of worship seemed unclear in the new universe of science and in the new expanding urbanized and industrialized society of the late nineteenth century. All through his life Fiske reacted to these problems. He began as a religious radical, trying to combine the insights of Transcendentalism with the coherent world view of science. Fiske modified the expression of his religious views, but he never significantly changed his basic ideas. The great popularity of his later religious books stemmed more from alterations in American religion than from changes in his work. Although orthodox denominations never adopted as extreme a response to such problems as did Fiske, the desire for a rational support for religion permitted believers to react to the positive tone of his statement while ignoring the less explicit negative implications of his views.

The writing of history, too, felt the effects of the growing prestige of science, and many historians tried to accommodate their work to physical or biological models. Historians reacted as well to a growing uncertainty about the role of America that manifested itself in the years after the Civil War. As the pace of urbanization and industrialization advanced, the United States seemed to diverge more and more from the ideal picture of its future formulated in the early years of the Republic. In his historical writing Fiske presented a view of the meaning of the American experience which was attractive enough to his contemporaries to make him the most widely read historian of his generation. His technique altered from the sociological approach of his youth, when he depended heavily on concepts drawn from Herbert Spencer, to his multivolume Colonial history, with its richly detailed filio-pietistic rendering of the American past. Although his presentation changed markedly, Fiske still derived his interpretations from sources extraneous to history—that is, from science and philosophy. He drew listeners who found these ideas, especially his definition of Americanism that identified it with New England elements in American life and thought, a meaningful and satisfying interpretation of their own experience.

Fiske was a popularizer, but he was not a popular writer in the twentieth-century sense of the term, for he never reached a mass audience. Fiske achieved financial prosperity through the appeal of his historical works (the chief money-makers) to a limited, not to a mass, audience. He attracted to his lectures primarily educated people, those who were at the top of the social and cultural hierarchy of the country, and those who desired to imitate the behavior of this leading group. Who bought Fiske's books is harder to determine than who turned out for his lectures, but it seems probable that the core of the book audience was similar to, if not identical with, the lecture audience. Although a limited group, there were enough such people on the expanding economic and educational scene of late nineteenth-century America to provide lucrative rewards for Fiske.

The belief that the entire evolution of the world had purposefully prepared for the rise of New England, and that the future would see the spread of its ideas over all the globe—this was the basic concept that informed all Fiske's historical writing. Fiske tried to support his ideas by using an evolutionary frame and arguing that the latest dominant group (namely, his own) was the goal toward which the whole cosmic process had been directed. But any such identification of final goal and purpose with an already existing entity necessarily entailed a denial of the continuity of the evolutionary scheme. To defend his position Fiske argued that evolution could and would show no further advance. He did not make this explicit in his histories, but in his religious essays he flatly stated that there would be no further evolution beyond man. Combining his views in both fields, his readers could conclude that history had reached the fulfillment of its progress in the nineteenth century, that the future would merely see the intensification of current trends, rather than a modification and growth out of the present. But Fiske found himself less and less in sympathy with the trends of his own day, with its growing cities and great industries built on immigrant labor. The vision of America which Fiske presented tended to be an idealized version of the nonindustrial New England of his boyhood. Ironically, he came to celebrate the same small-town New England from which he had fled as a youth. His emotional reaction to the world around him had led Fiske in the end to an implicit denial of the philosophical ideas of evolution which he tried to popularize in all his works.

The appeal of Fiske's religious thought paralleled that of his historical ideas. Again Fiske attracted a limited, though highly significant, group—not the masses. The bulk of the American population, both in cities and in rural areas, belonged either to immigrant churches or evangelical sects. These groups were least affected by the religious trends about which Fiske spoke; they therefore paid little attention to him. The churches that drew into their orbit the social and cultural leaders—the Unitarian, Congregationalist, Presbyterian, and Episcopalian—showed the most interest in new religious ideas.

What was most striking in the reception of Fiske's thought was the way ideas which seemed radical when first presented, became attractive, with only slight alterations, to groups that desired to take a moderate or conservative attitude towards religious change. This happened in all the denominations to which Fiske came to seem an outstanding defender of the faith. Even the Unitarians had split in the sixties, with the majority of the church rejecting the ideas that attracted Fiske—the de-emphasis of supernatural elements and almost total ignoring of the Christ figure, stress on God as immanent in the universe, the use of evolution to explain the true nature of religion, and limitation of religion primarily to an emphasis on morality in this life that would be rewarded by immortality in the next. By the end of the century, the relatively undogmatic Unitarian Church was able to adopt most of this position. The problem was harder, and therefore the shift even more noteworthy, in orthodox churches which wished to hold on to some dogma and were especially concerned to retain the central figure of Christ. Yet even they adopted ideas similar to Fiske's, though endeavoring to extend them further and to find a way for Christ to function in an orderly universe ruled by an immanent God. Fiske's emotional assertion that he had proved how evolution supported all the essentials of religion, often made in churches where elements of dogma were considered part of that essence, made it possible for these groups to feel that Fiske supported their position.

That Fiske's pale affirmations could seem a major support for faith indicated the great distance orthodox denominations moved in the last forty years of the nineteenth century. Fiske's popularity was thus a measure of religious change. Its significance went far beyond the small number of believers involved, for it was the dominant minority of the country that responded to these ideas and to Fiske. By accepting "modern" views they turned this approach to religion into a challenge the rest of religiously inclined America had to meet.

Today Fiske's philosophical and religious writings are almost forgotten. Twentieth-century catastrophes have made Fiske's easy optimism, a facet of his character that pleased his contemporaries, seem naïve; it is more difficult now to believe in a guaranteed happy ending both in this life and in the hereafter. Fiske's histories have fared better. Not only do scholars still discuss his thesis on the "Critical Period," but his emphasis on New England elements in American life continues to attract sufficient readers to keep some of his volumes in print sixty years after his death.

But it would be an error to evaluate Fiske in terms of what he directly contributed to the twentieth century. For we may apply to Fiske the words which O. W. Holmes, Jr. intended for Fiske's master, Herbert Spencer: "He was in fashion once, therefore he filled a need. Our fashion is not more respectable than any other. If a man has his time of being in fashion he has all that anyone has, and has proved his claim to be a force shaping the future." [25]

Fiske's best work drew its power from the way it met the needs of his own age. His outstanding talent for popularization, his ability to restate other men's ideas in clearer and more easily understood language, combined with his own emotional need for reassurance that led him to stress the kindest aspects of the topics he covered, ideally fitted him for his task. Although he turned to such work reluctantly, once engaged in it he did it better than any other writer

[25] *Holmes-Laski Letters,* Mark DeWolfe Howe, ed., 2 vols. (Cambridge, Mass., 1953), p. 652.

of his time. In his works on evolution, in his religious essays providing a means of retaining faith while adjusting religion to an altering world, and in the vision of the destiny of America that informed his histories, Fiske rendered an irreplaceable service in providing his generation with ideas and concepts that permitted intelligent Americans to achieve a workable intellectual accommodation with the rapid social and intellectual changes of the nineteenth century.

NOTES ON SOURCES

INDEX

NOTES ON SOURCES

The footnotes of this study indicate the primary sources of factual information. Secondary works have been cited only when a statement in the text leans particularly heavily upon them or where they are only relevant to a specific section. This does not exhaust the debt to the authors whose works have been consulted. The notes which follow briefly discuss those works whose facts and opinions, whether accepted or rejected in this book, have affected the treatment throughout. An even more extended annotation can be found in the footnotes and in the bibliography (pp. 509–556) of the doctoral thesis on which this study is based; a copy of the thesis is on deposit in the Harvard University Archives, Cambridge, Massachusetts. For convenience, after indicating the location of Fiske manuscripts and listing his books, the printed works mentioned will be taken up under four headings: Reminiscences and Evaluations of John Fiske, History, Science and Philosophy, and Religion.

I. SOURCES ON JOHN FISKE

A. Fiske Manuscripts

The Henry L. Huntington Library and Art Gallery, San Marino, California, holds the most important collection of Fiske manuscripts. This includes more than one thousand letters from Fiske to his wife and mother, as well as important groups of letters to Shepherd Gilbert, Ginn & Co., Henry Holt, Henry A. Richmond, George Litch Roberts, James G. Wilson, and Herbert Spencer, along with letters to Fiske from

Spencer, T. H. Huxley, Charles Darwin, and others, miscellaneous memoranda, and manuscripts of Fiske's essays, lectures, and books. Unfortunately, many of the letters have been mutilated, with entire sections cut away and words or sentences removed with ink eradicator.

The Library of Congress has some sixty letters from Fiske to his wife and mother, supplementing the collection in the Huntington Library, as well as an important group of letters to Manton Marble, and scattered items in other collections, of which those in the J. Franklin Jameson Papers proved most valuable.

The Harvard University Archives contain useful material on Fiske's education and teaching career in the official records of various college bodies, class reports, and in the Charles W. Eliot Papers. The letter books and records deposited in the Houghton Library of Harvard University by the Houghton Mifflin Company, covering the activity of that firm and its predecessors to 1900, clarify Fiske's relations with his publishers. The Charles Eliot Norton, William Dean Howells, Thomas Bailey Aldrich, Prescott Hall, and Horace Scudder collections, all in Houghton Library, contain relevant letters, while scattered items of lesser value occur in other collections.

The Princeton University Library holds a group of letters from Fiske to Laurence Hutton and some miscellaneous items among its collections. Fiske's correspondence with Marshall S. Snow and William Greenleaf Eliot is now in the Archives of Washington University, St. Louis, Missouri. The University of California at Los Angeles, which purchased Fiske's library in 1926, has some Fiske letters, along with scrapbooks and volumes annotated in Fiske's hand. Minor items turned up in the collections of the Boston Public Library, the Cornell University Archives, the Missouri Historical Society, the Johns Hopkins University Archives, the University of Southern California Library, and the William L. Clements Library of the University of Michigan.

B. Books by John Fiske

Tobacco and Alcohol. I. It Does Pay to Smoke. II. The Coming Man Will Drink Wine. New York: Leypoldt & Holt, 1869.

The Class Room Taine. History of English Literature by H. A. Taine, Abridged from the Translation of H. Van Laun, and Edited with Chronological Table, Notes, and Index by John Fiske. New York: Holt and Williams, 1872.

Myths and Myth-Makers. Old Tales and Superstitions Interpreted by Comparative Mythology. Boston: J. R. Osgood and Co., 1873.

Outlines of Cosmic Philosophy. Based on the Doctrine of Evolution, with Criticisms on the Positive Philosophy. 2 vols. Boston: J. R. Osgood and Co., 1874.

The Unseen World, and other Essays. Boston: J. R. Osgood and Co., 1876.

Darwinism, and other Essays. London and New York: Macmillan and Co., 1879. (Revised and enlarged edition, Boston: Houghton, Mifflin and Co., 1885.)

The Presidents of America. A Series of Original Steel Engravings . . . by H. W. Smith. With Biographical Sketches and an Introductory Essay by John Fiske. Boston: E. F. Thayer and Co., 1879.

The Destiny of Man Viewed in the Light of His Origin. Boston: Houghton, Mifflin and Co., 1884.

Excursions of an Evolutionist. Boston: Houghton, Mifflin and Co., 1884.

American Political Ideas Viewed from the Standpoint of Universal History. Three Lectures Delivered at the Royal Institution of Great Britain in May 1880. New York: Harper & Brothers, 1885.

The Idea of God as Affected by Modern Knowledge. Boston: Houghton, Mifflin and Co., 1885.

Appleton's Cyclopaedia of American Biography. Edited by James Grant Wilson and John Fiske. 6 vols. New York: D. Appleton & Co., 1887–1889.

Washington and His Country. Being Irving's Life of Washington, Abridged for the Use of Schools, with an Introduction and Continuation, Giving a Brief Outline of United States History from the Discovery of America to the End of the Civil War. Boston: Ginn & Co., 1887.

The Critical Period of American History, 1783–1789. Boston: Houghton, Mifflin and Co., 1888.

The Beginnings of New England. Or the Puritan Theocracy in Its Relation to Civil and Religious Liberty. Boston: Houghton, Mifflin and Co., 1889.

The War of Independence. Boston: Houghton, Mifflin and Co., 1889.

Civil Government in the United States. Considered with some Reference to its Origins. Boston: Houghton, Mifflin and Co., 1890.

The American Revolution. 2 vols. Boston: Houghton, Mifflin and Co., 1891.

The Discovery of America. With some Account of Ancient America and the Spanish Conquest. 2 vols. Boston: Houghton, Mifflin and Co., 1892.

Edward Livingston Youmans, Interpreter of Science to the People. A Sketch of His Life with Selections from His Published Writings and Extracts from His Correspondence with Spencer, Huxley, Tyndall and others. New York: D. Appleton & Co., 1894.

A History of the United States for Schools. With Topical Analysis, Suggestive Questions and Directions for Teachers by Frank Alpine Hill. Boston: Houghton, Mifflin and Co,. 1894.

The Presidents of the United States, 1789–1894. By John Fiske, Carl Schurz, [etc.]. . . . Edited by James Grant Wilson. New York: D. Appleton & Co., 1894.

Old Virginia and Her Neighbors. 2 vols. Boston: Houghton, Mifflin and Co., 1897.

A Century of Science, and other Essays. Boston: Houghton, Mifflin and Co., 1899.

The Dutch and Quaker Colonies in America. 2 vols. Boston: Houghton, Mifflin and Co., 1899.

Through Nature to God. Boston: Houghton, Mifflin and Co., 1899.

The Mississippi Valley in the Civil War. Boston: Houghton, Mifflin and Co., 1900.

Life Everlasting. Boston: Houghton, Mifflin and Co., 1901.

Essays, Historical and Literary. 2 vols. New York: The Macmillan Co., 1902.

New France and New England. Boston: Houghton, Mifflin and Co., 1902.

The Historical Writings of John Fiske. Standard Library Edition. 12 vols. Boston: Houghton, Mifflin and Co., 1902.

The Miscellaneous Writings of John Fiske. Standard Library Edition. 12 vols. Boston: Houghton, Mifflin and Co., 1902.

The Writings of John Fiske. Edition de luxe of 1,000 copies. 24 vols. Cambridge, Mass.: Printed at the Riverside Press, 1902. [Text identical with Standard Library Edition.]

Studies in Religion. Being the Destiny of Man; the Idea of God;

Through Nature to God; Life Everlasting. (*The Miscellaneous Writings of John Fiske*, IX) Boston: Houghton, Mifflin and Co., 1902.

Colonization of the New World. (*A History of All Nations*, XXI) Philadelphia: Lea Brothers & Co., 1902.

Independence of the New World. (*A History of All Nations*, XXII) Philadelphia: Lea Brothers & Co., 1902.

Modern Development of the New World. (*A History of All Nations*, XXIII) Philadelphia: Lea Brothers & Co., 1902.

How the United States Became a Nation. [The "Continuation" from Fiske's *Washington and His Country*.] Boston: Ginn & Co., 1904.

The Discovery and Colonization of North America. [The "Introduction" from Fiske's *Washington and His Country*.] Boston: Ginn & Co., 1905.

Unpublished Orations. Limited edition of 489 copies. Boston: Printed for Members Only; The Bibliophile Society, 1909.

Clark, John Spencer, *The Life and Letters of John Fiske.* 2 vols. Boston: Houghton Mifflin Company, 1917. [The most useful edition of Fiske's letters.]

The Personal Letters of John Fiske. With an introduction by H. H. Harper. A limited edition printed for members of the Bibliophile Society of Boston. Cedar Rapids, Iowa, 1939. [Consists primarily of travel letters.]

The Letters of John Fiske. Edited by his daughter, Ethel F[iske] Fisk. New York: The Macmillan Company, 1940. [This is the most extensive printing of letters, but Mrs. Fisk edited so extensively, altering her father's language and combining parts from several letters to make one of her items, that her book cannot be used in conjunction with the footnotes of this study.]

For full bibliographic descriptions of Fiske's books, see *Bibliography of American Literature,* compiled by Jacob Blanck, vol. III (New Haven, 1959), 159–179.

C. Articles by John Fiske

Most of Fiske's essays were republished in the volumes listed above. Bibliographic data on the few significant articles which Fiske never reprinted are given in the appropriate footnotes of this book. A full listing of all Fiske articles in newspapers and magazines that could be located, along with data on later publication in book form, appears on pp. 521–533 of the thesis copy in the Archives of Harvard University.

II. Selected Reminiscences and Critical Evaluations of Fiske

Although scattered items of interest appear in the obituary notices and book reviews cited in the footnotes, the most useful reminiscences are found in articles by friends and acquaintances, such as [anonymous], "John Fiske's Simplicity," *Atlantic Monthly,* 88:717–718 (November 1901); Charles Fisk Bound, "Personal Reminiscences Concerning John Fiske" (manifold copy in Houghton Library, Harvard University); John G. Brooks, "John Fiske," *Review of Reviews,* 24:175–178 (August 1901); John Spencer Clark, "Introduction" to Fiske's *American Political Ideas* (Boston, 1911), pp. xi–lxxv [Clark's two-volume *Life and Letters of John Fiske* also contains valuable personal memories of Fiske, whom Clark knew from Fiske's days at Harvard]; Samuel M. Crothers, "John Fiske," in *Later Years of the Saturday Club,* M. A. DeWolfe Howe, ed. (Boston, 1927), pp. 273–278; Samuel S. Green, "John Fiske," in American Antiquarian Society, *Proceedings,* n.s. 14:421–428 (October 1901); Franklin H. Head, *John Fiske* (Chicago, [1902?]); Henry Holt, *Garrulities of an Octogenarian Editor* (Boston, 1923), pp. 321–351; James K. Hosmer, *The Last Leaf* (New York, 1912), pp. 168–178; William Dean Howells, "John Fiske," *Harpers Weekly,* 45:732 (20 July 1901); Laurence Hutton, *Talks in a Library* (New York, 1905), pp. 343–355; F. W. Osborn, "John Fiske as a Scholar," *Education,* 22:206–208 (December 1901); Thomas Sergeant Perry, "John Fiske: an Appreciation," *Atlantic Monthly,* 89:627–637 (May 1902); and William R. Thayer, "A Sketch of John Fiske's Life," *Harvard Graduates' Magazine,* 10:33–38 (September 1901). Some interesting, if inaccurate, apocryphal tales were gathered in the [anonymous], "Fiske Anecdotes," *Bookman,* 14:10–11 (September 1901). The most interesting interview of Fiske, by Wilder D. Quint, appeared in the New York *Times Saturday Review* of Oct. 15, 1898. T. S. Perry's *John Fiske* (Boston, 1905), intended as a brief biography, is most valuable today for the memories of Fiske it contains.

Almost all the obituary notices and book reviews cited in the footnotes contain some indications of contemporary critical opinion of Fiske. Among more extended considerations of Fiske's value, the laudatory and inaccurate Elbert Hubbard, "John Fiske," in *Little Journeys to the Homes of Great Scientists,* 17:135–151 (December 1905), needs to be balanced by more accurate works, such as Rollo Ogden's "John Fiske, Popularizer," *Nation,* 73:26–27 (July 11, 1901), and Josiah Royce's "Introduction" to the 1902 edition of Fiske's *Outlines of Cosmic Philosophy,* I, pp. xxi–cxlix, still the best discussion of Fiske as a philosopher.

The spectrum of religious reaction to Fiske can be sampled in Lyman Abbott, *Silhouettes of My Contemporaries* (Garden City, N.Y., 1921), pp. 81–99; Henry A. Brann, "Dude Metaphysics," *Catholic World,* 42:635–641 (February 1886); John W. Buckham, "American Theists," *Harvard Theological Review,* 14:267–282 (July 1921); Paul R. Frothingham, *All These* (Cambridge, Mass., 1927), pp. 45–70; Henry Collin Minton, "Christianity and the Cosmic Philosophy," *Presbyterian and Reformed Review,* 10:1–24 (January 1899); and Edmund T. Shanahan, *John Fiske on the Idea of God* (Washington, 1897).

Highly laudatory critiques of Fiske's contributions to history were William G. Brown, "The Problem of the American Historian," *Atlantic Monthly,* 92:649–661 (November 1903); and H. Morse Stephens' two articles, "Some Living American Historians," *World's Work,* 4:2316–2327 (July 1902), and "John Fiske as a Popular Historian," *World's Work,* 5:3359–3364 (April 1903). Professional historians were more critical. The most influential were C. M. Andrews' thorough and balanced discussion in "John Fiske," *Yale Review,* n.s. 7:865–869 (July 1918); G. L. Beer, "John Fiske," *Critic,* 39:117–118 (August 1901); and A. B. Hart, "The Historical Services of John Fiske," *International Monthly,* 4:558–569 (October 1901).

More recent studies of Fiske were of lesser value for this work than the evaluations by his contemporaries. Among items solely devoted to Fiske, James Truslow Adams's sketch in the *Dictionary of American Biography,* VI, 420–423, neatly summarizes the standard scholarly view of Fiske; Henry Steele Commager, "John Fiske: an Interpretation," Massachusetts Historical Society, *Proceedings,* 66:332–345 (1936–1941), emphasizes the period before 1880; Russel B. Nye, "John Fiske and His Cosmic Philosophy," in Michigan Academy of Science, Arts, and Letters, *Papers,* 28:685–698 (1942), is a solid, thorough summation; H. Burnell Pannill, *The Religious Faith of John Fiske* [Duke Studies in Religion, I] (Durham, N.C., 1957) summarizes Fiske's statements on religion and considers their place in the Christian tradition; L. C. Powell, "John Fiske, Bookman," in Bibliographical Society of America, *Papers,* 35:221–254 (1941), has interesting information on Fiske as a book collector and author, drawn largely from the U.C.L.A. Library collection of Fiske material and manuscripts; Gustav Reese, *Evolutionismus und Theismus bei John Fiske,* Inaugural-Dissertation zur Erlangung der Docturwürde der hohen Philosophischen Facultät der Friedrich-Alexanders-Universität, Erlangen (Leipzig, 1909), does little more than paraphrase the four books on religion Fiske wrote between 1884 and 1901; Jennings B. Sanders, "John Fiske," in *The Marcus W. Jernigan Essays in American Historiography,* William T. Hutchinson, ed. (Chicago, 1937), pp. 144–170, carefully assesses Fiske's histories in terms of his biases and attitudes to current events.

III. History

The pace and direction of change in American historical thought can best be sampled in the writings of historians active in these years, especially those who led the shift to a professional orientation of the discipline. Much information of value can be gleaned from the reviews in the periodicals cited in the footnotes to chapters ten and eleven. Letters and essays of historians are also revealing. Those that proved most useful for this study are Henry Adams, *The Education of Henry Adams* (Cambridge, 1918), *The Degradation of the Democratic Dogma* (New York, 1919), and *The Letters of Henry Adams,* W. C. Ford, ed., 2 vols. (Boston, 1930–1938); *Historical Scholarship in the United States, 1876–1901, as Revealed in the Correspondence of Herbert Baxter Adams,* W. S. Holt, ed. (Baltimore, 1938); C. M. Andrews, "These Forty Years," *American Historical Review,* 30:225–250 (January 1925); William A. Dunning, *Truth in History and other Essays* (New York,

1937); *The Life and Letters of Edward Augustus Freeman,* W. R. W. Stephens, ed., 2 vols. (London, 1895); *An Historian's World, Selections from the Correspondence of James Franklin Jameson,* E. Donnan and L. F. Stock, eds. [American Philosophical Society, *Memoirs,* XLII] (Philadelphia, 1956); and James Ford Rhodes, *Historical Essays* (New York, 1909).

Most secondary accounts of the course of history, as well as biographies of historians active in the United States during these years, mention Fiske; few add much to the view of him that became general shortly after his death. They are of more value in forming a picture of how history altered in the latter part of the nineteenth century, especially: H. Hale Bellot, *American History and American Historians* (London, 1952); Eric F. Goldman, *John Bach McMaster* (Philadelphia, 1943); W. Stull Holt, "The Idea of Scientific History in America," *Journal of the History of Ideas,* 1:352–362 (June 1940); Michael Kraus, *The Writing of American History* (Norman, Okla., 1953); M. A. DeWolfe Howe, *James Ford Rhodes* (New York, 1929); Richard B. Morris, "The Confederation Period and the American Historian," *William and Mary Quarterly,* 3rd ser., 13:139–156 (April 1956); J. H. Randall, Jr. and G. Haines, IV, "Controlling Assumptions in the Practice of American Historians," in *Theory and Practice in Historical Study: a Report of the Committee on Historiography* [Social Science Research Council, Bulletin 54] (New York, 1946), pp. 15–52; W. P. Randel, *Edward Eggleston* (New York, 1946); Edward N. Saveth, "Introduction," to *Understanding the American Past* (Boston, 1954) and his *American Historians and European Immigrants, 1875–1925* (New York, 1948), especially pp. 32–42 on Fiske.

The interesting attempt of Harvey Wish in *The American Historian* (New York, 1960) to treat Fiske as a successful popularizer, did not come to my attention until this book was already in type.

IV. Science and Philosophy

One of the most valuable keys to Fiske's youthful ideas lies in the works which influenced him in his early years. Those most significant in forming his vision of the world are cited in the footnotes of the first three chapters. The most influential single writer was, of course, Herbert Spencer, almost all of whose work was eagerly read by Fiske. Spencer's *Autobiography*, 2 vols. (New York, 1904) and *The Life and Letters of Herbert Spencer*, David Duncan, ed., 2 vols. (New York, 1908) are indispensable sources. His later views on religion are conveniently indicated in *The Nature and Reality of Religion: a Controversy between Frederic Harrison and Herbert Spencer*, with introduction and notes [by E. L. Youmans] (New York, 1883). The best study of Spencer's ideas is by a disciple turned critic, Hugh Elliot, *Herbert Spencer* (London, 1917.)

The writings of leading scientists cited in the notes to chapters two and five, especially those of Louis Agassiz, Charles Darwin, Asa Gray, Sir Charles Lyell, and T. H. Huxley, proved very valuable; the collections of letters of all these men help trace the spread of Darwinian ideas on evolution.

Nineteenth- and twentieth-century views of the relation of biology to ethics are explored in T. H. and Julian Huxley's *Evolution and Ethics, 1893–1943* (London, 1947), containing the Romanes lectures of both grandfather and grandson, along with a historical survey of the problem by Julian. C. M. Wilkins, *A Review of Systems of Ethics Founded on the Theory of Evolution* (New York, 1893) and Robert Mackintosh, *From Comte to Benjamin Kidd; the Appeal to Biology or Evolution for Human Guidance* (New York, 1899) help fill in the nineteenth century picture. G. G. Simpson, *The Meaning of Evolution* (paperback edition, New York, 1951) supplements Julian Huxley on recent trends.

The impact of science on philosophy comes out clearly in the writings of nineteenth-century thinkers. The most illuminating items used include John Dewey, *The Influence of Darwin on Philosophy* (New York, 1910); William James, *Memories and Studies* (New York, 1912), *The Letters of William James*, Henry James, ed., 2 vols. (Boston, 1920); Josiah Royce, *Herbert Spencer* (New York, 1904); Andrew Dickson White, *A History of the Warfare of Science with Theology*, 2 vols. (New York, 1896) and his *Autobiography*, 2 vols. (New York, 1905); Chauncey Wright, *Philosophical Discussions* (New York, 1876) and *The Letters of Chauncey Wright*, J. B. Thayer, ed. (Cambridge, Mass., 1877).

The most extensive discussion of the effect of Darwin upon Americans is Bert J. Loewenberg's unpublished Ph.D. thesis (in Widener Archives, Harvard University), "The Impact of the Doctrine of Evolution on American Thought, 1859–1900," and his three articles, "The Reaction of American Scientists to Darwinism," *American Historical Review*, 38:687–701 (July, 1933), "The Controversy over Evolution in New England, 1859–1873," *New England Quarterly*, 8:232–257 (June 1935), and "Darwinism Comes to America," *Mississippi Valley Historical Review*, 28:339–368 (December 1941). A. H. Dupree, *Asa Gray* (Cambridge, Mass., 1959), provides much useful material on these problems. Richard Hofstadter's stimulating *Social Darwinism in American Thought* (rev. ed., Boston, 1955) clearly demonstrates the wide impact of Spencer's ideas upon the United States. *Evolutionary Thought in America*, Stow Persons, ed. (New Haven, 1950), contains many valuable articles.

Although almost every survey of American thought devotes several pages, or even a chapter, to Fiske, few add much to the contemporary evaluations cited in section II of this note. The most informative were those which related religious change effectively to the new trends in philosophy, especially Morris R. Cohen, *American Thought* (Glencoe, Ill., 1954), H. S. Commager, *The American Mind* (New Haven, 1950), Ralph H. Gabriel, *The Course of American Democratic Thought*, 2nd ed., (New York, 1956), and Herbert W. Schneider, *A History of American Philosophy* (New York, 1946). Philip P. Wiener, *Evolution and the Founders of Pragmatism* (Cambridge, Mass., 1949) includes a chapter on Fiske, although he does not fit into the school of thought being discussed. Confusing Fiske with pragmatism destroys the relevance of an intriguing attempt at a Marxist critique of Fiske: Harry K. Wells, *Pragmatism: Philosophy of Imperialism* (New York, 1954), pp. 41–50.

V. Religion

Printed sources relating to American religious developments in the nineteenth century are very voluminous. Those most important for an understanding of Fiske's early ideas are cited in the footnotes to chapter one, those relevant to the religious reception of Darwin in chapters two and five, those on the development of American religion from the Civil War to 1900 in the notes to chapters eight, nine, and eleven.

The files of religious periodicals cited in chapter nine proved indispensable. Nothing more eloquently reveals the confusion, turmoil, and emotional impact of the rapid religious changes of the period than the day-to-day accounts of events, and the attempts to explain the positions reached, that these journals contain. Though frequently the materials found there, except for reviews of Fiske, did not lend themselves to quotation or specific citation in this work, they have affected the views expressed in all sections dealing with religion. They well repay the effort and time needed to consult them. In addition, each of the volumes of sermons, essays, memoirs, autobiographies, and biographies written by Fiske's contemporaries referred to in the notes contributed useful facts and sometimes valuable insights into the matters in connection with which they are cited.

Among more general contemporary attempts to evaluate religious developments, the most useful are Comte Eugene Goblet d'Alviella, *The Contemporary Evolution of Religious Thought,* J. Moden, trans. (New York, 1886), which includes firsthand observations of radical religious groups in England and America by this Belgian admirer of Herbert Spencer; John Wright Buckham, *Progressive Religious Thought in America* (Boston, 1919); George Park Fisher, *History of Christian Doctrine* (New York, 1896); Frank Hugh Foster, *A Genetic History of the New England Theology* (Chicago, 1907), a history of pre-Civil War religion written while the author was in process of shifting from orthodoxy to modernism, with traces of both approaches, as well as his *The Modern Movement in American Theology* (New York, 1939), a sympathetic treatment of religious liberalism after the Civil War; and Arthur Cushman McGiffert, *The Rise of Modern Religious Ideas* (New York, 1915), which traces the concepts Fiske helped to popularize.

Among recent surveys, Kenneth Scott Latourette's *The Great Century, A.D. 1800–A.D. 1914, Europe and the United States* [*A History of the Expansion of Christianity,* IV] (London, 1941) has the most useful summary of the events and tendencies of the period, while Herbert W. Schneider, *Religion in 20th Century America* (Cambridge, Mass., 1952), helps relate nineteenth-century changes to later developments.

Francis P. Weisenburger, *The Ordeal of Faith* (New York, 1959) collects much biographical material that illustrates the impact of religious changes, 1865–1900, upon the lives of those involved in them. H. Richard Niebuhr, *The Kingdom of God in America* (Chicago, 1937), and Winthrop S. Hudson, *The Great Tradition of the American Churches* (New York, 1953) contain many striking insights in their disenchanted critique of nineteenth-century theological changes. More general histories of religion in America tend to be somewhat thin on the matters of greatest interest to this study.

Many monographic studies proved rewarding. Aaron I. Abell, *The Urban Impact on American Protestantism, 1865–1900* (Cambridge, Mass., 1943), Charles H. Hopkins, *The Rise of the Social Gospel in American Protestantism, 1865–1915* (New Haven, 1940), and Henry F. May, *Protestant Churches and Industrial America* (New York, 1949), ably depict the response of Protestantism to industrial changes. Timothy L. Smith, *Revivalism and Social Reform in Mid-Nineteenth Century America* (Nashville, 1957), argues stimulatingly, if not always convincingly, that the origins of later religious attitudes to social reform can be found in pre-Civil War evangelicalism. Windsor H. Roberts, *The Reaction of American Protestant Churches to the Darwinian Philosophy, 1860–1900* (Chicago, 1938), concisely states denominational positions on evolution.

The most useful among the many recent biographies of religious leaders include Arthur S. Bolster, Jr., *James Freeman Clarke* (Boston, 1954); Ira V. Brown, *Lyman Abbott* (Cambridge, Mass., 1953); Mary E. Burtis, *Moncure Conway* (New Brunswick, N. J., 1952); H. S. Commager, *Theodore Parker* (Boston, 1936); Barbara M. Cross, *Horace Bushnell* (Chicago, 1958); D. R. Sharpe, *Walter Rauschenbusch* (New York, 1942); Paxton Hibben, *Henry Ward Beecher* (New York, 1942, first ed., 1927); and Israel Knox, *Rabbi in America: the Story of Isaac M. Wise* (Boston, 1957).

On radical religion, Stow Persons' *Free Religion: an American Faith* (New Haven, 1947), provides an illuminating account of the Free Religious Association, while Sidney Warren's *American Freethought, 1860–1914* (New York, 1943) is also useful. On the development of Judaism, Nathan Glazer, *American Judaism* (Chicago, 1957), Beryl H. Levy, *Reform Judaism in America* (New York, 1933), and David

Philipson, *The Reform Movement in Judaism* (New York, 1907), are all valuable. Paul W. Spaude, *The Lutheran Church Under American Influence* (Burlington, Iowa, 1943), and Abdel Ross Wentz's thorough and informative *A Basic History of Lutheranism in America* (Philadelphia, 1955), describe developments in that denomination. John T. Ellis, *American Catholicism* (Chicago, 1956), is the best brief survey of its subject, but tends to skip over internal conflicts and must be supplemented by Robert D. Cross, *The Emergence of Liberal Catholicism in America* (Cambridge, Mass., 1958) and Thomas T. McAvoy, *The Great Crisis in American Catholic History, 1895–1900* (Chicago, 1957). Alec R. Vidler, *The Modernist Movement in the Roman Church* (Cambridge, England, 1934), a study of modernist trends in European Catholicism, done by an Anglican sympathetic to the rebels, provides a striking contrast with what happened in America.

Index

Harvard Historical Monographs

*Out of print

1. Athenian Tribal Cycles in the Hellenistic Age. By W. S. Ferguson. 1932.
2. The Private Record of an Indian Governor-Generalship. The Correspondence of Sir John Shore, Governor-General, with Henry Dundas, President of the Board of Control, 1793–1798. Edited by Holden Furber. 1933.
3. The Federal Railway Land Subsidy Policy of Canada. By J. B. Hedges. 1934.
4. Russian Diplomacy and the Opening of the Eastern Question in 1838 and 1839. By P. E. Mosely. 1934.
5. The First Social Experiments in America. A Study in the Development of Spanish Indian Policy in the Sixteenth Century. By Lewis Hanke. 1935.*
6. British Propaganda at Home and in the United States from 1914 to 1917. By J. D. Squires. 1935.*
7. Bernadotte and the Fall of Napoleon. By F. D. Scott. 1935.
8. The Incidence of the Terror during the French Revolution. A Statistical Interpretation. By Donald Greer. 1935.
9. French Revolutionary Legislation on Illegitimacy, 1789–1804. By Crane Brinton. 1936.*
10. An Ecclesiastical Barony of the Middle Ages. The Bishopric of Bayeaux, 1066–1204. By S. E. Gleason. 1936.
11. Chinese Traditional Historiography. By C. S. Gardner. 1938. Rev. ed., 1961.

12. Studies in Early French Taxation. By J. R. Strayer and C. H. Taylor. 1939.

13. Muster and Review. A Problem of English Military Administration 1420–1440. By R. A. Newhall. 1940.

14. Portuguese Voyages to America in the Fifteenth Century. By S. E. Morison. 1940.*

15. Argument from Roman Law in Political Thought, 1200–1600. By M. P. Gilmore. 1941.*

16. The Huancavelica Mercury Mine. A Contribution to the History of the Bourbon Renaissance in the Spanish Empire. By A. P. Whitaker. 1941.

17. The Palace School of Muhammad the Conqueror. By Barnette Miller. 1941.*

18. A Cistercian Nunnery in Mediaeval Italy: The Story of Rifreddo in Saluzzo, 1220–1300. By Catherine E. Boyd. 1943.

19. Vassi and Fideles in the Carolingian Empire. By C. E. Odegaard. 1945.

20. Judgment by Peers. By Barnaby C. Keeney. 1949.

21. The Election to the Russian Constituent Assembly of 1917. By O. H. Radkey. 1950.

22. Conversion and the Poll Tax in Early Islam. By Daniel C. Dennett. 1950.*

23. Albert Gallatin and the Oregon Problem. By Frederick Merk. 1950.

24. The Incidence of the Emigration during the French Revolution. By Donald Greer. 1951.*

25. Alterations of the Words of Jesus as Quoted in the Literature of the Second Century. By Leon E. Wright. 1952.*

26. Liang Ch'i Ch'ao and the Mind of Modern China. By Joseph R. Levenson. 1953.*

27. The Japanese and Sun Yat-sen. By Marius B. Jansen. 1954.

28. English Politics in the Early Eighteenth Century. By Robert Walcott, Jr. 1956.*

29. The Founding of the French Socialist Party (1893–1905). By Aaron Noland. 1956.

30. British Labour and the Russian Revolution, 1917–1924. By Stephen Richards Graubard. 1956.

31. RKFDV: German Resettlement and Population Policy. By Robert L. Koehl. 1957.

32. Disarmament and Peace in British Politics, 1914–1919. By Gerda Richards Crosby. 1957.

33. Concordia Mundi: The Career and Thought of Guillaume Postel (1510–1581). By W. J. Bouwsma. 1957.